Dec. 1999

D0306990

To T
love
Sharif

Developing Language in the Primary Classroom

Sarah Tann

CASSELL

Cassell Educational Limited
Villiers House
41/47 Strand
London WC2N 5JE

First published 1991

British Library Cataloguing in Publication Data
Tann, Sarah
    Developing language in the primary classroom.
    1. Great Britain. Primary schools. Curriculum subjects:
    English language. Teaching
    I. Title
    372.60440941

ISBN 0-304-31986-4
    0-304-31983-X (paperback)

Typeset by Fakenham Photosetting Limited, Fakenham, Norfolk
Printed and bound in Great Britain by Biddles Ltd, Guildford and King's Lynn

Contents

Acknowledgements

I would like to express my thanks to students and colleagues at Oxford Polytechnic for the ideas and inspiration which they have sparked. In particular I have appreciated input from Angela Baker and Barbara Phillips and especially from Margaret Armitage (from Freelands School).

My thanks also to the P.A.G.E. team in Oxfordshire, Jenny Monk, Sylvia Karavis and Pat Davies, for their examples of a linguistic analysis of children's chronological and non-chronological writing.

I am also grateful to Thomas Nelson and Sons for funding the part-time secondment which enabled me to work regularly in schools over one academic year. Special thanks to the staff and children in Windmill First School, Sandhills Primary School and Chinor Primary School.

Thanks are due to Scholastic Publications Ltd for permission to use data (appearing in Chapter 2) which had earlier been used in *Teacher Handbooks: Talking and Listening* edited by D. Wray (1990), and to Cassell for material (appearing in Part I) adapted from Activities in *Reflective Teaching in the Primary School* by A. Pollard and S. Tann (1987).

Introduction

We are now in the new ERA of the 1988 Education Reform Act. The decade of the 1990s is witnessing the implementation of a national curriculum and a national system of assessment and testing. Contrasting with all this nationalization and centralization is the localization of management and financial controls, which gives the governors of individual schools greatly increased responsibility for staffing, resourcing and monitoring all these changes.

Such widespread change engenders debate and discussion at all levels: 'unalterable truths' are challenged, 'myths' questioned, ambiguities aired, yet many central issues of purpose and value are still left unexamined. Inevitably the large number of simultaneous changes can bring conflict, uncertainty, stress, instability, demoralization and a sense of crisis. But the situation can also be seen as one of tremendous challenge, providing the opportunity to achieve greater clarity and a stronger sense of professionalism as colleagues work together to develop the necessary school policies on the plethora of new initiatives.

What has happened to 'language' in all this? First, the terminology has changed. The notion of 'language across the curriculum' and of every teacher being 'a teacher of language' was enshrined in the Bullock Report (DES, 1975). This stressed the fundamental role of language in all learning, and its phrase, 'language across the curriculum', reflected a way of teaching and learning: a pedagogy that encouraged learners to take greater responsibility for and play a more active part in their own learning. It also underpinned a method of organizing and managing the classroom that involved greater use of collaborative groupwork. Now, however, we have a subject called 'English', which is part of a core curriculum that includes Maths and Science.

Secondly, the emphasis has changed. The shift from 'language' to 'English' may signal an attempt to refocus attention on what is uniquely English and thus be a move away from language as a service subject, which assists learning in all other areas of the curriculum. This change could lead to a re-conceptualization of English: it may herald a move away from a 'language in use' focus towards reinstating the traditional specialist approaches to literature and linguistics. The definition of both these areas is problematic, but, if there is to be such a shift, there is a need to clarify the boundaries of English.

1.   WHAT ENGLISH? ALTERNATIVE CONTENTS

Traditionally, the first component of English relates to reading and responding to literature. At primary level 'literature' effectively means 'books', and these might be ones considered by an individual teacher to be 'good', ones that are 'popular', or it might be 'all' texts. At this level the choice of books is influenced strongly by wishing to motivate children to read and by wanting them to experience success. Choice is also dependent on what is available in the library, at home, through commercial book clubs, or perhaps through family reading groups. Recently 'texts' have sometimes included non-book material, as in the oral or visual texts central to media studies.

The second component, linguistics, is concerned with the study of the language itself: its structures, functions and development. This may extend to considering the variations in the English language relating to purpose, audience, context, and variation over historical periods or geographical areas, including regional differences or foreign loan words. It may also include comparisons with other languages.

A third aspect of 'English', one that was much stressed in the 1960s, emphasizes English as being concerned with language as a means of personal development through writing, talking and drama, using verbal, para-verbal and non-verbal modes.

A fourth aspect comprises a utilitarian approach to language – a vocational bias, sometimes referring to the subject as basic English: instrumental reading for information retrieval and information recording (both verbal and graphic). This latter feature has never acquired the academic status of the other components and seems to be the main feature of the 'service' aspect of English. All these strands are apparent in the final documents for English in the National Curriculum.

2. WHY ENGLISH? DIFFERENT RATIONALES

The Cox Report (DES, 1989) identified five main aspects of English that justify its key place in the curriculum (2.20–2.27):

(i) *Adult needs*: the responsibility of English teachers is to prepare children for 'the language demands of adult life' so that they can communicate, in the spoken and written mode, 'clearly, appropriately and effectively'.

Such a goal is certainly not new, and was prevalent in the debate when the 1870 Education Act was passed. However, the education then had to be circumspect and relevant to working needs, so that the new social class of pupil intake should not become too 'uppity'.

(ii) *Cultural heritage*: the responsibility of the school is to 'lead children to an appreciation of those works of literature that have been widely regarded as the finest in the language'.

This goal also has a long pedigree. It has been voiced strongly, for example, in the 1930s, by such scholars as F. R. Leavis and T. S. Eliot. Such sentiments are often considered to relate to an elitist and conservative tradition in English teaching.

(iii) *Personal growth*: the role of literature, language and learning is to develop 'children's imaginative and aesthetic lives'.

This is sometimes associated with some forms of the 'progressive' movement which dominated the rhetoric of the 1960s. It still has considerable current credence and has been absorbed into mainstream approaches.

(iv) *Cross-curricular*: the responsibility of all teachers is to help children with 'the language demands of all subjects' so that English is both a subject and a medium of instruction.

Here, the emphasis is on facilitating learning and of not allowing language to become an impediment. This focus led to a valuable analysis of registers and specialist subject languages and to a continuing re-examination of the complex relationship between language and learning. However, there has been criticism to the effect that such a model focuses on training children in the existing communication patterns (some of which pose barriers) rather than challenge them.

(v) *Cultural analysis*: the role of English is to help children towards 'a critical analysis of the world and the cultural environment in which they live'.
   This represents a viewpoint which regards English in a much wider communication context. It embraces verbal and visual media, changing structures and constructed meanings, values and attitudes of different communicators.

3. HOW DO WE ACQUIRE LANGUAGE? MODELS OF LEARNING AND TEACHING

There are three main alternative models to explain how children acquire language:

  (i) *Imitative, behaviourist theories* (S–R) propounded by B. S. Skinner, based on the notion that children learn by copying what they hear around them. In teaching terms this leads to repetitious exercises and drills.
 (ii) *Innate theories*, associated with N. Chomsky, who suggested that as human beings we have a Language Acquisition Device (LAD) enabling us to deduce underlying rules of language so that we can generate new statements. In teaching terms this could lead to faith in osmosis: just 'bathe children in language' or 'leave all to discovery'.
(iii) *Interaction theories*, associated with J. S. Bruner, who suggested that the quantity and quality of the social context, the Language Acquisition Support System (LASS), were vital in supporting the child's efforts. In teaching terms, what is crucial is the nature of the language environment and how it provides important structures or 'scaffolding' to help the child. Appropriate intervention is positive when it takes place in a natural, purposeful context to improve understanding. Recent research has helped to identify many of the contributory factors to such a support system.

   The importance of social context to the learning and use of language is strongly emphasized in the (initially suppressed) work of Soviet theoreticians such as M. M. Bakhtin and V. N. Volosinov in the 1930s. Such work, now released, underpins a fourth model, which Edwards and Mercer (1987) call the 'cultural-communicative' approach. Volosinov (1973) argued against the European tradition that 'objectified' language by focusing on structures and forms from whence were derived meanings. Instead, he emphasized the ways in which meanings were created through dialogues and understandings were achieved through participants' interactions and responses. Further, Bakhtin (1986) believed that meaning not only derived from current utterances but from knowledge of previous utterances and from knowledge of the participants and the situation.

All this potentiality for meanings exists within the language context. The possibility of learning from such a context can be enhanced by adult intervention in what Vygotsky (1962) terms the 'zone of proximal development': that area of meaning in which children are moving implicitly, but which an adult can help to confirm, extend and make more explicit.

It is also important to remember that 'acquiring language' is a lifelong process. 'Linguistic competencies' develop early (for example by the age of 3 most children are talking in whole sentences and by 7 have mastered most agreements and irregular past tenses, though passives and relative clauses are often not confidently used before they are 12). However, 'communicative competence' (Hymes, 1972), which is the appropriate use of language in an ever-widening range of situations, and 'analytic competence' (Bruner, 1975), which is the ability to reflect on and be aware of language, continue to develop throughout life.

Given this diversity of theories about how children learn language, the range of competencies and contexts, and the long-term process of language learning, it is difficult to know on what to base a theory of teaching. Each of the theories about language learning depends a great deal on context, whether highly structured, 'naturalistic', or 'scaffolded'.

In addition there are contexts in which historical and cultural conventions and practices impinge on the individual's use of language. Also, personalized contexts exist dependent on an individual's social and personal experiences. Such 'personal history' is embedded in a social context, although the individual's response may be unique. All these aspects need to be considered by a teacher charged with the responsibility of furthering the development of children's language in a classroom context.

However, since theories about how children acquire language emphasize learning in a social context this book is based upon an interactive approach. Hence, it is important to examine teachers' own language use in the classroom, as well as the roles and the strategies they employ for intervention and 'scaffolding' at different stages of children's development. This entails the need

- to be aware of the relationship of purposes, audiences, developmental processes and use of language – whether speaking or listening, reading or writing;
- to consider the social context of the classroom and to plan carefully the managing, modelling and monitoring of language provision and the children's progress.

Finally, it is important to consider the support needed for the teachers. At the time of writing, English is taught in the primary school by generalist teachers who, in some schools, are supported by a postholder or consultant for 'English'. Given the rapidly changing demands, present and future teachers will need new background knowledge on which to base their professional action and new skills to implement and evaluate it.

This book is an attempt to meet some of these needs in mainstream schools. Each of the three parts – Oracy, Reading and Writing – attempts to review relevant current knowledge: spelling and handwriting are discussed in their general literacy context. Each section provides suggested activities (which can be adapted to suit individual needs) and further reading (which can assist in the reflective process), so that users can develop a basis of theoretical knowledge to inform classroom practice. The first chapter of each section emphasizes theoretical knowledge and the second chapter of each section emphasizes related classroom practices. Such insights form the basis for professional decisions and help to ensure the entitlement of each child to develop their full potential as a language user.

Part I

Oracy

Chapter 1

Teachers as Talkers and Listeners

INTRODUCTION

Chapter 1 will introduce the concept of 'oracy', review its origins and implications and argue the need to connect the rhetoric of oracy (the goals for developing active listeners and talkers in the primary classroom) with the reality of current practice in primary classrooms.

The first section examines the why, how and where of 'talking to learn' and the aims of oracy in the classroom. Section two reviews current classroom practice and questions how far the aims are being implemented, while the third section identifies key pedagogical issues (management, motivation, modelling, matching and monitoring) and examines how they can improve the coherence between rhetoric and reality. Each of these pedagogical issues will be revisited in the subsequent chapters in the context of the teacher's role in developing English in the light of the National Curriculum programme of studies and attainment targets.

1.1. ORACY IN THE CLASSROOM

The term 'oracy' was coined by Andrew Wilkinson in the 1960s. The new word sounded analogous to 'literacy' and may have helped to encourage the use of a similar frame of reference. Both terms were aspects of communication and learning: in the case of 'oracy' it highlighted 'talking to learn'. The term may also have helped to stress that listening and talking are as important as reading and writing.

It is useful to consider what might have prompted this re-assessment of the role of oracy and what the subsequent implications might be.

(i) Changing perceptions

By the 1960s demographic and economic post-war expansion had created a concomitant need for expansion in education, both for children of statutory school age and for those wanting to continue education beyond the minimum period. There was also the political desire to improve the quality of education and also the money to fund research in relevant areas.

Based on contemporary research results, there was a shift away from the model of learners as passive recipients of knowledge – empty vessels to be filled. Instead, learners were regarded as active participants, who made knowledge 'their own' often through practical investigations and discussion. In the classroom it led to the notion that the learner was no longer to be dependent on listening to the teacher-expert and reading a textbook, i.e. experiencing a 'transmission' mode of learning, which was heavily dependent on verbal means of communication and, in particular, on literacy. Instead, classroom activities developed in two complementary ways.

First, drawing upon Piagetian stages of cognitive development (sensori-motor, pre-operational, concrete operational and formal (logical) operations), and upon Brunerian modes of learning (enactive, iconic and symbolic), initial learning was based on practical, concrete experiences. Second, learning was encouraged in a social context (drawing upon Vygotskian principles) where 'talking to learn' became an important means of developing understandings, through an 'interpretative' mode of learning. These changes led to a growing interest in the processes of learning rather than just the end products. Furthermore, talking became recognized as an essential part of that process of learning, instead of just a means of testing the accuracy of what had been learnt.

The processes involved in talking to learn had a further advantage for the teacher. Such talk gave access to the child's learning strategies, allowing the teacher to monitor the learning and identify where and why the child might be having difficulty. Hence this mode of learning helped teachers gain a better understanding of how children learn.

(ii) Changes in organization

The notion of 'oracy' in the classroom had far-reaching pedagogical implications. It implied that both the teacher and pupils should act as both speakers and listeners and that the listeners should contribute by talking. The assumption was that learning took place in an interactive context with all participants constructing meanings together. Consequently the teacher's role needed to be that of an enabler.

Such a fundamental reconceptualization of learning led to the need to consider ways of reorganizing the classroom. Clearly, a 'new look' was needed in those classrooms where learning was previously considered to be the result of something teachers did to pupils, i.e. the teacher talked (taught, transmitted knowledge) and the pupils listened (learnt, received and remembered). Rows of desks facing the spot from which the teacher stood as fount of all knowledge were no longer suitable in an environment where it was intended that children, in small groups, would design, carry out and report on practical activities as a means of constructing and sharing their understandings.

In order to improve this match between the physical environment and the theoretical perspectives, primary teachers needed to experiment with alternative forms of management, in terms of classroom layout as well as the organization of the children and of the timetable. This resulted in tables grouped together to provide surface space for practical work, bays where on-going investigations could be held over extended periods, and separate activity areas for art work, maths, and so on.

The children also needed to be grouped in different ways for different task purposes. Individual work, group activities and whole-class sessions could each be used to promote specific learning goals. The increase in collaborative groupwork, an approach unfamiliar to many teachers, involved careful consideration of group size and composition (in terms of intellectual, social and language abilities, gender, race, personality and compatibility) in relation to the demands of the particular task.

Further, if children as active learners also became active in learning to design and plan their own tasks, this would result in a substantial change in the role of the teacher. The teacher could expect to share control over task developments though still retaining responsibility for the overall learning programmes. When children take more responsibility for negotiating their learning this is likely to result in greater integration of classroom tasks and a wider range of timing and duration of those tasks. There may well be less emphasis on the extensive use of subject-based activities and compartmentalized timetabling and more emphasis on flexible alternative arrangements. One consequence of this for the teacher is that much of the time spent in pre-planning assignments (so often undertaken by teachers each 'holiday' and adjusted each night in preparation for the following day) becomes redundant. Instead, teachers can have more time to analyse and monitor the learning that has been undertaken by the children during that day or week.

Modelling

The language, as well as the physical environment, had to change to accommodate the new theoretical perspectives. Hence, where previously teaching might have depended on telling followed by testing through the means of question-and-answer sessions, a shift to an alternative teaching style was needed based on different patterns of interaction.

However, for talk to become an established tool for learning the teacher needs to know which kinds of talk are most effective. Research on how children 'learn to talk' concluded that by the time children enter school at 5 years they have acquired almost all the basic rules of language, though obviously some specific grammatical points are refined later. But how children 'talk to learn' remained a much less understood area.

Barnes, Britton and Rosen (1969) were in the forefront of investigations into the way children use language in learning contexts, the effect of teacher presence and the ability of children to make knowledge 'their own'. Researchers studying how children

learn to talk had focused on vocabulary, syntax, length of utter-
ance and sentence structures. The interest in talking to learn led to
the analysis of discussion sequences and 'discourse'. Researchers
recognized the complexity of oracy, i.e. how the social context
affects linguistic, interpersonal and thinking skills. In order to
develop 'talking to learn', the task remains to clarify what these
skills are and to decide how they might be taught.

The extensive classroom research of the 1970s and 1980s showed
how teachers dominated classroom talk. Researchers stressed the
need to adopt other strategies that would encourage children to
enquire, explore, explain and evaluate ideas through discussion.
Teachers would need to adopt and encourage a more tentative and
formative style of talk. The children would also need such a style if
they were to use language to learn, find out and discover, rather
than using it for producing answers.

(iii)   Changes in monitoring policy

The Bullock Report (DES, 1975) marked a watershed in professional attitudes to language. Although for some teachers it said
little that was new and for others did not say enough, it legitimized
classroom practices that some had already pioneered and others
had regarded suspiciously as 'progressive'. Above all, it encouraged a much broader view of the role of language within and
beyond the school. In particular, the Report reaffirmed the convic-
tion that every teacher was a teacher of language, that language
was developed across the whole curriculum (not just in English)
and that language was 'for life'. In fact, 'language-across-the-cur-
riculum' was a doctrine about learning and not just a statement
about 'English'.

The recurrent social and political concern about standards that
are always alleged to be falling, has resulted in renewed initiatives
to monitor and assess children's language abilities. However, the
debate about standards is never conclusive because there is never a
clear definition of what aspects of language are being compared;
nor is there any clear measure of previous standards. A particular
problem is that societal expectations are constantly changing and
the view of 'adequacy' therefore fluctuates. Sharper definitions are
emerging as a result of the research in the 1970s and 1980s. This

has shown a considerable shift in focus from structures to functions and styles. In addition, more attention is being paid to the relationships between language, purpose and audience, with a concomitant emphasis on appropriateness instead of the previous obsession with accuracy.

But the question of assessment still looms large. Concern that it might be inadequate led to the establishment of the Assessment of Performance Unit (APU), as recommended by the Bullock Committee, in 1974. The APU refined the language categories and developed new procedures for assessing language skills. These procedures used classroom-based activities that were hoped to be less disruptive of classroom work, less artificial and more useful than previously used tests in helping teachers to diagnose children's learning needs.

Subsequently, during the radical shake-up of most aspects of education initiated by Conservative Secretaries of State for Education, Sir Keith Joseph and Kenneth Baker, a further change was proposed in 1987: namely, a national system of testing with public reporting of schools' results at Key Stages of 7, 11, 14 and 16 years of age.

The suggested assessment system was two-pronged: informal teacher appraisal and formal national Standardized Assessment Tasks (SATs). However, the development and administrative cost of such large-scale testing was never calculated; neither was it considered how much time teachers would need for setting up and marking such tests. By April 1990 the new Secretary of State for Education, John MacGregor, was already having second thoughts.

The increased emphasis on oracy, and particularly on testing, aroused fears in many teachers who felt ill-equipped for the task. Concern over how to raise awareness – particularly about 'oracy' – and to support teachers wanting to try out alternative ways of developing and monitoring in their classrooms led to the launch of the National Oracy Project in 1987. It would seem that, 25 years after the term 'oracy' was coined, its central role in an active, constructivist approach to learning has at last been recognized. So, by the 1990s, considerable progress has been made in identifying the components of talking to learn and in establishing a basic curriculum for oral language development.

However, there is a danger that the intangibility and fluidity of talk will lead some to try to pin it down so that it is teachable and, more significant, testable. It is the very tentativeness of talk which is essential to exploratory and interpretative learning. In order to play its role in such learning, talk needs to be allowed to infuse the curriculum, not to become a separate section. It is also important to accept that talking to learn needs to be taught: it rarely happens without guidance. We need to be able to analyse and be more aware of what we are doing. We need to be able to manage our classrooms, our time and our children so that we make time for talk. We need to model oracy, to motivate children, and their parents, to recognize the potential of 'talk' for serious learning. But, above all, we need to be able to monitor the achievements, experiences and opportunities for talking to learn. These areas will be addressed in the remainder of this chapter.

FURTHER READING

The following two books give an overview of all three language areas in the primary school focusing on general policy components and practical ways of raising school awareness. They are particularly intended for post-holders.

Ashworth, E. (1988) *Language in the Primary School*. London: Croom Helm.

Dougill, P. and Knott, R. (1988) *The Primary Language Book*. Milton Keynes: Open University Press.

The books below highlight current research findings in oracy in the primary school.

Corson, D. (1988) *Oral Language across the Curriculum*. Clevedon, Avon: Multilingual Press.

Jones, P. (1988) *Lipservice: The Story of Talk in Schools*. Milton Keynes: Open University Press.

MacLure, M. *et al.* (1988) *Oracy Matters*. Milton Keynes: Open University Press.

Wilkinson, A. *et al.* (1990) *Spoken English Illuminated*. Milton Keynes: Open University Press.

The following books include excellent sections on pre-school oracy (and literacy) experiences.

Garton, A. and Pratt, C. (1989) *Learning to Be Literate*. Oxford: Basil Blackwell.

Gibson, L. (1989) *Literacy Learning in the Early Years*. London: Cassell.

1.2.   THE PRACTICE OF CLASSROOM TALK

A considerable body of classroom research exists showing that teachers do most of the talking in the classroom. This fact is in itself of consequence when we consider the rhetoric on the role of talk in promoting learning. It is of even greater consequence when we establish the nature of classroom talk: what kinds of talk there are, who teachers talk to, why they talk so much and to what purpose. We also need to examine the consequences of teachers' verbal domination on children's perception of learning, on their perception of the teacher's role, and on their self-perception and the learner's role.

(i)   Patterns of classroom talk

Research in America in the early 1970s, most notably by Flanders (1970), established what has come to be known as the 'two-thirds rule'. This means that for two-thirds of class time there is talk, and two-thirds of it is by the teacher! Subsequent research in Britain confirmed Flanders' findings (e.g. Galton, Simon and Croll, 1980; Bennett *et al.*, 1984). More detailed analysis, in the ORACLE project, revealed the nature of that teacher-talk (Galton, Simon and Croll, 1980). It was found mostly to be task-orientated, such as giving information (often to the whole class), instructions (often to a group) and feedback (most often on an individual basis). The ORACLE project found that 44.7 per cent of teacher utterances were statements of which 15.4 per cent were information-giving, 28 per cent were task directions or instructions and a further 14.5 per cent related to class routines. Twelve per cent of utterances were questions of which 95 per cent elicited closed answers. Other findings revealed that when there was individual teacher–pupil exchange this was most often of a question-and-answer type, using closed questions demanding only a low-level cognitive response. The exchange was more likely to be undertaken in order to check children's understanding or recall, or sometimes to prompt a child to check their own working procedures as part of a feedback contact.

A common result of these quick-fire sessions was that the exchange developed into a game of 'guess what's in the teacher's mind' and inhibited any genuine exploration or collaborative con-struction of understandings (Barnes *et al.*, 1969). Children learn that teacher-talk is to promote testing rather than learning. They rarely experience models of discussion and are therefore unclear as to the purposes, processes and conventions of such a talking and learning context.

In addition to the content of the talk, it is pertinent to note its direction. For instance, how much is of an I–R–F pattern (*Initiation* by the teacher directed to the class in general or to an individual, who *Replies*, followed by evaluatory *Feedback* from teacher)? How much is of an A–A pattern (individual child *Asks* teacher who then *Answers* inquiry)? To what extent is there talk from teacher to child which is then picked up by other children before the teacher contributes again? And how much talk is there between children, without the teacher's presence?

Apart from the nature of the talk which takes place in class-rooms, it is also very important for teachers to be aware to whom it is directed. Amounts of contact have been found to vary in rela-tion to race (Galton, 1986), gender (Clarricoates, 1981; Spender and Sarah, 1980), and ability (Croll and Moses, 1985). These researches also reveal differences in who initiates the talk (the children or the teacher) and under what circumstances. For example, boys receive a greater share of the teacher's attention, both negative and positive, especially in oral situations. The posi-tive attention is mainly task-orientated in contrast to the social attention which the girls receive. We need to consider what effects these factors of the 'hidden curriculum' have upon the self-esteem of children of both sexes.

Further, the APU (1988) noted that whilst girls achieved better on most language measures, on oracy boys equalled or occasion-ally surpassed them. We need to be cautious in how we respond to these tentative findings. Whilst girls may need to be encouraged to become more articulate in oral situations it should not be at the cost of denying boys the main language mode in which they can express themselves.

ACTIVITY

Patterns of Talk

Tape or video part of a learning session
Then consider:

(a) *How much talking is there and who is doing it?*
Estimate the proportion of teacher-talk time and the time spent by children talking to each other/to the teacher.

(b) *How is talk distributed amongst the class?*
Was more talk directed towards boys or girls, or more able or less able children?
Were more initiations made by the teacher, or the children (which ones)?

(c) *What is the talk about?*
How much time was spent on discipline/control; setting task/ supervising; exploring issues/ideas?
Were the different purposes for which talk was used evenly spread amongst the class, or were some children the target of control talk and others the target for exploratory learning?

FURTHER READING

The following books are based on research which reveals more about classroom interaction and the role of the teacher. The first is a seminal collection of three essays representing some of the early results of such research and is specifically focused on groupwork.

Barnes, D., Britton, J. and Rosen, H. (1969) *Language, the Learner and the School*. Harmondsworth: Penguin.

The following contains further examples of a wide range of findings in specific contexts and also deals with research issues in collecting and interpreting classroom data.

Adelman, C. (ed.) (1981) *Uttering and Muttering*. London: Grant McIntyre.

The remaining titles take a more general view of classroom interaction.

Edwards, A. D. and Westgate, D. P. G. (1987) *Investigating Classroom Talk*. Basingstoke: Falmer Press.
Galton, M., Simon, B. and Croll, P. (1980) *Inside the Primary Classroom*. London: Routledge & Kegan Paul.
Richards, J. (1979) *Classroom Language: What Sort?* London: George Allen & Unwin.
Stubbs, M. and Hillier, H. (eds) (1983) *Readings on Language and Classrooms*. London: Methuen.
Wilkinson, L. C. (ed.) (1982) *Communicating in the Classroom*. New York: Academic Press.

(ii)   Opportunities for oracy in the classroom

If we accept that oracy is an important medium for active learning then we need to consider how we can create appropriate contexts for such talk within a classroom environment. The physical features of the classroom themselves can enhance or inhibit talk. For example, background noises, distortions and distractions need to be reduced. Hard surfaces such as lino, concrete, paint and plaster reflect sound and create echoes, as do high ceilings. Such environments are acoustically poor as well as being bare and unwelcoming. Classrooms need to be at least partially carpeted or have cork-type tiles, to have drapes as background to displays, soft board on the walls and smaller spaces within the room, created by use of room-dividers made of sound-absorbent materials.

Furthermore, a considerable amount of any verbal message is conveyed by para-verbal and non-verbal means (intonation, pace, volume, gesture, facial expressions). Because of this, a supportive environment for talk should allow participants to see each other, so that faces can be 'read' as well as voices heard. In addition, seating is linked to status, so the relative location of participants can confer or deny 'leader' status.

The average size of primary classes is a further physical factor which can affect opportunities for talking and listening. If a class contains over thirty children, at whatever age, it is difficult to find the time to give children much individual attention, even with additional help (for example, voluntary help from parents and support from welfare assistants for specific children).

(a)   Using questions

In order to maximize learning through an oral context it is essential for teachers to consider how they can use productive language strategies in their classroom. The ORACLE research findings (Galton, Simon and Croll, 1980) showed that teachers who were more successful in encouraging and developing children's thinking and learning were those who, compared to other teachers, used a higher proportion of time on whole-class sessions where higher-order, open-ended questioning techniques were employed in a discussion situation. Questions were used to encourage further investigations, to explain findings and explore suggestions. Such teachers were classified as 'class enquirers'. These teachers made relatively less use of questions which demanded recall or instant application of knowledge or tested understandings.

In terms of general classroom practice questions account for a considerable amount of teacher talk. The greatest single category of such questions are closed questions used for checking understanding or testing knowledge (and for gaining attention). However, as noted above, questions can be used for many different purposes. They can provide immediate feedback on how participants are thinking as well as on what they know. They are, therefore, a useful way of helping us to understand the learning process.

It is important for teachers to remember that how they *ask* the questions – the actual form, the accompanying para-verbal features such as tone of voice, the non-verbal features such as body stance – can contribute to how children interpret the status of the question: whether it is being 'fired' at them, is designed to 'find them out' or shows signs of teacher interest and curiosity. In addition pseudo-questions (e.g. Would you like to do some maths now? or Why don't you put some blue on the sky?) really function as hidden directives: the child is expected to comply. Children often hesitate before answering because they are confused by the mismatch between the form and the style of the question.

Further features of teacher questions have been noted. For example, teachers rarely ask questions to which they do not already know the answer. It has also been noted that, on average, teachers only allow two seconds between asking the question and then repeating, or re-phrasing, or re-directing the question to another child. This will hardly encourage children to view questioning as a means to thinking or exploring ideas! No wonder that children usually offer an answer based on trying to guess what is in the teacher's mind. Children try to interpret cues provided in the wording of the questions, tone of voice and facial expression. In this way, they learn the art of 'right answerism' (Mehan, 1974; French and MacLure, 1983).

How teachers *listen* to the responses alerts children to the teacher's purpose in asking the question. Teachers typically evaluate each response either by comment ('Good', 'No', 'Not quite') or by repeating or re-phrasing it to confirm or correct the answer. This particular I–R–F pattern is unique to classroom life. In everyday conversation it would not be appreciated!

Such a form of handling responses tends to turn the situation into a testing one, even if this is not intended. Other strategies might suit teachers' purposes better. For example, participation might be encouraged by:

- pausing longer in waiting for a reply
- not evaluating each response
- collecting and holding responses for the children to sort and decide upon.

It is important, therefore, to adopt an appropriate pace, accept and not prejudge responses, probe, prompt and provide time to think. Listening can teach much about children's thinking. It is also important to vary the range of strategies so that questioning can be used for exploratory purposes in a more open discussion situation (see pp. 26–29). Moreover, the purpose of any question–answer session should be stated and so should any shifts in purpose (e.g. from checking comprehension to exploring suggestions). If children understand what is expected of them they can contribute more confidently.

With regard to questioning and listening, teachers need to become more aware of their intentions and strategies and the reactions of their class. Monitoring oral classroom behaviour in this way not only raises awareness but provides data that can be analysed and acted upon. Being aware of one's use of these strategies could be a first step.

ACTIVITY

Analysing Questions

A checklist can be devised relating to a particular feature of teacher questioning, e.g. purposes, form and style, responses. This can be used to 'tally' the quantity and quality of questioning used. In addition, codes could be used, to replace a simple tally, in order to indicate the distribution of strategies over a class of children, e.g. ability, gender, race. The following lists could provide a framework for such checklists.

Purposes

(i) *Pedagogic*
(a) *closed questions* (low-level cognitive demand):
● to ask for information for testing and feedback
● to give on-the-spot solutions: for practising application
● to classify/compare: for encouraging closer analysis

(b) *open questions* (higher-level cognitive demand):
● to develop interpretation, speculation, imagining
● to synthesize information and ideas
● to focus on possible contradictions or discrepancies in evidence
● to evaluate and make decisions – encouraging judgements
● to transfer understandings to new situations – for flexibility

(ii) *Psycho-social*
● to show interest in and value for group members
● to encourage shy members to contribute
● to develop respect for other's views
● to implement routines and procedures
● to assert control/discipline.

Forms

(i) *Monosyllabic elicitation:*
- a question that can be answered in just one word: useful for testing purposes but not to generate discussions without a string of further questions which can then seem like an interrogation.

  e.g. Did you have a nice class trip? Yes.

(ii) *Direct question:*
- short and simply constructed question with a single focus that can encourage participation but can also be very threatening (if you don't know the answer), but can be used for many purposes to obtain simple facts, invite speculation, elicit opinions or interpretations.

  e.g. How could you make an alarm for this?

  What makes a good book?

  How do you think the explorers felt when they arrived?

(iii) *Indirect question:*
- long, composite question which contains a number of leads and can be useful for initiating discussion but can cause bewilderment as to where to begin.

When monitoring the responses and how they are handled, here are a few things to look out for.

How often are children's responses in the form of subsequent questions?

Does this mean that a) the teacher did not have/keep attention? b) the instructions weren't clear?

How long do we pause in waiting for a reply?

Why are the children so keen to get the answer 'right'?

How often do we provide opportunities for exploring issues and individual experiences, where every response can be valued?

FURTHER READING

Both the following books, though based on research in secondary schools, are also relevant to primary schools:

Brown, G. and Edmundson, R. (1984) 'Effective questioning' in Wragg, E. C. (ed.) *Classroom Teaching Skills*. London: Croom Helm.
Kerry, T. (1982) *Effective Questioning*. London: Macmillan.

(b) Giving information and instructions

This mode of discourse, sometimes referred to as 'expository', is another common pattern of teacher talk in the classroom. The teacher explains what the children are to do and gives instructions, or explains what she wants them to know and gives information. It is a monologue (with some questioning to check understanding) and can be a useful mode of discourse at the start of a learning session and, with a little modification, at the final report-back stage.

The listener's role is essentially receptive. This does not mean passive because listeners need to make sense of what they hear, so as to check their own understanding and seek clarification if necessary. It is often also reactive, i.e. children are required to do something in response to the instructions or information.

The speaker needs to remember the difference between written and aural modes. In a written context the input can be re-read, chewed over, viewed as a whole and responded to after due consideration. Listening to oral instructions or expositions involves attending to a linear set of information and processing it immediately for, as listeners, they have little control of the rate of information-flow. To expect children to respond at once to questions or to contribute further ideas, as teachers often do, is to ask a great deal of them.

Hence, the immediacy of an aural situation is very much to the advantage of risk-taking, confident, extrovert children and to the disadvantage of reflective, less confident, introvert children. Further success in this kind of listening is also related to many other variables: the physical environment, the degree of familiarity of the place/content/speaker and whether the listener is interested or the speaker interesting. These factors all need to be considered by the teacher.

It is easy to create confusion unintentionally by changing expectations during the mode of communication. For example, in classrooms there is a frequently used sequence of aural/oral

ACTIVITY

Planning Expositions

In using expositions, the teacher can help to make the task of 'listening' easier. This can be done by clarifying the speaker's purpose and the listener's role, so that expectations are clear.
The speaker could:

- give a clear and consistent signal to gain attention
- wait till s/he knows that the children are listening
  (e.g. by looking at the speaker)
- clarify purposes of the session and the speaker/listener roles
  identify what the children will listen to (focus/topic)
  suggest how they are to respond/react
  (e.g. by offering ideas/information, moving to act upon instructions, remembering to do/not to do something)
- distribute attention across the whole group
  (e.g. using non-verbal eye-contact, gesture)
- signal the beginning of the substantive exposition and each new point ('The first point is . . . Then we'll . . .')
- deliver the exposition using lively/varied tone, and 'chunk' it into memorable-sized bites
- summarize the information/instructions/issues before moving to the next phase
- make sure that listeners don't have to listen to too much at once, or for too long without varying the mode
  (e.g. moving from exposition to question-and-answer)
- encourage the children to give feedback (verbal/non-verbal) to check for understanding (which ones volunteer, which ones are called on . . . why)
- allow questions/points to be raised
- assign the children to tasks (and groups)
- identify necessary resources
- disperse the children to their activities.

Such a checklist could be used to monitor teacher expositions and identify strengths, weaknesses and patterns of oral behaviour in the classroom so that such sessions can be reviewed.

interchange that begins with a 'discussion'. It may start with the teacher eliciting children's knowledge and experience, focusing on the selected topic and stimulating their interest in the planned activity. The session then shifts to an 'expository' mode when the teacher provides information and instructions about the activity. This is followed by a 'question and answer' session to check on the children's understanding (and attention) before they disperse to undertake the tasks.

These shifts involve different expectations about the role of the speaker and the listener. For instance, during 'elicitation' some calling out is welcomed as evidence of enthusiasm, but it is frowned on during the 'checking' session. Named 'elicitations' may be a reward for a child wanting to contribute in response to an open general invitation, but naming a child for a 'question' may be seen as a threat or a control mechanism.

Having become aware of some of the difficulties that children have in being good listeners it is important to act upon such understandings. In particular, if we expect children to listen attentively to teachers, teachers should provide an appropriate model of listening skills and demonstrate strategies for positive responsive interaction. After all, how often and for how long do teachers listen – really listen – to children?

FURTHER READING

These two books, though based on secondary school research, are relevant to the primary classroom.

Brown, G. (1978) *Lecturing and Explaining*. London: Methuen.
Wragg, E. C. (ed.) (1984) *Classroom Teaching Skills*. London: Croom Helm.

(c)   Handling class discussions

The main key to success in handling a discussion is to be clear in one's own mind as to its purpose. The teacher's role is a dual one. First, the teacher needs to enable the whole group to discuss together (which requires a high level of managerial control to maintain the task goals). Secondly, the teacher needs to enable individual children to use the opportunity to develop their discussion skills (which requires a monitoring role in order to meet individual needs). Hence, on the one hand teachers often encourage contributions from those children who will have something useful to add, to keep the discussion moving. On the other hand, teachers need to encourage less regular or confident contributors to join in without allowing others to become restless.

In contrast to exposition sessions, which are essentially explanatory, discussion sessions are essentially exploratory. The role of the teacher is to elicit the children's experiences, responses, ideas and imagination in order to encourage them to build on these and use them in subsequent work. The discussion is open-ended and open to everyone to contribute, though the teacher should gain and keep attention, and clarify the purpose of the session.

In addition there are also discussions which are action-orientated, in which, after initial exploration, decisions have to be made and the ideas acted upon. The teacher needs to provide guidance so that children can take greater responsibility in discussion where they are planning their own learning processes. For example, when children are beginning a new investigation teachers should help them to:

- identify what they already know;
- what they want to discover;
- how they will try to find out;
- how they will organize themselves to complete the task.

Whole-class discussions form an important context in which a teacher can model positive discussion strategies, and also identify, label and reward such strategies so that children learn to recognize them and use them consciously (Tann, 1987). In this way discussion strategies can be explicitly taught, in a real context. A 'metalanguage' to describe them can be developed, giving participants a common language in which to discuss discussions. For example, teachers can, in the course of the discussion, say 'Can anyone think of some other alternative *ideas*'; 'That was a good *example*'; 'Let's *focus* on this idea a bit more'; 'If you *follow that through* . . .'; 'Are we *making progress* on this?'

The modelling of strategies that contribute to positive discussion is important. This might include inviting others to contribute ideas/information/experiences, comparing these and identifying similarities/differences, commenting or extending, modifying or focusing, querying and clarifying, seeking evidence and explanation, challenging or even rejecting.

Such skills take a long time to develop and need to be regularly used and discussed. Teacher support will be essential in the early stages as well as when a new task or new grouping makes new demands. It is, therefore, important for teachers to organize the class so that they can be free to support the discussion group. This usually means either having another adult (a parent or assistant) in the class to supervise some of the children or engaging the rest of the class in familiar activities that should not require a great deal of teacher attention.

Knowing exactly what is demanded in terms of time and organization for successful group activity is essential if confidence in groupwork is to develop. The teacher must ensure that the groups understand what is expected of them so that they can learn to monitor their own progress. De-briefing is also important, both in terms of the task and of the discussion itself. The management of such a supportive environment is a demanding, though rewarding, task for the teacher.

FURTHER READING

The following books report recent research which shows how adults and teachers can provide support for young children's conversational and discussion skills, both in the home and in school.

Bruner, J. S. (1983) *Child Talk*. London: Fontana.
Garton, A. and Pratt, C. (1989) *Learning to be Literate*. Oxford: Basil Blackwell.
Tizard, B. (1984) *Young Children Learning*. London: Fontana.
Tough, J. (1981) *A Place for Talk*. London: Ward Lock/Schools Council.
Wells, G. (1986) *Meaning Makers*. London: Hodder & Stoughton.
Wells, G. and Nicholls, J. (eds) (1985) *Language and Learning: An Interactional Perspective*. Lewes: Falmer Press.

ACTIVITY

Managing Discussions

Selections from the following checklist can be used to monitor discussion sessions. By varying the selections the monitoring can be used to focus on different aspects. It is helpful to tape record such sessions – or invite a colleague to monitor, as it is difficult at first to discuss and monitor simultaneously!

The teacher should:

- distribute attention carefully in order to give 'air-time' to as many children as wish to contribute;
- invite others to join in (especially those who don't volunteer) even if it is only to ask if they agree;
- ensure interchange and response to each other's comments from acceptance, to modification, extension and challenging;
- encourage children to empathize with each other, and provide sensitive support;
- encourage participants to generate alternative ideas, open out, extend/lift ideas being offered;
- encourage clarification through questioning and using details, elaboration, evidence, explanations, reasoning;
- encourage focusing/funnelling through further probing of ideas, their relevance, appropriateness;
- encourage hypothesizing, predicting, follow-through;
- encourage comparison, classification, sequencing, prioritizing;
- reorientate the discussion if it appears to be getting 'stuck';
- provide information if necessary to move the discussion along;
- review the progress of the discussion;
- evaluate the success of the discussion.

. . . . so that the participants make meanings together, and learn to learn in a group.

1.3.   PLANNING CONTEXTS FOR CLASSROOM TALK

(i)   Managing for oracy: grouping

The ORACLE research cited earlier analysed further features of primary classroom life which have relevance to managing the work in the primary classroom (Galton, Simon and Croll, 1980). Of particular interest, were the findings relating to the organization of time spent on different areas of the curriculum. The investigators found that basic literacy work (mostly writing, with only 2 per cent oral work) accounted for a third of learning time; a further third was spent on number work and a third on topic work, including art and craft activities.

The research also showed how children were organized in order to do the work. It pinpointed the need to distinguish between the ways in which the children were seated (often in groups around a table or cluster of desks) as opposed to the way in which they worked. It was found that 90 per cent of the teachers never used collaborative groupwork. The few who did employ this organizational form did so in art and craft and topic work in about equal proportions. Very few used collaborative groupwork for basic subjects. Where this did occur it was usually in maths, for occasional 'practical' sessions, in 'streamed' ability groups. Hence the unique learning context that collaborative groupwork can provide was denied to most children. Yet it is precisely such mixed-ability collaborative groupwork which has been found to be of such value in the primary classroom in developing 'talking for learning'.

There is a growing body of research showing how advantageous groupwork can be to both high- and low-ability children (Barnes and Todd, 1977; Sharon, 1980; Swing and Patterson, 1982; Webb, 1982). So why do we find it so rarely being practised in primary classrooms?

It seems that teachers are not sure when and how to use groups, or how to monitor the outcomes. Groupwork is frequently avoided because teachers are not sure about the precise purposes of such groups, or about what kinds of provisions should be made. They are also unsure about how to intervene during the process of such groups, and how to identify the end products. Each of these will now be examined.

Purposes of groupwork

Groups can be used for many reasons; the reason will determine the size and composition of the group.

(a) Short-term groupings can be used as 'buzz groups', to generate as many different ideas as possible in, say, a three-minute period. The openness of such a group could be encouraging to a shy child, though the pace at which it might operate could be frightening to a reflective child. The group can be quite large (perhaps eight to twelve), so that plenty of ideas can be generated which can then be sorted and acted upon in smaller, more leisurely groupings.

(b) Groups of about four to six children can be used for medium-term ventures, such as a specific problem-solving task, or alternatively as a forum for sharing thoughts and ideas, for example, in response to a story or poem or to provide critical support for each other's writings. In such groups children can try out ideas (oral rehearsal), sound out audience needs and thereby find ways of clarifying ideas and learn to sort and sequence ideas to improve coherence.

(c) Longer-term groupings can be used for more extended investigatory projects. This might involve a group of children working on the same (or set) of related activities over a period of time. This type of groupwork can be particularly advantageous in topic work.

(d) Finally, the whole class can become a short-term group, which gathers to discuss and prepare for an activity or to share problems that have arisen or results that have been discovered. The whole class can also be used as a feedback group to report on the progress of individual or group activities.

Provision

Problem-solving and investigatory groups should be encouraged to use a wide variety of materials and modes of learning so that children with different abilities can all be given a chance to make a positive contribution. The group's task needs to be designed to include various ways of exploring the problem, using, for example:

● visual and graphic resources

- oral/aural resources
- own recalled experiences
- own imagination and ideas.

Clearly, each of these types of provision makes particular demands of the children. By carefully preparing the task, a teacher can ensure that it is so structured that it provides an opportunity for each child to participate. A similar range of media for presenting the outcomes of the group's activity needs to be considered (oral talk/tape, drama play/puppets, written or visual formats, e.g. 2-D pictures/charts, 3-D models, etc.).

When considering provision it is important to identify the type of task being set (Phillips, 1985) in terms of whether it is

- operational,
- experiential,
- expositional,
- hypothetical, or
- argumentational.

These distinctions highlight the types of demands made upon a group and may help a teacher to anticipate what kind of difficulties might arise and therefore what kind of provision is needed.

Processes

Children need to become aware of the progress of their own discussions in order to help them to monitor their success and choose appropriate strategies. Tuckman (1965) suggests that four stages can be identified in the life-cycle of a discussion:

- forming (establishing roles and 'getting started')
- storming (handling the confusion and possible conflict relating to 'getting settled')
- norming (developing group conventions or 'getting going')
- performing (when the group are 'getting on with it').

However, whilst 'getting on with it' there are further stages which could be described as an

- initial stage of exploring the task itself (characterized by suggestions which generate ideas and some instant responses)

- developmental stage (characterized by elaborating ideas through clarifying, explaining, expanding by comparing and analysing, justifying and evaluating ideas before following one through)
- concluding and review stage (characterized by the group examining their own results and reviewing the success of the task and of their collaborative abilities).

Each of these stages makes different demands and will be characterized by different kinds of talk. It is also necessary to recognize that the pace of the contributions will vary. Finally, it is important for the participants to realize the positive role that silent thinking can play, for without such 'space' for reflection and consideration a 'discussion' can easily generate more heat than light.

The use of a range of policies for grouping can play an important part in providing contexts in which different oracy strategies will be demanded. Obviously different children have different needs and teachers need to monitor the varying provisions within their classroom so that they can be sure that they are providing a full range of opportunities for developing talking and listening. Criteria listed in this section could form the basis for a checklist of provision.

FURTHER READING

The following references discuss some of the general issues involved in planning and managing groupwork.

Tann, C. S. (1988) 'Grouping and the integrated classroom' in Thomas, G. and Feiler, A. (eds) *Planning for Special Needs*. Oxford: Basil Blackwell.

Waterhouse, P. (1983) *Managing the Learning Process*. London: McGraw-Hill.

The next three titles relate to infant, junior and middle-school age ranges respectively.

Willes, M. (1983) *Children into Pupils*. London: Routledge & Kegan Paul.

Phillips, T. (1985) 'Beyond lip-service' in Wells, G. and Nicholls, J. (eds) *Language and Learning: An Interactive Perspective*. Lewes: Falmer Press.

Barnes, D. and Todd, F. (1977) *Communication in Small Groups*. London: Routledge & Kegan Paul.

(ii)   Motivation and matching

Success is important for every child, particularly for those who don't often get a chance to succeed. It is crucial, therefore, to ensure that a variety of appropriate organizational contexts and different modes of learning are provided so that children can be more likely to experience success.

Children who are less confident with the printed word may perform better in a group context using an oral mode. Those who are reflective, or those who are less socially confident, may prefer an individual or pair context and a (slower) experimental task. Those who are risk-takers, impulsive or extrovert may find the context of a group initially frustrating and become dominating and impatient, but could learn to find the discipline of working with others a productive restraint, for example, if the task requires the physical help of participants (e.g. in constructional activities).

In schools where talking to learn is not firmly established there may be an initial problem in developing positive attitudes towards learning through talk, so that it is not considered a 'soft option' or 'mere chat'. Children frequently perceive learning as 'acquiring facts, which are written down', not as 'exploring ideas, through discussion', but this view can only have come to them from adults, so it is parents, governors, teachers and heads who, above all, have to be encouraged to take a positive view of oracy.

Talking to learn, especially through collaborative groupwork, imposes very particular demands on both the participating children and the teacher. The children need extensive oral language and considerable social skills. There will also be the cognitive demands engendered by the task on which the group is engaged.

Apart from matching context and mode to facilitate success, it is also important to ensure that the tasks are at the appropriate level of learning for individual children. Bennett (1984) identified five different levels and purposes of activities which were set for children in the classroom:

● incremental tasks (to acquire new skills/knowledge)

- restructuring tasks (to advance and use known skills)
- enrichment tasks (to apply known skills to new contexts)
- practice tasks (to reinforce skills assumed to be known)
- revision tasks (to reactivate skills assumed to be known)

A classroom teacher could use this set of variables to analyse the tasks that are planned for the classroom and thus maximize a suitable match between task and child. It is equally important to analyse the activities that children instigate in order to anticipate when support might become necessary.

Pacing of activities is as important as variety in encouraging positive attitudes and developing skills. Otherwise, just as the session is beginning to close and the important group de-briefing is about to begin, children who have already finished their activity may become restless. This affects the children's willingness to review what they have done and evaluate their individual and group achievements. To support such a process, a formal system of verbal report-back (live or on tape) could be introduced, or comments could be 'logged'. If the children know what to do next and there is a strategic use of positive stand-by activities and/or any available adult help, this can make all the difference in achieving a successful use of discussion in the classroom.

(iii) Monitoring and recording

Two forms of monitoring are crucial to the classroom teacher. In the first instance monitoring exactly what learning is being offered in the classroom facilitates planning. This kind of monitoring of classroom provision is now a requirement of the National Curriculum. It is intended to help the teacher who is planning a programme for learning to match classroom activities to each child's diagnosed needs. The analysis of tasks in terms of the criteria (i.e. Attainment Targets and skills, attitudes, knowledge and understandings) that a teacher hopes a child will achieve provides a management framework. This helps to keep track of what learning opportunities are offered. That same set of criteria can also be used as a monitoring framework to keep track of how well individual children have achieved.

Such frameworks can be constructed in a grid formation, listing the learning components (or Attainment Target strands) across the top of the page and the activities (for a management record) down the side. For individual progress records, the same format can be overlaid by a page with children's names down the side instead.

Some teachers prefer a 'wheel' format of concentric circles. This reduces the apparently hierarchical or linear assumptions about learning, though components are still separated and thus 'ordered' into specific rings within the concentric circles. Whatever format is devised, it should make it possible to record information quickly and to read the information contained in it, so it can be used to 'inform' (School Examinations and Assessment Council, SEAC, 1990) the planning of the next set of matched tasks.

The second kind of monitoring concerns what learning actually takes place, as noted in an individual child's progress record or profile. For both types of monitoring it is necessary for the teacher to listen, look and learn and to find ways of managing time in the classroom for monitoring. For example:

- listening to the children's talk provides a unique insight to how the children think, for oracy helps to make their learning process accessible,
- conferencing about children's work can help to show their perceptions and reactions to the task, to themselves, to their achievements: oral 'miscues' can reveal children's understandings in any of these areas,
- talking about books (rather than just listening to them read) can indicate how much they have understood and how well or meaningfully they have read and also whether they can read 'between the lines' and 'beyond the lines' in a critical and responsive fashion,
- making time to observe children working in a group, making a model, browsing in the book corner, using a reference book, or drafting stories provide further insights into children's attitudes, skills and knowledge.

Ways of 'creating' time for monitoring is a key goal of classroom management. SEAC (1990) suggests scrutinizing classroom practices in order to encourage the children to be less teacher-dependent. This should involve:

- reviewing the storage and accessibility to children of materials,
- examining classroom routines,
- reassessing the size and sequence of curriculum units and making sure the children know what they need to do next,
- greater use of whole-class public discussion on the purpose, process, problems and products of activities so that peer-tutoring (mutual help) is encouraged and effective.

Having gained time for monitoring, it is necessary to clarify the purposes for which one is observing the children:

- formative (to help plan 'what' the next activity should be)
- diagnostic (to guide 'which' kind of help is most needed)
- summative (to show 'where' the child is going)
- evaluative (to provide general information on 'how well' the child is doing).

These different purposes also relate to different audiences – child; class teacher (or supply); colleagues (e.g. transfer between schools); parents – though many types of assessment will be useful for more than one audience. This issue of purpose and audience needs to be considered when deciding the suitability of different forms of recording the information collected through monitoring.

If teachers monitor successfully along these lines they can learn a great deal about individual children. But it involves careful class management so that the necessary time is made available on a regular, though not necessarily frequent, basis for every child. To maximize the effectiveness of such precious time for observation, it is important to be highly selective and to consider:

- which particular child(ren) e.g. 1–4 children
- why and with which language objectives in mind e.g. 3–6 criteria
- what will count as evidence and will therefore be monitored
- how it will be recorded and later used
- when the observation will take place and
- what the other children will be doing meanwhile

Initially it may be helpful to plan brief periods of observation time, e.g. just 2–5 consecutive minutes. And to enable the teacher to 'sample' what is happening at different stages the times could be varied: for example, to coincide with the beginning, middle and end of an activity. Clearly, children behave very differently at different times: some work better early in the day, others later; some are slow to warm up, others quick to give up.

There are many possible alternatives when it comes to deciding upon observational practices. On some occasions it is preferable to observe one child a day on all activities. On others it may be preferable to observe all the children working on the same selected target attainment criteria. The important step is to have made the decision on positive grounds so that the time spent observing will be of maximum benefit.

Apart from the concerns regarding how to observe, there are also the issues relating to how to record. Although checklists may prove a simple format to use, they can rarely be constructed so as to tell the whole story. Many teachers prefer to supplement them with a 'long hand' comments section.

Another extension is to encourage children to make self-assessments and record those. For younger children, a teacher can record the child's appraisal comments, or children can represent their views by pictorial means. This is most often achieved by using a range of 'smiley' faces (mouth curving upward for a positive evaluation, mouth straight for mixed evaluation, and downward-curving mouth for negative evaluation). For older children logs can be kept, to which teachers and parents can respond so that they become interactive dia-logs.

The ILEA Language Record, suggested by the Kingman and Cox Reports, proposes a detailed approach that includes a structured framework within which open-ended comments can be made under broad headings. This document also includes a section for background information about the home and the child's language experiences. Sections are included for interviews with the child's parents and conferences with the child, as well as the teacher's comments.

In order to collect data that can be used reliably as a basis for such comments it is important to engage in a range of alternative approaches to collecting useful classroom information about individual children. In a busy teaching situation it is easy for information to be impressionistic, sporadic and incomplete. It is important to try to collect data that is:

• descriptive (rather than judgemental)

- dispassionate (not based on supposition and prejudice)
- discerning (so that it is forward-looking)
- diagnostic (so that it can lead us into better action).

Monitoring of children's learning is a crucial part of the reflective cycle in which every teacher needs to engage, so as to 'inform' their planning (see Figure 1). There is a danger that this process of

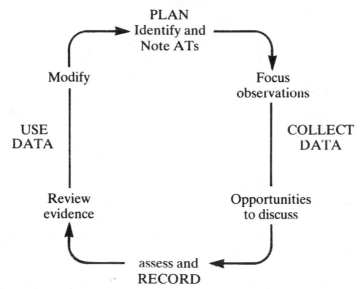

Figure 1

plan–collect–record–use becomes very laborious and turns into an end in itself. The more the children are encouraged to self-monitor the more the burden is shared and the more it becomes, in itself, a real learning experience for all parties concerned. Any improvement in monitoring and, therefore, in matching is going to feed positively into motivation and individual progress. It is developing this kind of approach to classroom monitoring which is fundamental to success in managing the primary classroom. Monitoring is not the antithesis of teaching: it is a prerequisite.

CHECKLIST OF MONITORING PROCEDURES

The following alternatives are suggested as methods of HOW to collect data:

- *Systematic observation*: using a schedule/list of behaviours to inform you about how a child works, which can be checked off every time the listed behaviour is seen
- *Field-notes*: long-hand notes to describe what the child(ren) does in as much detail as possible (quoting examples of what is said and done)
- *Questionnaires*: these can assess children's perceptions of what they enjoyed/found difficult or would like to do more of
- *Conferencing/Interviews*: longer periods of in-depth discussion with a child
- *Video and/or audiotape*: of children/teacher in the classroom, to analyse at leisure later, perhaps with the children, as part of their self-analysis
- *Children's logs*: diaries which children can keep of how they respond to particular learning tasks
- *Analysis of children's work*: and of course the analytic marking of children's work so that the patterns of 'miscues' can be seen in context, rather than isolated 'mistakes' noted and corrected.

FURTHER READING

Hook, D. (1983) *Studying Classrooms*. Deakin, Victoria: University of Deakin Press.

Jagger, A. and Smith-Burke, M. T. (eds) (1985) *Observing the Language Learner*. Newark, Delaware: International Reading Association.

SEAC (1990) *A Guide to Teacher Assessment*. London: Heinemann.

Stubbs, M. and Robinson, B. (1979) *Observing Language*. PE 232, Bk 5. Milton Keynes: Open University Press.

CHECKLIST OF RECORDING METHODS

There are also a number of different ways in which the data collected, when analysed, can be marked up on a child's Record Sheet. Individual teachers, schools and authorities have a range of preferences. The following suggestions indicate alternative ways of HOW to record data:

- *Grids*: shaded differentially to indicate different levels of achievement
- *Wheels*: also shaded (these may be preferable because they appear to be less linear in their assumptions about development)
- *Rating scales*: very simple to fill in and easy to read but lack the opportunity for nuance unless very lengthy and cumbersome
- *Checklists of selected behaviours*: also shaded (these can become cumbersome)
- *Folders of the child's work*: chosen by the child, the teacher, the parents with brief comment as to why it was chosen (including tapes of stories composed, reports given, or discussions held)
- *Running record or diary* of 'significant' changes (or continued lack of change), which could be attached to a folder
- *Summative report* made by teacher (including child and parent) about things a child likes or doesn't like, needs help on and main achievements and areas for attention.

These methods can of course be used in combination. For suggestions concerning WHAT criteria might be used in any of these forms of recording information, see the final sections of Chapters 2, 4, and 6.

Chapter 2

Children as Talkers and Listeners

INTRODUCTION

This chapter will focus on interactive teaching and learning in the context of oracy. The framework for action assumes that children are active learners who play a crucial part in their own, and others', learning process. It also assumes that the teacher plays a key role in modelling strategies, supporting the children's strategies and helping to make their understandings explicit.

Because there is now a statutory curriculum within which all State schools must operate, it is sensible to discuss classroom action in terms of the Orders for English, the given Attainment Targets and their supporting Programmes of Study. Although these are enshrined in law, it is still important to consider them critically and challenge them where necessary. Further, the Orders do not describe all that must be taught, only the minimum. Nor do they prescribe *how* English should be taught but only *what* should be taught.

The first section of this chapter outlines the key targets for oracy. The second section discusses ways of developing oracy in the primary context, using the framework of the 'strands' identified in the Working Party Report (1989, para 15.19):

- assimilate and act appropriately on information, explanations and instructions (transactional);
- collaborate and participate positively and with understanding in general discussion (collaborative);

- communicate imaginatively and effectively as performers and readers (dramatic);
- put forward and properly support statements of personal feeling, opinion or viewpoint (personal and persuasive);
- develop and express an awareness of varieties of spoken English and the relationship between spoken and written language (awareness).

2.1. TARGETS FOR DEVELOPING ORACY

The National Curriculum, as expressed in the Statutory Orders for English, has one oracy component comprising both talking and listening. The rationale for this is stated as being due to the reciprocal and integrated nature of the processes of listening and speaking.

The Attainment Target for Oracy proposes the following aim:

> The development of pupils' understanding of the spoken word and the capacity to express themselves effectively in a variety of speaking and listening activities, matching style and response to audience and purpose.

A range of audiences are suggested (Statements of Attainment, levels 1–5), which are deemed to be progressively more demanding:

- child as participant in a group situation (with/without a teacher)
- child with a teacher on a one-to-one basis (conferencing/feedback)
- child with a peer partner
- child with a known adult
- child as a member of a group reporting to a group, class or school with teachers and unknown adults.

Each of these audiences makes different social demands on a child and requires different types of confidence. The particular nature of each context also demands a range of speaking and listening styles.

It is a gross over-simplification to imagine that the size of the group alone determines the level of demands made upon the participants. Other factors which need to be taken into account include social, language and task demands. For example:

- relationships within the group – its composition;
- degree of formality of the occasion;
- familiarity with the group members and with group processes;
- familiarity and interest in the task – its content,
  e.g. degree of abstraction, controversiality, complexity;
- purpose of the task – to 'exchange' or 'impart',
  e.g. exploratory and formative ↔ explanatory and summative;
- appropriateness of 'style' – register, delivery;
  e.g. officious ↔ conversational; flamboyant ↔ stolid; cooperative ↔ confrontational; serious ↔ flippant . . .;
- appropriateness of 'response' to speaker or listeners
  e.g. respectful ↔ sarcastic; courteous ↔ rude,
  where expectations may include didactic monologue or brief interchanges or extended discussion.

Typical classroom activities involve a wide range of contexts which may embrace many of these features. For example, in being part of a group, though not necessarily a vocal member, there is still the need to listen, follow, respond and carry out any agreed action in a collaborative context. Speaking in a one-to-one situation may or may not be perceived as threatening, depending on the social relationships and the task in hand. Talking with a peer partner in an informal situation, probably in a conversational style, may be less threatening, though it still provides the challenge of handling the social as well as the cognitive task demands. Talking with a known adult is likely to require a slightly different kind of language register because of what might be a semi-formal situation. However, talking as part of a group initially requires informal though purposeful decision-making, perhaps followed by a more formal presentation to a larger audience.

The English Working Party (DES, 1989) identified specific purposes or strands, for which oracy should be developed. The communicative functions of these strands can be summarized as transactional, collaborative, dramatic, personal and, also, an awareness of language and an ability to evaluate and reflect upon it. However, this separation of functions is 'simply an organizational device', for it is recognized that

> ... language development is not linear but recursive, with pupils returning repeatedly to the same aspects of competence and reinforcing their skills on each occasion. In addition, what is difficult will vary from different individuals and according to circumstances: some topics will themselves vary in difficulty; some people will perceive the difficulty of the same task differently; and circumstances may make an otherwise easy task seem very hard (para 15.20)

Finally, the Cox Report recognized the 'intimate links between dialect and identity' and the 'damage to self-esteem and motivation which can be caused by indiscriminate "correction" of dialect forms' (para. 15.15):

> All children should be supported in valuing their own dialects and in using them where appropriate to context and purpose, but they should be able to use Standard English when it is necessary and helpful to do so in speaking as well as in writing. (para 15.15)

> In general terms, we advocate that there should be explicit teaching about the nature and functions of Standard English in the top years of the primary school. (para 4.38)

> The teaching of Standard English should ... focus on the differences between written and spoken English ... then it need not reject the language of the home. ... No-one uses written Standard English as his or her native dialect. (para 4.39)

> Teaching Standard English should draw upon (pupils') knowledge of other dialects. The aim is to add Standard English to the repertoire, not to replace other dialects or languages. (para 4.43)

It would seem from these statements that Standard English is viewed primarily as a written form, identifiable by its vocabulary and grammar: its constructions which 'ensure the intended meaning is expressed with precision and clarity', the way 'sentences can be linked together' and the way 'ideas can be introduced and given prominence'. It is anticipated that by gaining competence in written Standard English pupils will gain 'sufficient knowledge to be able to convert this into competence in spoken Standard English when appropriate'. Further, these competences will be gained, not by correcting the speech of pupils in any general way, but rather by setting up situations in which it is 'natural to use

ACTIVITY

Attitudes to Language

Questionaires and rating scales can encourage respondents to challenge and pinpoint the views which are usually kept implicit.

Answer the following questions and share your answers with a colleague. Think of the classroom implications of your views.

Are you satisfied with your profile?
How does it relate to school policy?
Does it accurately reflect your classroom practice?
What changes do you think should be made?

		Agree				Disagree	
1.	Poor grammar and spelling should always be corrected.	1	2	3	4	5	6
2.	It is confusing for young children to use two languages in school.	1	2	3	4	5	6
3.	Working-class children can communicate just as well as middle-class children.	1	2	3	4	5	6
4.	The first task for all children is to learn good English.	1	2	3	4	5	6
5.	We should always use books with positive images of all nationalities.	1	2	3	4	5	6
6.	Dialects are bad English.	1	2	3	4	5	6
7.	We are doing a disservice to our children if we don't teach them to use good English.	1	2	3	4	5	6
8.	No one should use expressions which are racist/sexist, e.g. 'a black mood', 'boys' games'.	1	2	3	4	5	6
9.	The more languages that are spoken in the classroom the greater the teaching resource.	1	2	3	4	5	6

Standard English' such as role play, drama and media work, producing news programmes, class panel discussions or debates (paras 4.49–4.52).

The section on Standard English touches on a very sensitive area. The Cox Report rightly associates 'language' with 'identity': it is this which makes it so sensitive. Many believe that Standard English is needed for access to certain kinds of jobs and organizations and that it carries social status and is therefore associated with 'class'. The same people argue that children are entitled to have access to a full range of opportunities in adult life and therefore teachers are perpetuating discrimination if they do not extend children's language repertoire. However, others, while recognizing that dialect often relates to discrimination, believe that to accept this is to support the status quo, and that, rather than extend children's language repertoire, schools should challenge the attitudes which sustain such a system.

FURTHER READING

The following books examine aspects of the multilingual school.

Edwards, V. (1983) *Language in the Multicultural Classroom*. London: Batsford Academic.

Hill, D. (1976) *Teaching in the Multiracial School*. London: Methuen.

Houlton, D. (1985) *All Our Languages*. London: Edward Arnold.

Johnson, K. and Morrow, K. (eds) (1981) *Communication in the Classroom*. London: Longman.

Miller, J. (1983) *Many Voices*. London: Routledge.

Saunders, M. (1982) *Multicultural Teaching*. London: McGraw-Hill.

Stubbs, M. and Hillier, H. (eds) (1983) *Readings on Language and Classrooms*. London: Methuen.

Trudgill, P. (1975) *Accent, Dialect and the School*. London: Edward Arnold.

2.2. PROGRAMMES FOR ACTION

The transition from home to school

Children have already mastered an enormous linguistic repertoire before coming to school. They understand and use language for many different purposes. However, the language world of the school is often quite different from that of the home. Classroom language has a form of its own and has specific functions which are unique. For such reasons many of the skills the children have acquired at home are positively dysfunctional in the school context.

Research findings have produced conflicting evidence concerning the nature of language in the home. Whilst earlier work in the Bernstein tradition found marked differences in the 'codes' used by working-class and middle-class homes (Robinson, 1981), recent work by Wells (1981), Heath (1983), Tizard and Hughes (1984) has demonstrated the richness of the home language environment – across all socio-economic categories – compared to that of the school, due partly to the greatly reduced adult–child ratio compared to that which exists in primary schools. Not only is the language environment different, but the language functions and contexts are different. These researches showed that language in the home was usually concerned with remarks about the here-and-now in a descriptive running-commentary style, was often related to giving instructions or making requests about an ongoing activity and was frequently accompanied by gesture and action. Further evidence of the differences between home and school can be found in Lindfors' (1980) research which identified distinct patterns in children's questions: pre-school/kindergarten children asked 45 per cent social questions, 33 per cent curiosity, and 23 per cent procedural, but primary children asked 14 per cent social, 19 per cent curiosity and 66 per cent procedural questions.

However, in the school situation, the function of language is often related to activities which are about to commence in the near future, or to stimulating recall of something in the past, speculating about events or encouraging evaluation and reflection on a current activity. Hence the role and character of language is different and the demands made upon the language users are different to those of the home. Furthermore, the child's role as a language-user alters.

One particular example of these discontinuities has been identified by Heath (1982) who found specific differences in the use of questions in the home compared to those in school. At home, questions were more likely to focus on comparing rather than naming: and were more likely to ask for personal responses ('Was that nice?', 'Did you like it?') rather than for definitions ('What is it?'). Thus home questions are more likely to focus on feelings/ emotions/people rather than on identifying objects. Questions at home were also less likely to be of the type where the answer was already known (i.e. pseudo-questions). Further, at home children were less likely to have experienced questions as hidden directives such as 'Would you like to put on your painting apron?', or statements like 'I'm hungry' (said in a messy classroom at 11.55 am), or commands as invitations ('Have a drink').

Talk at school has often been regarded as de-contextualized, divorced from real-life purposes (or re-contextualized into the particular environment of a school setting). School language is also associated with telling rather than showing, hence relying more on verbal communication. It carries a greater burden of transmitting information, with subsequently less support from accompanying para-verbal communication such as gesture, activity and similar aspects of visual communication. Further, the purpose of language at home is 'getting things done', whereas language at school often seems to be for the sake of eliciting talk or assessing the child.

One of the major differences between home and school, consistently highlighted by research, is that classroom situations are often evaluative (Jackson, 1968) and the social and language conventions are very different from those in a domestic conversation. In the classroom adults frequently ask children what they are doing or how they did something, in order to discover the children's thinking or feelings, and to check on their understanding. If the same number or kind of questions were asked of children, or of other adults, in a domestic conversation it would be inappropriate and even offensive. In school children soon learn to accept such questioning as peculiar to the 'culture' of the school. However, we need to be aware of the difficulties some children may have in adapting to such a 'culture', particularly those who may feel uneasy with the language of the school, perhaps because they come from very different linguistic and cultural backgrounds.

In terms of the role of the child as a language user, Willes (1983) found that on entering school, children had to learn not to talk and not to take the initiative: in fact to learn to become pupils. Children very quickly learn that their role is a passive one, and primarily that of a listener. As it is the teacher who largely controls language in the classroom, much depends on the ability of the teacher to help to make participation easier. We need to analyse some of the demands made upon children as talkers and listeners and to discuss ways in which a teacher might try to develop oracy.

(i)   Transmitting information and instructions

(a)   Transmitting information: describing an event, telling 'news'

Children already bring with them considerable experience of such activities from their home environment, where they have recounted daily happenings to a parent or grandparent. Yet the expectations of a similar activity in school is significantly different. Research by Michaels and Collins (in Romaine, 1984) indicates a number of ways in which the language demands of the home and the school differ.

The most common communication context when children are the 'speakers' is during Newstime. Teachers' purposes in holding such occasions are that children should gain confidence in talking in a different context and to a larger audience. They also use this opportunity to try to develop the children's vocabulary, by encouraging the child to describe very explicitly the object they have brought in (which everyone can see), or their visit to a fairground (to which most of the rest of the class also went). The children, however, have different reasons for offering to speak. They want to be the star of the show for a while and to tell the class of their own particular personal experience (which may not be of interest to others). Hence, the demand for explicitness is puzzling to the child, who is often put off by the teacher's interruptions and requests to describe items in more detail.

Teachers need to question why children are asked to perform in this way and what the speaker or listener learns from it. Perhaps the speaker feels valued, by the teacher at least, and can gain confidence in speaking in public. Perhaps they also get better at speaking – at speaking up and delivering the information (the Programmes of Study mention 'audibility'). They may get better at structuring and sequencing the information ('explaining and presenting ideas'), at anticipating the listener's needs and making information clear ('reflect on their use of language', 'adjust their language and its delivery to suit their audience', 'help the listener').

However, it is easy for a child to pour forth an unstructured stream of consciousness which is difficult to channel or stem. In such cases it is hard to identify what either the speaker or listeners gain.

The teacher for whom communicative 'competence' and situational 'appropriateness' are clearly defined goals is better placed to help the children attain them. In order to help achieve such goals, teachers can prompt the child, by saying, 'When did . . . happen?', 'What do you think you need to tell everyone first so that they will understand it better?'. With such preliminary preparation children can be encouraged to organize their thoughts in order to help their audience, so that listeners understand when and where the incident took place, what happened to whom, why and with what consequences. With this type of support and scaffolding, children should be able:

- to 'describe an event' (AT 1, level 2) and
- 'relate real/imaginary events in a connected narrative'. (level 3)

But what is the listener's role? Is it to attend to the speaker, and value what they have to say? Is it to show interest non-verbally (by looking and listening, by facial expressions) and verbally (by responding and becoming an active participant)? Listeners can be encouraged to be active participants by a speaker, and by whoever is leading the session. For example, others can be invited to compare the information with something similar which they have done recently; or be invited to suggest what they might have done or felt; or encouraged to ask questions for further clarification. Listeners can be shown how to use key words such as 'why' (causes/purposes), 'how' (process), 'so what'/'what then' (significance) and relate personal reaction and feelings (evaluation). This can help both the speakers and the listeners become more aware of the listener's needs. Such development will enable children to be able:

- to listen with an increased span of concentration to other children and adults, asking and responding to questions and commenting on what has been said. (AT 1, level 3)

Researchers have identified marked differences between the conversational styles of talk and the formal style of 'a talk' as in Newstime or Report-back (Tannen, 1984). It would appear that teachers are encouraging children in formal skills which are highly appropriate to literacy: they are in fact asking for an oral presentation in a literary mode. The more formal type of school 'talk' illustrates such literary criteria. In addition to precise vocabulary, clear structure and explicit linkages to promote coherence, teachers often expect a linear, single-focus, logically-sequenced delivery – in what is termed a 'topic-centered' style (Tannen, 1984). In the school context it is the teacher who decides what is relevant to the topic, and even decides who is relevant to the task by selecting particular children to contribute. This teacher-controlled, 'topic-centered talk' is in stark contrast to a conversational style of 'talking' where the content is negotiated by the contributors and the course is often more rambling or 'rhapsodic', multi-focus and tangential. This conversational style can be described as 'topic-associated'.

The more structured form of presenting information to a teacher or group of peers is a feature of classrooms across all areas of the curriculum. It is enshrined in curriculum documents in other core subjects, Maths and Science, which also have stated targets involving oracy (DES, 1989). For example, children should

in Maths: talk about their own work and ask questions, make predictions from their experience, describe current work and review/check the results;
in Science: describe and communicate their observations, ask questions and suggest how and why, sequence main features.

The foundation subjects such as History and Geography also include sections on 'asking [historical/geographical] questions', 'demonstrating sensitive awareness', 'synthesis and communication of ideas', graphical presentation, as well as qualitative response. Recognition of the role of communication across the curriculum is important. These skills of discussion and investigation, of collaborative groupwork and final presentation can be developed in all 'subject' areas and in all activities.

(b)   Receiving and transmitting instructions

In many classrooms children are often cast in the role of listeners. This emphasis on receptive listening can reinforce a passive role for the child. Hence it is particularly important to involve the listeners in a more active way and encourage children to perceive listening as a reactive or even interactive situation. These skills can be developed and enjoyed by very young children, especially if presented in the form of traditional games such as Chinese Whispers, Simon Says, Pass the Portrait (where child A describes a person to child B who tells child C who draws it for child A . . .) and frequently feature in published materials such as *Listen, Think, Do*.

Speakers can help listeners by making the purpose clear and by structuring the instructions (in ways similar to those outlined in the section on exposition, p. 24). They should also make clear to listeners what role they can play and what they can actively do during the process of listening to the instructions. For example, listeners need to be alerted to the need to focus their attention; to be warned that this information is relevant and important to them. The listener needs to know what the instructions are going to be about – in general (e.g. school trip, wet lunch hour, time to tidy up), what they have to do during the instruction-giving (e.g. listen, take down details, ask about anything that has been left out or forgotten) and when they are supposed to respond (e.g. immediately (by lining up), at home (by asking for a signature), or tomorrow (by returning their library book)) and what they are expected to do next.

Apart from 'preparing' the listener in this way, the speaker can also encourage children to participate in constructing and giving the instructions. Many classroom instructions are routine, or could be deduced from the situation. Hence children can be invited to think for themselves and for each other and suggest what the instructions should be. In order to encourage independence and interdependence the teacher can invite the children to explain and remind each other, or to decide collectively. This takes up more time, of course, and is not for emergency situations, but it can turn teacher-given routines into a children's learning activity.

Identifying verbal or non-verbal 'response' as part of the listener's role may help to emphasize a further aspect of listening as being an active experience. It has been estimated that 65 per cent of social meaning is conveyed non-verbally (Stephens and Valentine, 1986) and that 62 per cent of an effective listener's time is spent looking at the speaker. By the end of the primary years children learn the functions of facial reactions and can interpret them as well as the average adult. Their ability to control and use non-verbal behaviour (gaze, body posture and movement, distance, signifying noises such as 'ums') also develops with age, but more slowly.

This listener-response element of interaction is often difficult. Listeners are so busy trying to follow the verbal flow as it emerges, bit by bit, that it is quite hard to reflect on the whole to see if it 'makes sense'. Research has shown (Dickson, 1981) that younger children usually blame themselves if they don't understand: they fail to realize that the message itself might be at fault and that it could be altered and improved. Even if they do recognize this it may be difficult for them to identify what specifically was ambiguous. It may therefore be difficult for them to ask an appropriate question.

However, if listeners can identify at least part of the confusion and can ask for clarification, it is then the task of the speaker to be able to rephrase or elaborate. Young children usually find it difficult to rephrase and tend to repeat what was originally said. Hence the skill of asking questions in an active, interactive situation is one that has to be encouraged and developed.

Children, who have had successful experiences of conversational situations and who understand alternate turn-taking on the criteria of wanting to add something, find that on entering school the game has changed without the rules being explained. Willes (1983) asks 'How is it that a 5-year-old who speaks when he wants to becomes a 6-year-old who waits to be nominated'. Children also learn that what they say (and who they are) is constantly being evaluated. Being a pupil 'entails feeling secure enough to risk making mistakes (in the public forum of the classroom) and recognizing negative evaluation on the part of the teacher even if it is implicit'.

An alternative type of listening situation, requiring more active participation of the listener, is one which allows children to conduct an interview. This could, for example, be on a school trip or when a visitor comes to the school. Children may prefer to formulate a questionnaire of items to ask a speaker. During the interview, the children will need to listen carefully to extract information and be flexible in their questioning. For example, if in answering one question the speaker goes on to develop a related point the children may not recognize that this in fact answers a subsequent question: instead they may ask the pre-planned question, expecting to receive a further answer.

The aim of following instructions and information may also require children to listen and take notes. This is a particular form of reactive–extractive listening. Although not a common demand for primary age children, it can be a very useful skill to begin to acquire. It is important for the teacher to prepare the listeners by helping them to decide what information they need, how to note it, and what to do with it.

Making notes, being encouraged to jot down key words or phrases to remind listeners of what they have heard or just read in a paragraph, is a very demanding activity. Brief phrases may only be a few words which do not demand too much of the physical labour of writing. But successful note-taking requires the ability to analyse, select and summarize. Children may often find it easier to represent the information by a labelled diagram or annotated picture which allows them to undertake the cognitive demands of selecting and sorting, and to imagize specific aspects to aid recall, before they have to try to find words for it.

Despite the fact that 'transmitting' information and instructions is often considered to be the domain of the teacher, with the concomitant passive and receptive role for the children, it is important to remember that all communication and learning is active. This means that the teacher needs to find ways of helping children to understand the active nature of learning, even when there is little verbal interaction. Hence, it is important to extend the parameters of communication to include para-verbal and non-verbal means, and to emphasize the constructing of meanings rather than just their reception.

FURTHER READING

All these titles contain detailed research evidence relating to young children's communicative competence. Understanding such evidence helps in making realistic demands of children in the classroom.

Dickson, W. P. (1981) *Children's Oral Communicative Skills*. New York: Academic Press.
Lindfors, J. W. (1980) *Children's Language and Learning*. London: Prentice Hall.

ACTIVITY

Identifying Listening

How do we tell if children are listening? How well do they listen? Record/observe a range of individuals (including the teacher) during normal teaching–learning situations in a classroom. What difficulties do you notice children have when:

- talking to the class,
- reporting back to the class,
- discussing in group/class,
- speaking to other adults,
- chatting to friends.

What do you do to try to model strategies for each?
How do you support/extend/reward children's strategies?
How do you encourage children to be alert to different modes of interacting?
Note the types of listening called for and the contexts.
Note behaviours that might indicate that they heard/understood.
e.g. Did they:

> look at the speaker,
> look around,
> appear to follow,
> answer questions,
> offer contributions,
> take turns,
> show awareness of others' needs?

Did they:

> jot down phrases or words,
> attempt verbatim reports,
> make visual representations,
> listen carefully,
> talk about it afterwards,
> pay no attention?

Robinson, W. P. (1981) *Communicative Development.* New York: Academic Press.

Tannen, D. (ed.) (1982) *Spoken and Written Language.* Norwood, NJ: Ablex.

Tannen, D. (ed.) (1984) *Coherence in Spoken and Written Discourse.* Norwood, NJ: Ablex.

Willes, M. (1983) *Children into Pupils.* London: Routledge & Kegan Paul.

(ii)   Collaborative group discussions

In a teacher-controlled environment, children learn to take their cues from the teacher, in fact to become teacher-dependent. Examination of classroom interaction (Flanders, 1970; Galton, Simon and Croll, 1980) between teacher and pupil reveals a typical pattern of teacher question, pupil-answer, teacher-evaluation, or pupil-query, teacher-answer, or pupil-suggestion (initiation) and then teacher-evaluation (feedback).

This poses particular problems in encouraging the development of discussion skills. In such an interactive context the children need to communicate with each other and not just the teacher. They also have to learn to take the initiative and become more responsible for the course of the discussion. Instead of relying on the teacher to develop the discussion, the children have to employ a broader notion of 'response' – interaction/modification/extension/explanation – not just 'reply' or answer.

The teacher, however, plays an important role in developing children's discussion strategies, by modelling them herself and identifying and rewarding those used by the children (Tann and Armitage, 1986). However, Cook-Gumperz (in Wilkinson, 1982) found that teacher–pupil interaction differed with different (literacy) ability groups: the lower the ability of a group the less likely the teacher was to encourage contribution in a disciplined and productive way and therefore the less likely the children were to acquire the necessary (oracy) skills for discussion purposes.

A further set of differences emerges where children come from more than one cultural background and where interactive strategies and, in particular, adult–child interaction patterns are different (Keiffer and DeStefano in Jagger and Smith-Burke, 1985). It highlights the point that different people say things in different ways, and indeed in different ways on different occasions. Hence accents, dialects, registers, styles of talking all 'say' something themselves. It is not only what you say, but how you say it that contributes to communicative competence and comprehensive effectiveness.

The social, linguistic and cognitive skills and attitudes which are necessary to groupwork are not easily acquired by chance. They may be picked up through osmosis, if they are consistently modelled by an adult, in whole-class or small group discussions. More effectively, the skills and attitudes need to be identified, labelled and discussed by both the children and teacher. A meta-language for discussing discussions can help to clarify expectations and heighten awareness of each other's contributions. However, organizing a class, so that such skills can be modelled and prac-tised, is itself difficult to achieve in busy, crowded classrooms. A continuing policy for oracy which is applied consistently through-out the school is vitally important.

Small group discussion skills can often be modelled by the teacher in a whole-class situation. For young children, the sessions 'on the carpet' at the beginning of the day for 'News' or general instructions and information, or during the day in 'Report-back' sessions, or at the end of the day at 'Storytime' are all occasions when comment and discussion is likely to emerge.

It has already been noted how such sessions can become oppor-tunities for active participation by increasing the number of chil-dren that take a positive verbal role. Even if at first only a few children join in voluntarily, the others can benefit by listening and learning vicariously. This benefit will be increased if it is made explicit when the session becomes a 'discussion' (as opposed to 'information transmission'), meaning that the roles of listener and contributor are more fluid and interchangeable. Children can be overtly reminded to 'listen to the person who is speaking', to 'take turns'. They can be encouraged to respond to each other (rather than talk at the teacher), and also to provide a context, put events in a clear order, explain, give details, etc.

By such modelling in a whole-class situation the children can acquire the words for discussing discussions. When small group-work is set up, children can use this metalanguage, thus becoming more independent of the teacher, who in turn can feel more confi-dent when leaving children to work on their own in groups.

Developing discussion skills

Reception and infant children on entering school can already talk purposefully and confidently to a variety of people, in groups of different sizes for different reasons and in different ways. However, although many children arrive at school as skilled communicators (Tizard and Hughes, 1984; Wells, 1986) others clearly do not. But with a clear school policy and sufficient time invested in talk, in talking about talk and using it to learn about things which are important to the children, the whole class can begin to become effective talkers during their first year and begin to be explicit about the necessary strategies and skills.

How can children become good talkers? How can a teacher help children to develop as talkers? What are we aiming for? How can we monitor their progress? From the start discussion has to figure prominently. However, it takes time to develop a 'class of talkers'. One strategy is for the whole class to meet together two or three times a day for periods of about 20 minutes each. First thing in the morning, at register time, there is a chance for anyone to tell everyone some important news. The chief skill here, for the speaker, is to remember that the rest of the class doesn't know about the speaker's problems with a baby brother and why last night was so exciting. So the speaker has to learn to start before the 'beginning', to give the background before the event last night. The listeners have to learn to follow the story and get inside the speaker's head so as to fully appreciate its significance and be able to make sympathetic and supportive comments.

During an exchange of news the children, initially, need to be reminded of the Golden Rules, which they could devise. For example:

Don't all talk together.
Don't interrupt anyone.
Listen to the person who is speaking.

At first, the teacher may field the contributions and direct the discussion. She may call on the children who are 'bidding' for their turn (usually by putting up their hand). She may sometimes call upon shy children who look as though they might want to add something. To encourage listening the teacher needs to ask another child to comment on what a speaker has said: What do you think? What would you have done? Something like that happened to you the other day, didn't it? To encourage the children to clarify or extend their contributions, she may ask further specific questions (for clarification) or general open ones (to encourage further reflection, elaboration or exploration of ideas). Finally, she can indicate that she values their views and news by listening to them herself and by creating opportunities for the rest of the class to listen also. It is also helpful to identify and label a particular skill thus helping children to recognize it in practice: 'You *explained* that beautifully'; 'That's a very good *reason*'. The contribution can also be rewarded by praise indicated by tone of voice and expression: 'That's a marvellous *idea*'.

Another way to develop a 'classroom of talkers' is to have an ongoing project about which every child can speak because each is participating in this common investigation. An important feature of such a way of working is to let the children take greater responsibility for the planning and decision-making processes. It takes longer this way and there is less, immediately, to show for it (less to put up on the wall), but it allows the children to do all the thinking and talking 'for real'. It has practical outcomes upon which the children can take action and with that opportunity comes interest, involvement and motivation!

For example, a class which was working on 'sight' was going into town to the new shopping complex which had lots of 'distorting' glass. The children planned the trip. They knew they would be going in a mini-bus, but they had to decide how many would fit in, how much it would cost, which route to choose, how long it would take, what equipment they would need to take (pencils, etc.) and what to order for class lunches.

In planning this trip the children had to identify the problems, calculate the capacity of the bus, the distance, the cost. They had to make and complete a questionnaire of class needs. They had to draw conclusions ('We'll have to go twice'); give reasons ('Diesel is cheaper'); quote sources of evidence ('My dad says'); ask questions to clarify ('What'll it cost?'); and ask questions for points of information ('Who can we ask?') or to direct attention to issues ('What about lunch?'). They also predicted ('The driver should know'), empathized ('You can't disturb him, it's not fair'), used analogies to support suggestions ('We always use maps on holiday'), compromised on decisions about food ('O.K. we'll have to ask everyone') and collaborated through listening and contributing throughout.

By the end of their first year they were already remarkably competent in discussion skills. These skills had been modelled to them by their teacher, they had been practised with their teacher and the children were now able to use them in groups on their own. However, the class was not yet at a stage where they found it easy to make the skills explicit.

Children's views on being a good talker can reveal important misconceptions. For example, Scott (1989) found children believed that a 'good talker' was someone who talked a lot, who talked loudly or who wasn't boring. Quantity seemed to take precedence over quality. In class, it was thought that 'talking stops you working', 'you mustn't talk if you're doing something important like Maths or English' and 'it's alright if you do it quietly'. Finally, these children felt that talking was important so you could help people, and that it was a nice thing to do 'with friends', 'if you're worried', 'bored' or 'lonely'.

Clearly, in such classes there is a lot of work to be done to help children understand that talking is a form of learning, that it is 'important' in itself and being able to talk is only a very small part of learning to discuss. Nevertheless, if young children are introduced to such ideas from the earliest ages they soon show remarkable maturity in this demanding area of language.

However, by the time children are in the top infant class, many can be explicit concerning their own and others' discussion skills. They can also prove to be highly committed to discussion as a means of planning and decision-making, especially for issues which are of vital concern to themselves, such as the setting up of lunch-time clubs. Observation of a class of 6- and 7-year-olds showed how awareness of discussion strategies can lead to the development of those strategies. Such top infant children can be very accomplished as participants in discussions. They can demonstrate the ability to take turns, listen to each other to get ideas, give clear instructions and explanations, put their own views with evidence or justification where necessary, ask others to explain or elaborate if they do not understand a point made previously. They can also hypothesize and evaluate.

Despite such developed skills, a teacher's presence can still be an important factor in maintaining 'discourse conventions'. For example, where the teacher's presence does not inhibit them and the discussion involves issues which are of real concern to the children, they can still get carried away by the excitement generated in these discussions.

The children found that being an active contributor was less of a problem than being an active listener. After much deliberation, the criteria for a good listener – and discusser – were established. They were listed in the order of probable occurrence thus:

- explain well
- listen to other people
- take turns to talk
- wait until the other person finishes
- say things which help other people
- keep to the subject
- share ideas with the rest of the group
- give suggestions and ideas
- be careful how you say things so that other people don't get upset
- ask each other questions so as to make things clear
- sort out and test ideas
- choose one idea together
- try not to be bossy in the group.

Having decided what they ought to do in a discussion (the aims) the list was photocopied for each child. The children then moved on to considering how they could get better at doing any of these things (the strategies). Pairs of children undertook to write down helpful tips. Each tip was written on a card and then all the tips relating to one of the criteria were contained in a plastic zip-bag. The bags were used when the children felt they needed to work on a particular strategy. For example:

To explain well:
    wait till everybody is listening
    make things clear
    ask a friend for advice
    make notes to help you to remember
    put your ideas in order
    speak well so other people can hear
    choose your words carefully so others can understand.

To listen to others:
  ask someone to talk to you
  try to understand what they say
  remember what they say
  look at the person who is speaking
  make sure everyone is quiet.

At the end of the group task, the children were given time (sometimes 20 minutes) to reflect upon their discussion and, in particular, upon the criteria they had selected for special attention. At first this proved very difficult to do. However, the children soon became more proficient at assessing and being assessed on the skills. Gradually, some ground rules emerged to make the process easier; for example, 'always try to comment about something someone was good at first'.

Questions were raised about the validity of monitoring individuals whose performance depends on the group situation. For example, how could the group assess a member's progress in 'ask each other questions to make things clear' if they had not needed to do this because the others were explaining things so clearly?

The approach to discussion skills described above involved the children at every step. It was they who recognized that earlier discussions had not been constructive. It was they who had begun to identify the reasons for this and what might be done to improve them. It was the children who decided the criteria, in their own terms, and who (initially) chose to mark their own progress. Identifying the skills was itself a considerable achievement. But learning to implement them and then to expose themselves to peer assessment made heavy demands on their maturity. Yet in the space of a term these top infant children showed themselves well able to make an impressive start on exercising these very elusive skills, explicitly.

The children had shown themselves able to 'communicate' effectively in an oral mode, to 'reflect upon and adjust their language' in order to facilitate their own and others' 'comprehension' – all of which are listed in the Programmes of Study.

ACTIVITY

Analysing Discussions

In appraising discussion skills the following may be useful:

Do the participants take turns?
- or do they frequently talk-over or interrupt?
Do they invite contributions?
- re-direct contributions for further comments?
- give encouragement?
Do they listen to each other?
- are they willing to learn from each other, i.e. respond and react to each other's contributions?
- or do they indulge in 'parallel' talk, i.e. continue their own line of thinking regardless?
Does conflict emerge?
- or is harmony maintained (at all costs)?
- are the ideas disputed?
- is the speaker attacked?
Is conflict positively handled?
- by modifying statements
  rather than just re-asserting them?
- by examining the assumptions
  rather than leaving them implicit?
- by explaining/accounting for the claim
  rather than ignoring the challenge?
Do they elaborate rather than answer in monosyllables?
- by giving details of events, people, feelings?
- by providing reasons, explanations, examples?
Do they extend ideas rather than let ambiguity go unchallenged?
- by asking for specific information?
- by asking for clarification?
Do they explore suggestions?
- by asking for alternatives?
- by speculating, imagining and hypothesizing?
Do they evaluate?
- by pooling ideas and suspending judgement before evaluating and making choices?

ACTIVITY

Analysing Groups

Awareness of the group dynamics can lead towards understanding useful issues arising from groupwork. These can be used in planning future activities in the class.

When monitoring a group activity the following aspects can be noted:

What is the composition of the group – age, sex, personality, social/ linguistic/cognitive ability?

What was the seating arrangement – who sat next to whom, could everyone see each other?

Was there a leader, a scribe?

Was this challenged?

Did anyone not participate? How did the others respond?

In what ways did the group collaborate?

Was help needed/requested?

What teacher support was given?

In what ways was the group successful?

Did the group *feel* successful?

FURTHER READING

The first title focuses on the social skills needed in groupwork and the second reviews research on general features of discussion.

Bolton, B. (1979) *People Skills*. New York: Prentice Hall.
Brown, G. and Yule, G. (1983) *Discourse Analysis*. Cambridge: Cambridge University Press.

The following titles illustrate classroom practice in the middle-school years which might be adapted for primary classes.

Bligh, D. (1986) *Teach Thinking by Discussion*. Slough: NFER/Nelson.
Chilver, P. and Gould, G. (1982) *Learning and Language in the Classroom*. Oxford: Pergamon Press.
Ur, P. (1981) *Discussions That Work*. Cambridge: Cambridge University Press.

(iii)   Dramatic communication as performers and readers

A third strand in the development of speaking and listening skills is that of 'communicating imaginatively' as performers and readers. This is used in conjunction with the term 'drama'. The role that drama can play, however, varies according to its aims and its contexts. The National Curriculum documents list a range of benefits accruing from using drama in the primary school. These include belief that drama contributes to personal growth, by enabling children to express their emotions and by helping them to make sense of the world (para 8.4).

Drama, like groupwork, is a social activity. It can promote collaborative talk through the need to identify purposes, develop the logic of situations, present interpretations, take account of audience's needs, evaluate choices and take decisions. Drama also extends language skills, encourages an awareness of language in use, provides a chance to try out a variety of language functions and voice skills (paras 8.5, 8.6). This interpretation of 'drama' is far removed from a focus on 'performance' and 'theatre arts', though these are not ruled out.

If we use 'drama' in this wider sense it can fulfil a central role in helping the child to develop as an 'active meaning-maker'. If we accept that children learn best by doing and making, then drama encourages a physical and concrete mode of working. Further, children are used to 'playing' and to creating and exploring roles, relationships and situations using 'pretend games' as a means of trying out alternative choices. They are used to collaborating in this context and to the idea that 'play' has rules and thus some certainty, yet the outcome is unknown and involves some risks (Neelands, 1984).

The importance of drama as an enactive mode of learning is emphasized by Neelands when he argues that:

> For children, the world is still a new phenomenon. They rely upon their imagining and on data processed through their senses rather than through their intellects as a means of acting on and understanding new information and experience (1984:3).

Thus by acting on sensory experiences and engaging their imagination children can begin to make sense of the world. Neelands goes on to suggest that there are two forms of knowledge: the scientific, in which objectivity and impersonal truth are valued, and the vernacular, which is based on personal, intuitive and affective responses. Further,

> Whereas children need to be initiated into school forms of knowledge ['scientific'] they already possess as a result of out-of-school learning, a degree of mastery in vernacular forms of knowledge (1983:4).

Hence, if schools reject the vernacular they run the risk of rejecting children's own learning resources by which they can bridge the familiar with the unfamiliar.

These arguments in favour of using drama as a tool for learning also show the link between developing language in a collaborative context (section 2.2), developing language for personal expression (section 2.4), developing awareness of language varieties in action (section 2.5), and even in developing language not just for transmission purposes (section 2.1) but also for 'feeling their way into knowledge'. For example, drama can be used in recreating historical events, scientific discoveries, technological disasters and many more situations!

The move away from considering drama as primarily a 'performance' art to using drama as a 'tool for learning' is associated with work pioneered and developed in Britain by Dorothy Heathcote. Her emphasis was on 'feeling' and on encouraging children (and adults) to explore their internal, personal meanings – 'gut-reaction' – and find ways of transforming them into an objective generalized understanding through external action.

However, as Bolton (1979) argues, self-expression alone is not drama. Personal feeling must be transformed into a collective understanding through sharing and exchanging feelings, exploring and searching for 'congruence' (an empathy with others though not necessarily an acceptance) and transcending individual perspectives. Drama in this sense is not just pretend or 'having fun'. It is not sensational or sentimental but about establishing significances. It is about uncovering truths, changing our understandings, creating new links between our 'self' and the world in which we live through reinforcement, clarification and modification.

(a) Developing a framework for drama in the classroom

A wide range of factors – attitudes, concepts, interpersonal skills and resources – all make an important contribution to drama.

From the outset it is essential that the participants have positive attitudes towards drama and establish an atmosphere in which participants feel safe in what they do (confident, accepted, respected). It also needs confidence in knowledge already gleaned (about characters, crises, conflicts, conclusions).

Instead of encouraging the claim 'We don't make a drama out of a crisis' we should encourage the children to enact and explore crises. Further, we must examine the significances of what we experience through drama so that we learn from it (our feelings, actions and outcomes, and from our understandings at a personal, universal or analogous level).

Secondly, there are key concepts in 'drama' which participants should acquire through their activities. These include the notions of action and incident (time, place, situation), character (personality, viewpoint, response), also tension, conflict and surprise, and finally, meaning, interpretation and significance.

The notion of 'meaning' is a complex one, as children move between their internal and external meanings. Both are equally important, and children often need help both in clarifying their own understandings and in moving beyond their personal responses to wider universal themes. Some of these more common, but fundamental themes include hiding/escaping, winning/losing, finding/losing, being lost/being found, cheating/being cheated, reward/punishment, invasion/defence, stereotypes, idols. Such universal themes are ones which children will have experienced in the stories they have heard, books they have read, programmes they have watched. They may not have been helped to look for the significances behind the 'plot', and it is at this level that drama can be a tool for learning, for personal growth and for moving beyond individual experience.

Thirdly, because drama encourages the interaction between internal and external meanings, it makes considerable demands on social, language and intellectual skills in handling the affective responses of the participants.

Finally, resources for drama are an important factor. If we begin with children's experiences – their vernacular knowledge – there are many 'what if . . .' situations which drama could help them to explore. Further, there are the situations deriving from shared literary experiences of stories and poems such as nursery rhymes, fairy stories, myths and legends, folk tales, magic and mystery stories. There are also documentary experiences, historical or contemporary that children can enter and 'take on'.

In order to develop the attitudes, concepts and skills central to drama it is useful to employ a range of forms of drama. For instance, in some classrooms, there is a preference for preliminary 'warm-up' exercises. These may include:

- physical exercises (e.g. limbering up, stretching and bending)
- specific skill practice (external, action emphasis) (e.g. carrying a load with a partner, brandishing a sword)
- imaginative development (internal, mental emphasis) (e.g. 'You've found a strange carving in the attic . . .')
- social skills (working with others non-verbally, verbally) (e.g. conducting an interview).

Some forms of drama, as mentioned in the Programmes of Study, already exist in the classroom. These include children's 'make-believe' as they role play in the home corner, classroom shop or surgery, or in the playground. Such situations may be defined by the place (classroom shop) or the roles (doctors and nurses). Within these self-established confines the children are creating and enacting simultaneously and spontaneously.

Using these same skills, children can be encouraged to enter into 'dramatic-play'. Bolton (1979) suggests that it might be fruitful to begin with 'play-acting scenarios', where children don't have to be 'in role' but just 'pretend'. For example, the teacher may invent such 'What if' situations as losing Tom Thumb, having to programme/instruct robots to carry out precise tasks in the kitchen, or finding your teacher has shrunk like Mrs Pepperpot.

Another form of classroom drama involves children exploring their understandings of a text by entering into the dilemmas it poses. For example, they may imagine defending the community from the Iron Man. Or, children may explore characters from more than one text, who might meet in a 'text' created by the children themselves; for example, where Cinderella might meet the Three Bears and be rescued by the Seven Dwarfs.

Alternatively, children can be encouraged both to work 'in role' and then to reflect upon that experience 'out of role'. This existential framework (or 'living through') could be defined by a particular event. It might be a dilemma that has arisen in school – a theft, gas failure in the kitchens on the day of the Centenary Party, the excursion coach breaks down . . . The situation could be defined by a story or poem which the group or class have shared. With younger children it may be easier to begin with situations where there are few identifiable 'characters' and lots of 'crowd', as in 'The Pied Piper of Hamelin'. Or the situation could derive from a contemporary or historical event linked to known texts, e.g. a local news event, such as the collapse of the Big Wheel at the fun fair or the oil pollution on nearby beaches, linked to a class story (e.g. *Spotter Puff* by Patricia Drew); or the 19th-century potato famines linked to documents or a play (e.g. *Black Harvest* by Nigel Gray).

A further form of 'drama' is sometimes referred to as 'the mantle of the expert'. Here, each participant becomes an expert whose particular skills are needed by the whole group and who therefore has a unique contribution to make and a 'part to play'. The individual has to assume responsibility for a specific aspect of the group's activity but is also responsible to the whole group. This dramatic collaboration may sometimes be developed spontaneously, though the initial impetus may be planned and structured by the teacher. Alternatively, it can be researched and extended, in role, over a lengthy period of time. Again, the stimulus for such activities can be a practical experiential project initiated by the children. For example, in one school 6- and 7-year-olds organized themselves as authors, illustrators, editors, etc. and designed, produced and sold a book. Or the stimulus may be literary: in another instance, 8- and 9-year-olds responded to the dilemma in the *101 Dalmatians* by plotting an ingenious way of recovering the pups using the expertise of the key characters in the story. Or, the stimulus may be documentary, as when 9- to 10-year-olds planned the subjugation of Wales by means of a programme of castle building for Edward I using their expertise as architects, masons, miners, fletchers, armourers, cooks, tailors, etc.

Finally, there are forms of drama which can be categorized as performance-orientated and are rehearsed and staged. These are outside the scope of this chapter, but nevertheless can contribute to widening children's experiences – socially, intellectually, and in terms of the very differing voices and languages which might be used.

As is already evident in this section, drama links closely with other strands of oral language use. It links with other modes of language through story-telling. It is also linked with both reading and writing. In all these spheres, drama can embrace a private as well as a public, performance mode.

(b)   Oral storying

Reading is often associated with an image of an individual poring over a book, silently, alone. Or an individual reading aloud to a teacher. In the context of 'drama' it is appropriate to remind ourselves that reading can be public, shared and interactive.

Many children – and teachers – look forward to 'story time'. A great deal of pleasure can be derived from a good story well read. But not always! Much depends on the quality of the book, the range of tastes and the concentration span within the group. The quality of the reading is also important. Not all of us read aloud equally well. After all, teachers now have to compete with trained actors and the visual effects on programmes such as *Jackanory* and *Book Tower*.

There are considerable differences for both teller and listeners between story-telling, telling-a-story and reading-a-story. Story-telling derives from an oral tradition where books did not exist. Traditional tales were told, each time embellished and transformed. Also, new stories were created, possibly drawing from local incidents and current concerns. It is a method that breaks down the typical barrier between reader and listener, an imaginative, improvisation situation in which teller and listeners interact and construct a narrative together (Cook-Gumperz and Green, in Tannen, 1984). It is a weaving together of suggestions from any of the participants orchestrated by the teller. Since the method is interactive, it allows the teller to invite contributions for a particular purpose, for example, to determine the sequence of events ('What could happen next ...', 'Who will ...', 'What might they say ...'); or to make explicit the structure of the narrative (for example, cause/consequence, 'If they did that, then ...'); or coherence/relevance ('What could follow ...', 'What would make sense ...'); or be 'in character' ('Would they be likely to ...').

Story-telling is not a recitation of a story without using the book. In the early stages (to allow both the teller and the listeners to gain confidence) a book may be used as a starting point and its story elaborated until it is hardly recognizable! Or additional anecdotes can be woven into the text. The point of these procedures is to break down the isolation of the listener from the reader and their text. This isolation is illustrated by Sartre in his autobiographical book *Words* (1964), when he recalls the shock of his mother reading him a story:

> She lowered her eyes and went to sleep. From this mask-like face issued a plaster voice. My mother had disappeared: not a smile or trace of complicity ... And then I didn't recognize the language: it was the book talking – it was language all dressed up in its Sunday best (p. 30).

What he missed was the 'intimacy' of her previous story-telling.

Telling-a-story rather than reading it is another approach to breaking down the reader–listener barrier. In this situation the book does not come between you and the eye-contact which you can sustain with your audience. Telling-a-story also creates a more immediate storying bond with the audience through its greater visual directness. To be effective, though, such telling-a-story needs great care in the choosing, rehearsing and presentation (with or without props).

Ben Haggarty, a professional story-teller, suggests that children can learn to tell a story by listening to a story-teller and then re-telling that story to other children, who have not yet heard it (Montgomery and Robinson, 1989). These re-tellings are highly creative, for although certain words, phrases and gestures will be picked up and repeated, other parts will quite properly become 'fields for freewheeling improvisation'. Such re-tellings form a bridge between story-telling and telling-a-story.

It is the rich mixture of imitation and inspiration in telling that characterizes 'traditional' tales and allows for the variations between traditions. According to an Irish saying, a story enters tradition by passing through three sets of mouths and three sets of ears: the outcome will still be recognizable yet vitally different.

Even when reading-a-story we can find ways to break down the barriers between the reader and the audience. Participation can be encouraged by inviting the audience to name the characters in the story, or the street where they live. Or the reader can make time for the audience to create the relevant sound effects, for example, when the giant stomps up the stairs or the monster smacks his lips.

Another way to encourage participation is by inviting children to make predictions: 'What will happen next?' 'Why?' or 'How would you have reacted?'. This becomes a more sophisticated activity as the stories become more complex, the children learn to listen more precisely, and to 'read the clues' in the text or pictures, so that they can respond and talk about their books (AT 2, level 2). Such group talking and listening can encourage children to use inference and deduction in finding meanings beyond the literal (AT 2, level 3).

It is important, especially for the youngest children, to have rests in the span of concentrated listening. Many teachers successfully provide these with action-rhymes. These are short, repetitive and involve the children in reactive mime and interactive choruses. Nursery rhymes and favourite classroom poems can also encourage children to join in. Both the rhyme and the rhythm of poetry encourage children to predict what will come next so that they can participate more confidently and develop their 'appreciative' listening through refining their awareness of such aural patterns. Many children enjoy such recitation (which is now suggested in the programmes of story at Stage 1, AT 1, para. 4) whether it is done in a group or individually. It is also a good opportunity for children to perform their own rhymes and songs in other languages.

Making 'story time' an enjoyable period will encourage children to listen and respond positively to stories and poems (AT 1, level 1) and in addition, children can also enjoy, offering and discussing preferences and expressing opinions concerning what has been read (AT 1, level 2, AT 2, level 2). This process of analysis and evaluation can begin at a very early level and become an activity which readers adopt throughout their lives, in an increasingly detailed and satisfying way, as they go 'beyond the text' to their inner experience. Such discussion could relate to the plot, setting and characters, and also to the structure and style of the book (AT 2, level 3/4/5 and elaborated in the programmes of study).

ACTIVITY

Preparing a Story for Reading or Telling

1.0   Reading a story.

1.1   What kind of stories are suitable?

(a)   Stories which you like as well as the children. It is difficult to be enthusiastic and genuine about something you detest.

(b)   Stories to hold attention: lots of action and plenty of dialogue

(c)   Stories which will allow participation: chorus/repeated lines
      as each time the giant says Fee, Fi, Fo Fum . . .
   or, providing sound effects
      as when the giant goes, thump, thump, thump . . .
   Traditional tales, fairy stories, etc. were first oral stories and often have these features.

1.2   How can we present them?

(a)   Preparation of the text: check through and decide if and where you want to make cuts, summarize bits, substitute easier words, put in a little aside, pause to ask a question and get some listener response . . .
   Also, decide which pictures you are going to show, why and when,   e.g. before or after reading the related text (why), for decorative support or for discussion

(b)   Practice: in particular, the voices you intend to use, and the pace . . . (faster for action bits, slow for descriptive) and pitch and volume . . . (soft for sad, spooky bits, loud for. . . .)

2.0   Telling a story.

This is a good alternative as you can maintain eye-contact so much more effectively. This also helps to hold attention better. It comes across with more immediate impact. Again, a spell-binder.

2.1   Which stories?

(a)   Stories that you know well! A familiar favourite from your own distant youth . . .

(b)   Stories from your own experience (embellished if necessary)

2.2 How can we present them?

(a) To help the audience to listen, make it lively!

Use your voice to 'colour' it, extra emphasis to convey key points.

Use facial expressions and gestures to reinforce, clarify, extend understanding . . . . . but not too much or it distracts.

Use visual aids like pictures, props, puppets, cut-outs stuck on a background board with Blu-tack, or a felt/magnetic board if you have one. Puppets which need a piece of clothing changed, or a prop which has opening doors/drawers, etc., all invite active participation and are always enjoyed. (Decide carefully who is going to do the participation beforehand . . .)

(b) To encourage participation you can start a story-line in the knowledge that named children will continue it at a given signal. This might be appropriate if the story is related to events and characters the class have already been discussing and are familiar with . . . . your own class 'soap'!

(c) If you are a good story-fabricator, ask the children to suggest a list of people, places and things which you then weave into a story, or let the children take on the task. . . .

FURTHER READING

The following are all practical books that help increase understanding of the use of drama in the classroom.

Bolton, G. (1979) *Towards a Theory of Drama in Education*. London: Longman.

Evans, T. (1984) *Drama in English Teaching*. London: Croom Helm.

Neelands, J. (1984) *Making Sense of Drama*. London: Heinemann.

Montgomery, P. and Robinson, R. (1989) 'The development of oral story-telling', *English in Education*, Summer issue.

Rosen, H. (1988) 'Stories of stories: footnotes on sly gossipy practices', in Lightfoot, M. and Martin, N. (eds) *The Word for Teaching Is Learning*. London: Heinemann.

The two titles below are excellent discussions of story-telling and telling stories in class, with plenty of practical advice:

Colwell, E. (1980) *Storytelling*. London: Bodley Head.
Garvie, E. (1990) *Story as Vehicle*, Philadelphia: Multilingual Matters.

(iv)　Personal response, preferences, persuasion

In Attainment Target 1, levels 1–3, children are required to listen and respond to books and also to each other's stories (thereafter, response to books is included in the second Reading component – see Part II). This illustrates the interlocking of the different English components and the integral nature of language. It also demonstrates the inherent artificiality of dividing language into discrete components.

Discussions about books is but one activity where children can be invited to express their personal responses and individual preferences. Discussions can take place in a collective, whole-class context as well as in a more private (pair) context. An example of the whole-class context is when the teacher reads aloud at storytime and encourages comments from children. Responses can be modelled explicitly by the teacher by inviting specific kinds of comments. Viewpoints and opinions can be aired, explanations offered, justification and substantiation requested as well as other people's views noted. The teacher can help to establish the framework for such a discussion and its ground rules: the importance of relevance, of listening, of 'taking the role of the other'. Such ground rules can be carried over to the private, pair context.

There are also opportunities for children to engage in storycrafting activities in pairs, where they can be an initial audience for their partner's draft. In such a workshop approach, they are critical listeners to each other and thus become 'response partners' by providing a sounding-board and some constructive criticism. This is a very important role and requires sensitivity and tact. The response partner can participate at the beginning, middle or end of the story-making process. For example, at the very beginning of a writers' workshop, children can be asked to spend two minutes thinking what they might like to write about, before spending a further five minutes telling each other about their proposed stories. At this stage the response partner needs to attend carefully to the story outline and then comment. In many instances, the role of the response partner is primarily to serve as an audience for whom the speaker can rehearse their story. The partner can also provide support and encouragement, give opinions and preferences, identify ambiguities and possibly suggest places where clarification might be needed.

Some classes have developed guidelines such as:

- say two nice things e.g. which bits you liked
- next ask questions e.g. if you weren't quite clear in places
- then make suggestions about how to make the story clearer/better

Later, when the first draft has been written, dictated or drawn in picture sequence, the draft can be read to the response partner. Again, the partner needs to remember the three steps outlined above, for children can find partnering too threatening if responses are critical, or too cosy if blanket support is given. Understanding the notion of 'constructive criticism' is a sophisticated achievement and needs careful modelling and support. Partners rehearsing their drafts need to be able to listen to the comments made, understand the reader's perspective, be willing to consider changes and explain their own position. Response partners need to be able to justify their preferences or suggestions and explain how the ideas might be strengthened or developed. Both parties can, of course, agree to differ. Nevertheless, both partners need to 'take the role of the other' in order to be effective partners.

Articulating such guidelines can help children appreciate what their role as partner should be, what to listen for and how to respond.

However, there are definite differences between voicing such opinions in a discussion mode and using an argumentative or persuasive mode. Children in an observed junior class quickly identified these differences in terms of both goals ('In a discussion you try to come to an agreement'; 'You try to find out what the other person is thinking') and listener-response processes ('You've got to be willing to try to understand what they say'; 'You've got to be ready to give your own views, to add details, reasons'; 'You've got to know how to chip in'; 'You've got to show you're listening by your expression').

In the event of the discussion becoming a quarrel the children noted 'You've got to try and calm them down', 'Agree with them a bit', 'Listen to them, ask them to explain it again', 'Tell them to say it differently', 'Bribe them, get them drunk . . .'. These ideas (mostly) show a mature understanding of the social demands made of the listener, and the difficulties of achieving good discussions.

Children's idea of a quarrel is typically one derived from TV soap operas of opposing views and contrary assertions, with little evidence to substantiate them and probably a refusal to listen to the other's views. Their models for persuasion are usually advertisements, which aim to influence by showing partial and prejudiced evidence without any opportunity for alternative or critical views. As the APU (1988) and DES (1982) have noted, they have very little experience of argumentation, either in oral or written form. Children mostly read fiction and the small proportion of non-fiction books are normally factual, bland, uncontentious and rarely adopt an argumentative form.

The validity of argumentation rests on the premiss that the participants are equally at liberty to hold their own personal opinions and values and can legitimately put forward alternative reasoned propositions (Berrill in MacLure *et al.*, 1988). This relies on the further premiss that 'knowledge' and 'truth' are socially negotiated, that no person has sole access to truth, and that there is not any absolute 'right' or 'wrong'. Argumentation therefore depends on points being made which are substantiated by personal experience or public knowledge, not recourse to ''Tis or 'tisn't' or 'My Dad/the book says'.

Thus it is clearly a sophisticated mode, requiring a considerable amount of social maturity. Two modes of argumentation have been defined: exploring and advocating (Dixon and Stratta, 1986). Both modes assume an ability to 'de-centre' sufficiently to be able to recognize other views. Nevertheless we should remember that from a very early age children 'explore' opinions about 'pocket money', 'playing out', 'bed-times', and when they go to school may participate in book buying policy for the library or in deciding playground rules. They can also be encouraged to advocate 'reform of classroom routines', 'choice of class outing', 'identifying a charity to support' and decide their position concerning 'treatment of animals' (in zoos/circuses/the wild), pollution (playground litter to national policies) or conservation (local issues, etc.).

Dixon and Stratta suggest that a series of argumentation strategies should include:

- defining the component terms
- selecting a focus
- reviewing the evidence for and against
- examining the implications and consequences
- attempting a conclusion (often a compromise) or a redefinition of the position

Situations often demand both modes: the need to explore as well as a later need to decide, conclude and perhaps advocate. Primary children can also be initiated into the style of formal debates, where the mode is one of advocacy in an adversarial context. In this instance the speaker is expected to develop a 'line of argument' and persuade, while the listeners need to be able to follow that argument, and, hopefully respond.

Both modes of argumentation serve as an excellent basis for secondary and tertiary student essays and also for work-place negotiation in adult life.

Developing an argumentation style requires the use of specific structural, pragmatic and linguistic features. Phillips (1988) highlights the fact that the exploration mode – often an expression of personal opinion – depends on particularistic anecdote (a chronological, loose structure) from which generalizations (often clichés) may loosely be derived. It is characterized by hesitation, substitution, backtracking on ideas introduced earlier and is linked linguistically by listing devices such as 'and' as well as by propositional extension and elaboration.

In contrast, argumentation in a formal advocacy (debate) mode is more tightly structured and offers reasoned explanation of alternative viewpoints (logical structure). It may move from the general to the particular by compiling and applying ideas. Linguistic cohesion is based on 'so', 'that', 'in order to'. Further, Garton and Pratt (1989) suggest that additional pragmatic features are evident such as a focus on 'what you say/what you mean' distinctions in order to clarify the argument and also methods of resolving conflicts (e.g. ways of 'disagreeing courteously').

Dixon and Stratta also identify two further distinctions in 'argumentation': action-orientated and notion-orientated. In the context of the primary classroom, it is probably more appropriate to use an action-orientated focus, where a discussion will lead to a decision resulting in action. For example, children can discuss how to spend the class allocation of £40 for equipment to use during playtime (for whose storage and safe-keeping they are to be held responsible). Notion-orientated argumentation relates to opinions and beliefs for which there is no definite outcome or concrete result.

Given that children rarely experience argumentation it is important to provide them with clear strategies for positive participation. One writer in particular, Edward de Bono, has attempted to develop such a package. It has been produced by the Cognitive Research Trust (CoRT). De Bono has outlined a set of practical strategies to help children learn how to develop a 'line of argument'.

For example,

At the outset, children can do a:
CAF (Consider All Factors),
which encourages them to explore the issues and brainstorm for possible variables which might be relevant to the task.
APC (Alternatives, Possibilities, Choices)
Having established a pool of ideas the participants then sort out the original results of the brainstorming.

Followed by:
AGO (Aims, Goals, Outcomes)
to remind themselves of the aims of the task and help them to establish relevance and to 'stick to the task'.
OPV (Other People's Opinions)
to take into consideration others' feelings, viewpoints and opinions so that the outcome can be satisfactory for all the participants.
FIP (First Important Priority)
to encourage children to rank order aims, to 'prioritize' in the light of aims, viewpoints and ideas generated.

Then, the children should try:
C and S (Causes and Sequels)
which encourages an examination of the implications of the factors already identified.
C and C (Compare and Contrast)
which encourages analysis and categorization of the ideas.
FOC (Fact, Opinion and Contradiction)
to encourage evaluation and critical analysis.
PMI (Plus, Minus, 'Interesting')
to encourage evaluation and decision-making.

These steps and procedures are practical, concrete strategies which children can undertake. Pencil and paper graphic representations of the contributions can be made. These show the range of ideas and de-personalize them so that the discussion is issue-orientated not person-orientated. It also encourages the participants to be problem-orientated rather than solution-orientated and thus to explore the issues first rather than rushing to find a conclusion.

Such visual representation serves as a record of the progress of the discussion and thus as an aide-mémoire for the participants. It also provides evidence that the teacher can survey, review and appraise. Any such activity, if followed by a discussion of the argumentation process, can provide the basis for developing children's own awareness of the process and of their growing mastery of it. Thus it provides a framework for the metalanguage in which to discuss the discussion, debate or argumentation.

FURTHER READING

There are few writings available on the topic of argumentation, but the following are recommended:

Andrews, R. (ed.) (1989) *Narrative and Argument*. Milton Keynes: Open University Press.

Berrill, D. 'Anecdote and argument'; Phillips, T. 'On a related matter' both in MacLure, M. *et al*. (1988) *Oracy Matters*. Milton Keynes: Open University Press.

The following titles give specific support to strategies for developing discussion and argumentation skills:

de Bono, E. (1976) *Teaching Thinking*. Harmondsworth: Penguin.

Mason, B. (1989) 'It's in our CoRT now'. *Support for Learning* **4**(3), 175–80.

ACTIVITY

Developing Argumentation

1. Promoting argumentation makes heavy demands of the participants' social and language skills. In order for the session to be successful the activity should include at least some of the features below. Monitor the argumentation opportunities in your class for the following:

- open-endedness to allow a range of valid alternative opinions and actions,
- relevance to the children's experiences whether fictional or factual,
- controversial, so that there is personal commitment and exchange of views;
- have a concrete outcome, so that decisions have to be made and agreements reached
  e.g. about the content, presentation ...

2. Children need a 'scaffolding' of practical strategies to support them in their discussion. Ideally, labels for such strategies should come from the children, having emerged in the review stage of the discussion activity.

Observe the children's use of such strategies as:

collecting ideas	by	brainstorming
sorting ideas	by	explaining/listening
using ideas	by	looking for patterns (cause/effect)
applying ideas	by	following up, making
presenting ideas	by	oral, graphic, 3-D, or literate means ...

3. Children also need to record the stages of their discussion e.g. by making

an ideas web	(collation)
a flow chart	(sequencing)
or tables	(categorization)

This helps de-personalize discussion so 'ownership' is not disputed rather than content discussed. Also it serves as an aide-mémoire and a means by which the processes of discussion can be reviewed and evaluated by the children and the teacher. Display and discuss such records with the children as a means of raising awareness of their strategies and improving them.

(v)   Awareness of language

We know that babies play with sounds in their cribs and enjoy the feel of sounds in their mouths. This marks the beginning of what is often a lifelong fascination with words and language which, as teachers, we can encourage and support. The main research evidence for children's growth in awareness of language and of their metalinguistic development, is through their ability to spot mistakes and/or to correct them in given examples during experimental sessions. Clark (1978) has identified unsolicited self-corrections that young children make. This, she believes, illustrates an implicit awareness about language and an ability to reflect upon language-in-use, so that such 'repairs' can be made. Clark notes instances of children at 19 months making pronunciation repairs (phonological awareness), at 30 months making word order changes (syntactic awareness) and at two-and-a-half years making word agreement changes (morphemic awareness).

However, Tunmer and Merriman (1984) argue that metalinguistic awareness only occurs properly when children have reached the concrete operational stage of development (they suggest around 6–7 years). At this stage children are able to exercise conscious control over such corrections. A further source of evidence concerning children's metalinguistic awareness is through study of their word games and jokes (Chapman and Foot, 1977).

Emphasis in discussions about 'awareness of language' is very often given to the forms and functions of language, particularly to:

word structures and meanings:	affixes, homonyms and puns, semantic relations between words (synonym, antonym, collocation)
sentence structures:	syntax (word order, agreements) 'parts of speech'.

Further areas could include other language units, such as,

sounds (syllables, intonation, rhyme, pronunciation)
textual and discourse structures (paragraph, cohesion)
as well as language use in the social context.

Many of these features can be located in a literary as well as an oral context. Thus children can be encouraged to find examples of these features both in their reading and in their writing, and can then discuss the effects in a context which is relevant to them.

(a) Forms, functions and features of language

Surface features: sounds and spelling. Children's pleasure in language grows continually. For example, pre-school children frequently enjoy making up words, often to insult each other but also for the pleasure of experimenting. An adult in the 'home corner' would not be surprised to overhear (usually friendly!) exchanges like the following:

'You're a pooh-pooh.'
'You're a soo-soo.'
'You're a silly-billy.'
'You're a willy-wally.'

The techniques employed often rely on doubling word sounds or rhyming them. It illustrates Schultz and Robillard's category of 'phonological' humour, which is typified by the kind of distortions employed by the cartoon character 'Tweety Pie' in the phrase 'I tort a taw a puddy cat' (1980). Phonic play is often employed by authors writing for children of this age in choosing character's names e.g. Henny-Penny, Dame Wishy-Washy.

An example of this delight in language was observed in a class of 6-year-olds. They were fascinated when one of them noticed that they could spell their names backwards, sometimes making an alternative word, sometimes making something that was merely pronounceable: so Lee became Eel, Mrs Tan became Mrs Nat, Ben became Neb, Carol became Laroc and, to the delight of all, Miss Armitage became Miss Egatimra. Until the novelty wore off (in about a week) some of the children talked and wrote notes backwards to each other. It certainly generated enthusiasm for words and led to the investigation of palindromes such as Dad, toot, madam.

Despite the wealth of insight which can derive from the spoken word, it is often through discussion of written texts that we can more easily reflect upon words. Talking about words leads to the development of what Olson (1984) calls the literate person who 'is aware of language as an artefact': someone who studies language as well as uses it.

Listening to poetry and nursery rhymes provides tremendous pleasure in words, their melody and rhythms (Bradley and Bryant, 1988). Stories also provide a wealth of features to discuss, e.g. identifying new words and finding how to pronounce them, recognizing letter strings and syllables, finding prefix/suffix patterns. Children enjoy noting similar/dissimilar aural and visual patterns (such as in homographs and homophones and their role in puns), all of which leads to a heightened awareness of word structures.

Word structures. Other discoveries were made when top infants were observed exploring words, and can be illustrated in the following examples. Six-year-olds noticed some of their names could be divided into separate words:

Stephen = step + hen
Justin = just + (t)in

Having explored more of these a girl enquired, 'Do we call it an "outing" because we go out and then come back in again?'.

This developed into an interest in word compounds, referred to as 'word sums' by the children, who made up examples for each other. Some examples contained two known words forming a new word which was a sum of their meanings, e.g.

school + boy = schoolboy (where there is a semantic contiguity)

Others contained known words which when joined bore no relationship to their meanings, e.g.

car + pet = carpet (where there is no contiguity)

In yet others the components were familiar but not the compound, e.g.

handy + man = handyman (which the children claimed not to know)

A variation of this game, which directed attention to surface features of words, was a form of the traditional parlour game in which competitors try to make as many words as they can out of the constituent letters of a given word. One 7-year-old child called this 'Finding the locked-in words', e.g.

cupboard = cup, up, board, oar;
        or by choosing non-consecutive letters: pod, cub;
        or by reordering letters: rod, rap, etc.

Word building took a different form with a group of 9-year-old children. They had been on an outing to a local complex of buildings that included a church and quadrangle. Interest in words is demonstrated by the following exchange:

'Is a quadrangle like a triangle?'
'No silly. Triangles have got three something. Like tricycles.'
'So what's a quadrangle then?'
'Like quads, when you have lots of babies.'
'How many?'
'Lots.'

This led to the exploration of words beginning with uni-, bi-, (du-), tri-, quad-, etc. Children discussed the 'one-ish-ness' of 'universe' or (Manchester) 'United' or 'uniform'. They also found science fiction terms from TV programmes which included a 'uni-quad-mobile' which, I was told, is 'a car for one person which has four wheels and it goes on the moon'. Such investigations of wordroots and derivations led to considerable research into how and why new words are invented. Advertising is a constant source of invented new words. The children minted their own terms to describe the different processes they observed, e.g. 'add-ons', 'melting words into each other', 'crazy spellings'.

A focus on morphemes by other 9-year-olds led to interest in changing words by altering endings (adjective 'strong' to adverb 'strongly'; adjective 'happy' to abstract noun 'happiness'; noun 'beauty' to adjective 'beautiful'; noun 'jump' to verb (participle) 'jumping'). The formal descriptive terms were not used and it was hard for the children to find appropriate explanations for distinguishing '-ly' words, e.g. quick-ly, from semantically unrelated similarly ending words, like f-ly. The search for word endings was enjoyed in terms of identifying words by 'rhyme', not by linguistic category.

Another group of children were interested in the fact that words do not simply exist but are invented by people. This idea led to frequent questioning about the derivation of words. Comics provided a good source of invented action and onomatopoeic words. The fact that these often 'show' their meanings in the calligraphy led to further investigations of calligrams, typeface and different letter shapes in different historical periods. This led to the examination of the scripts of different cultures – another example of how surface features have a close relationship between the signifier (graphic symbol or letter shape) and referent (abstract or concrete object to which it refers).

(b) Acquisition of language

Children of primary school age very often have younger siblings or cousins who are at the stage of learning to talk and can be a language resource. Children are able to bring into school examples of 'babies' talk', as well as the 'baby talk' in which adults indulge when talking to babies. The school-aged children are adept at understanding their younger siblings' talk (as well the phrases of the doting adults). Moreover, children can usually expand the telegraphic sentences of younger siblings into full sentence structures which reflect 'how they would say things themselves'. This can provide a very natural way for children to make explicit their knowledge about 'sentences'. It gives them an opportunity to compare 'babytalk' with 'proper talk' which can lead them towards articulating 'what makes them different'. It can also lead to discussion about how children learn language and how they can best be helped.

A class of junior children also considered the situation of a newcomer to the school whose mother-tongue was not English. The question 'What English do they need most when they come to school?' generated a range of suggestions. It also raised the questions 'How do you teach someone a new language?' and 'Do children learn in the same way as babies?'.

The majority of suggestions for a 'basic English' resulted in a list of isolated words that were specific to being at school. For example the suggestions included a list of all the teachers' names, the new child's name, 'yes', 'no', 'hallo', 'goodbye', 'toilet', 'help', and a list of every sport or playground activity that a newcomer might be likely to want to join. Such an approach was challenged by others in the class; 'That's not how people talk . . . you should teach them the proper way first.' When the usefulness of single words was challenged it was defended: 'You just put words together if you want to.'

The children devised ways of making learning easier. Ideas ranged from memorizing items in order of likely need, to arranging contrasting pairs of words with picture clues which were funny 'because it's easier to learn funny things'. For example:

tennis 'bat'	cricket bat
music (descant) recorder	tape recorder
swimming trunks	elephant trunks

Another group began with basic sentences to meet basic needs, then planned how these might be taught. The sentences were initially grouped in sets according to meanings. One participant noticed that some of the sentences made a pattern. This observation resulted in regrouping 'because it would be easy to learn them if they are nearly the same'. The sentences, grouped according to similar structures, were as follows:

may I have the skipping rope
may I have the rubber
may I borrow the glue
may I go and change my book

can I join in
can I play with the polygons

shall I use colour pencils

where is the paper
when shall I open my eyes
what happens now
how do I do this

sorry I didn't mean to
please don't do that
I don't understand
thank you for letting me play

This led to questions concerning the difference between 'may I', 'can I' and 'shall I'. It was also noted that most of the basic list were in the form of questions. Some children pointed out that asking questions is one thing but understanding the answer is quite another. Others argued that this would not be a problem, 'because they can see what they are doing, whether you're stuck, whether you like it . . .'.

It was notable that the discussions did not throw up much specialist vocabulary. Instead the forms of words were discussed in terms of their functions, particularly their social functions and degrees of 'politeness'. This accords with Donaldson's assertion (1989) that 'children are concerned with what people mean, not with what words mean'.

Nevertheless, such considerations formed the beginnings of a growing awareness of the skills of children who spoke more than one language and allowed children to explore their own experience of issues relating to language acquisition in their own terms. It helped to generate a greater sympathy with the frustrations of trying to learn a new language in a busy classroom and a respect for the achievement. Hoffman (1989), a Polish migrant to Canada at the age of twelve, vividly expresses some of the frustrations:

> Linguistic dispossession is a sufficient motive for violence for it is close to dispossession of one's self. If one is perpetually in the entrophy of inarticulateness it is bound to be enraging . . . I had to form entire sentences before saying them so that my speech became deliberate, heavy, different. The language invented another me . . . I fell out of the net of meaning into the weightlessness of chaos . . . (p. 124).

(c)   Language varieties: generational, geographical, historical

Playground talk. Research evidence demonstrates children's ability to self-correct syntactic mistakes (such as '-ed' morphemes) at the early age of two-and-a-half years. Yet it is the 'psychological primacy of meaning' which is clearly dominant in such 'repairs' and even more obviously in the peer talk, words games and jokes (Schultz and Robillard, 1980).

Within their peer group children have a rich resource in the language that they use, particularly in the playground. This embraces both the 'oral traditions' of rhymes and chants that the Opies have recorded so extensively and also 'tangle talk' (e.g. 'One fine day in the middle of the night . . .'). In the area of oral traditions children show themselves to be excellent guardians of continuity.

Children are also very creative language users, as demonstrated in their use of superlatives and the changing 'slang' of the playground. Fashions come and go rapidly. What was 'great' becomes 'brill', then 'bad', 'wicked' (even 'well-wick'd'), perhaps even 'crucial' or 'storming'. Trying to decide the nuances of such 'in' words or their origins can give rise to heated debate which generates a more explicit appreciation of forms and nuance.

Nuance emerged as being of particular concern to the children. In trying to describe friends, family or people known to them, sensitivity to the connotations or word pairs (antonyms) such as fat–thin, ugly–handsome, thick–clever, nice–nasty was found to be very important. Word slides were devised. The children found it easier to arrange the words 'in order' when handling physical attributes, e.g.:

ginormous, giant, blubbery, big, podge/porky, large,
→ slim, slinney, thin . . .

These slides frequently moved from the denotative to the connotative, e.g.:

muscle, strong, weak, dumb . . .

The task became more difficult if the words were related to personality rather than physical attributes. The word slides generated synonyms, which demarcated the semantic field of each word in the pair rather than indicating the gradations of meaning between them, e.g.:

nice, kind, loving, grateful, laughing, surprising
→ nasty, horrible, spiteful, wicked, mean, hateful . . .

(They rarely used prefixes, such as 'un-', as a means of turning positive attributes into negative ones, e.g. kind and unkind.)

This kind of investigation into children's own language is a way of encouraging them to engage in fieldwork relating to their own experience of language. It develops their vocabulary and their awareness of words. It can involve consideration of the kinds of words parents and grandparents used at the same age. Further, where there is a mobile school population with parents changing jobs and moving house there may also be the opportunity for children to contribute dialect words from different localities. Even in an area of limited migration, children are exposed to language varieties through a wide range of TV programmes and presenters.

There are many features of Australian and American English that children can study (plenty of them watch *Neighbours* and *Dallas*!).

Geographical and historical varieties. Moving from the playground to the family can provide an interesting source of words to describe family relationships. These words are remarkably similar across a wide range of Indo-European languages. For example, the word for mother is 'matar' (Hindi), 'mutter' (German), 'mama' (Russian), 'mam' (Welsh) and 'mathair' (Irish). Words related to numerals also show a remarkable similarity (see, for example, Hawkins (1984) and Freeborn (1986)). Examining these similarities could perhaps help children to develop respect for other languages.

Another source from within the family is names, both 'family' (surnames) and 'personal' (first names). These too have meanings that can be explored and fashion trends that can be monitored. Nicknames, celebrity names, book character names are all 'labels' that can be investigated.

Moving outside the school playground, into the high street, there is further evidence of language varieties. Loan words such as 'launderette', 'menu', 'kebab', 'pizza', and 'anorak', 'sputnik' or 'shampoo' may be a surprise to children – though some are easy to spot by their 'un-English' spelling or pronunciation. When and why these particular words were incorporated into English is a matter upon which children can speculate and research. The children can also investigate English words which are exported to other languages.

Beyond the high street, there are of course place names which can provide a rich resource for investigating meanings. Any of these foci can serve to heighten the fact that words can be created, combined and changed to communicate changing needs. Children can even embark on creating their own code or language. Often this is done spontaneously in their friendship groups, or gangs, for 'secret languages' are a sign of belonging, of membership.

Playing with words. Words are an endless source of fascination, and humour, for many children. By the age of about eight many children are ready to stand back and look at words rather than be totally absorbed in using them. The lower junior age is often a period when children enjoy puns and jokes and become adept at manipulating words. This is not to say that younger children don't also play with words, but the play is of a different type.

Verbal jokes can often reflect children's linguistic understandings and agility more accurately than 'grammar exercises'. However, the understandings may be implicit rather than explicit, and the children may lack sufficient metalinguistic vocabulary to enable them to articulate the understandings they have. Brodzinsky (1977) suggests that sources of linguistic humour can include phonological, lexical, surface- and deep-structure. Rothbart and Pien (1977, in McGhee and Chapman, 1980) identify logical and situational incongruity as an important humour element, while Shultz and Robillard (1980) add semantic dimensions concerning rules of admissible word combinations and their deliberate violations (e.g. The rock walked down the hill), or word invention (e.g. Mr Sillyface) or word voidity (e.g. brillig), and also social rules concerning pragmatics and their violations, such as over-literality (e.g. 'Do you know what time it is?' 'Yes').

Perera (1987) illustrates a feature of children's ability to play with associations and meanings. She quotes an example of two 5-year-olds making models of Guy Fawkes. One said to the other: 'I'm going to call mine knife. They'll be Knife and Fawkes!'

Asking children to make their own joke books doesn't usually require much encouragement. Asking them to also collect jokes from younger children in the school can lead them to work out what makes a joke funny and whether children tell different kinds of jokes at different ages.

The jokes which children collect can, very tentatively, be classified to demonstrate different linguistic awareness at different ages. The jokes show children 'playing' with different aspects of language. For example, the following reflect an interest in surface features relating to sounds/sense (nonsense, puns, spellings):

What do you get if you cross a cow with a duck?
A cream quacker. (5 yrs)

What do vampire doctors say to their patients?
Necks please. (7 yrs)

What do you do to make a witch itch?
Take away her 'w'. (9 yrs)

Situational incongruity (literal, lateral, logical):

Why do witches fly on broomsticks?
Because Hoovers are too heavy. (6 yrs)

Why did the policeman cry?
Because he wanted to take his Panda to bed. (8 yrs)

What gets bigger the more you take from it?
A hole. (8 yrs)

Structural features (word boundaries, pronoun references, phrase modifiers):

Knock, Knock, Who's there? Justin.
Justin who? Just in time for tea. (7 yrs)

Teacher on phone: Hallo, I hear Jimmy is ill and can't come to school. To whom am I speaking?
Voice: This is my father . . . (10 yrs)

I got out of bed, grabbed a gun and shot the lion in my pyjamas. What was the lion doing in your pyjamas? (10 yrs)

There are plenty of 'sick jokes', political jokes, and currently topical jokes in the repertoire of older juniors:

Why did Michael Jackson call his latest album 'Bad'?
Because he didn't know how to spell 'pathetic'. (9 yrs)

And then there are jokes about jokes, which rely on the participants taking one step further back in their awareness of the games language play.

Waiter, waiter, there's a frog in my soup!
The fly is on holiday. (9 yrs)

Awareness, analysis and appreciation of English.   Increasing children's awareness of spoken language can be an important step in increasing the value they attach to their own and other's languages in all their glorious varieties. The programmes of study and attainment targets in the National Curriculum are based on an assumption about the importance of making explicit the implicit understandings that children already have concerning language. This is in the belief that explicit knowledge will enable them to realize their entitlement to language in terms of increasing pleasure in language and improving their use of English.

Olson (in Garton and Pratt, 1989) proposed that metalinguistic development was a product of learning to read and write, for when engaging with written language a child can reflect upon the structures. This accords with those who contend that learning about language should come through discussing the language which the child is using, rather than through separate artificial exercises.

Olson and also Donaldson (1978) argue that written language serves to develop logical thought. They found that learning to read developed children's thinking abilities, for reading extended their mental representations and thus their knowledge of the world. By using books children learned about learning, and by taking away language from a speaker and placing it in a text it made it easier for children to challenge the content. Hence literacy promoted cognitive development in general and encouraged metalinguistic understanding in particular.

To define the metalinguistic awareness that children should acquire the National Curriculum outlines a range of necessary knowledge. For the first time knowledge about oracy is given equal weight to knowledge about literacy. The required knowledge extends to the use of talk for different purposes (e.g. presentational, interactional or in play and drama), and for different audiences (e.g. peer, teacher, other adults). This knowledge relates particularly to styles of delivery, the ability to adjust talk for different occasions and processes such as discussion, problemsolving or planning. Using talk for learning, especially in collaborative situations, also entails a positive attitude to the value of talk and the value of the collaborative context. In addition, sharing readings and writings with peers and adults provides opportunities for talking about and studying the meanings of texts and words, which can not only enhance our understanding of literary texts and language but also enrich our oral language.

FURTHER READING

The following books provide considerable detail about the English language and its historical development:

Bradley, H. (1968) *The Making of English*. Harmondsworth: Penguin.

Freeborn, D. (1986) *Varieties of English.* Basingstoke: Macmillan.
Hawkins, E. (1987) *Awareness of Language.* Cambridge: Cambridge University Press.

These titles demonstrate how children acquire working knowledge of linguistic features from very early years and throughout their school life:

Early years:
Crystal, D. (1976) *Child Language, Learning and Linguistics.* London: Edward Arnold.
Olson, D. (1984) 'See! Jumping! Some oral language antecedents of literacy' in Goelman, H., Oberg, A. and Smith, F. (eds) *Awakening to Literacy.* London: Heinemann.
Wells, G. (1987) *The Meaning Makers.* London: Hodder & Stoughton.

Early, primary and middle years:
Garton, A. and Pratt, C. (1989) *Learning to Be Literate.* Oxford: Basil Blackwell.
Perera, K. (1987) *Understanding Language.* Warwick: National Association of Advisors in English.
Romaine, S. (1984) *The Language of Children and Adolescents.* Oxford: Basil Blackwell.

2.3. MONITORING ORACY

Oracy, with its ephemeral nature, is notorious for being the most difficult of the three language areas to monitor. To monitor talk is particularly difficult, for the meaning or significance of a contribution is not always immediately obvious. To monitor the talk while the 'monitor' is participating is even more demanding. However, to record the talk on audiotape only allows access to the speaker. It does not measure the listener's or the speaker's ability to read the responses. Neither will audiotape allow access to the non-verbal gestures accompanying the talk. Some of these omissions can be picked up if videotape is used instead but too much 'technology' in the classroom can become very intrusive and distort the context in which the talking is taking place. Moreover, the advantages of using audio- or videotapes can often be outweighed by the length of time it takes to replay and analyse, much less transcribe.

Other features of oracy compound these problems. Its context is almost always social. Hence the relationships between the participants are also important and have greater but more fluctuating impact than does the relationship between reader and writer.

Because speaking and listening are interdependent, even if the interaction is silent, this means that the performance of either party is significantly affected by that of the other. This makes it very hard to allocate individual 'marks' in what is essentially a joint enterprise.

Further, as meanings and understandings are constructed over time, judgements should be based on cumulative sequences of interaction rather than on single utterances (which may each have multiple meanings). This provides more useful evidence than a frequency count or analysis of the distribution of particular categories of talk which some researchers have undertaken for their own purposes.

It is clear that monitoring oracy raises very particular problems. Nevertheless, many of these difficulties are due to teachers attempting to do too much. At the moment there are more models of monitoring oracy from researchers than there are from teachers, as it is only recently that teachers have been required to undertake this form of monitoring. It is not feasible to monitor oracy in as much detail as some research projects have done, nor is it necessary, unless there is a particular worry about a specific child.

The main benefits from monitoring oracy come through the involvement of the participants in reviewing their own talk and in the subsequent discussion. For in discussing their talk participants are encouraged to reflect their own roles, purposes and strategies. It provides a natural forum for developing the metalanguage of talk and for increasing awareness of the participants' processes.

In each of the sections above, there are a wide range of variables which could be monitored. But as was pointed out in Chapter 1 (p. 35) it is essential to be selective and focused in terms of

- what is going to be monitored
- who will be monitored
- when and where
- why and how the information will be used
- how the information will be recorded

Having once settled these points, it is possible to 'eavesdrop' on a peer group or to interact with a group with particular objectives in mind. It is important to remember that it is only possible to sample children's talk relating to a few key areas. Initially the task of monitoring oracy is daunting, but, if teachers are selective and undertake regular 'soundings', the increasing experience will soon lead to a growth in confidence. The more teachers become familiar with the objectives and the terminology, the more they will find ourselves recognizing features to which they were not alert before.

There is so much talk already in primary classrooms and consequently, plenty of opportunity for talk to take place naturally and be monitored unobtrusively. As teachers refine perceptions it will become easier to take a more objective view of the strategies used, and not only to take account of the content. This will enable all those involved in monitoring to give differentiated help to specific children and thereby develop their oracy as well as their ideas.

ACTIVITY

Monitoring Oracy

Using the Attainment Targets in conjunction with the Programmes of Study, devise a set of indices by which you could distinguish what a child is doing during an activity, so that you have evidence on which to base an appraisal, in discussion with that child.

A checklist format (no longer than half a side of A4) can be a quick way to collect the 'bare bones'. The remaining half a side can be used for qualitative comments to help 'put the flesh on the bones'.

FURTHER READING

For a critical view and a defence of oracy in the National Curriculum, see:

Maybin, J. (1988) 'A critical review of the DES Assessment and Performance Unit's oracy surveys'. *English in Education* 22 (1).
Brooks, G. (1989) 'The value and purpose of APU oracy assessment. A reply to Maybin'. *English in Education* 23 (2).

The next title, from the APU, presents evidence about the standards of oracy in primary schools, as elicited by the tasks set:

MacLure, M. and Hargreaves, M. (1986) *Speaking and Listening: Assessment at 11*. Windsor: NFER/Nelson.

The following book demonstrates an alternative way of investigating oracy in schools:

Rosen, H. (1982) *The Language Monitors*. London: London University Press.

Forthcoming publications from the National Oracy Project, Newcombe House, London W11 3JB, will reveal more about developing and monitoring oracy.

Part II

Reading

Chapter 3

Teachers and Reading

INTRODUCTION

Despite the fact that this area of language is the best researched, there are still huge areas of debate and disagreement. It is important to clarify our own beliefs and conceptions of reading so that we can translate our knowledge into pedagogic principles to underlie our classroom teaching practice.

Chapter 3 begins by examining what we mean by 'reading' and briefly reviewing the main alternative methods of 'teaching' reading. The second section identifies different types of published resources used for developing reading and discusses some issues involved in the management of a reading environment to 'entice' children into books. The third section notes some current practices in primary schools that attempt to use additional human resources to motivate and support readers: parents at home, adults who come into the classroom or older pupils who act as tutors.

3.1. WHAT COUNTS AS READING?

Many definitions of reading have been offered and each implies subtle distinctions which can be reflected in different classroom practices. The conception of reading has typically been a very narrow one, focusing on the efforts of young children aged between 5 and 7, or on the early efforts of older (remedial) children. Research on the teaching and learning of reading adopted a strictly behaviourist approach, focusing exclusively on the component parts of learning in the belief that these could be hierarchically ordered and sequenced as the basis for a reading programme. These components were word recognition (sight vocabulary, phonic analysis, speed of reading), comprehension (extending vocabulary, interpretation and evaluation), and study skills (use of library catalogues, indexes, summarization).

Whilst this narrow definition prevailed, teacher training and in-service education were similarly focused. This trend continued until changes in professional thinking took place during the 1970s. In the 1960s the behaviourist approach to learning began to be challenged by the psycho-linguistic approach. This recognized children as active learners and agents in their own efforts to 'make sense' of their world, including the world of print.

In reviewing developments in reading, Southgate *et al.* (1981) quote one of the early writers and researchers of reading, Huey (1908), who recognized the strengths of an interactive, problem-solving approach to reading:

> Until the insidious thought of reading as word pronouncing is well worked out of our heads, it is well to place the emphasis strongly where it really belongs, on reading as thought-getting (p. 23).

Much later, Morris (1973) stated: 'Reading is thinking under the stimulus of the printed word.' However, 'thinking' is just as complex a concept as 'reading'. To change the terms does not clarify the activity, but it may lead to a re-examination of the concept. It can also lead teachers to articulate their aims and procedures for teaching reading so that a clearer statement can be made about reading and a more consistant policy adopted.

(i)   Purposes, skills and strategies

Extensive researches over many decades have identified a plethora of variables which are involved in what Clay has termed the 'patterning of complex behaviour' (1979). This includes variables such as alternative purposes, component skills and a range of strategies, all of which contribute to the act of reading. Each of these will be reviewed in turn.

It is important to clarify the particular purpose of reading on each occasion for it affects how the reader, the reading process and the text is viewed. This in turn will affect the provision, teaching and consequently the learning of reading. In general, there have been three main teaching approaches distinguishable by their implied purpose. In historical order, these are:

- 'decoding', where the purpose is to translate the written squiggles on the page into words which can be sounded aloud or read silently (receptive);
- 'reading for meaning', where the emphasis is on understanding the text (active);
- 'responsive reading' where the notion of reading extends to a recognition that readers bring their own understandings to the text and then respond to, interact and create meanings with the author and text (interactive).

These alternative definitions lead to different practices in the classroom. The decoding approach tends to emphasise basic skills that are believed to help children recognize words and letters and to match letter shapes to the sounds they represent. This allows children to 'sound out' the words, a practice sometimes referred to as 'barking at print' because the emphasis is on being able to decode the written word rather than on understanding or responding.

The second approach recognizes that the function of the printed word is to communicate meanings. Hence, the emphasis is on a concept of reading which embraces decoding as well as comprehending. The third approach focuses on reading as an interactive process that involves the author, text and reader in a dynamic activity. Through this, readers generate their own meanings in response to the author through the medium of the text.

Hence, if decoding is reading by 'ear and eye', then reading for meaning can loosely be thought of as reading with the 'brain', whereas responsive reading is reading with 'heart and mind' in order to create both cognitive and affective meanings and responses. The approaches are not mutually exclusive but part of the same continuum. Hence, in order to respond to text it is important to understand as well as decode.

In order to decode, a number of component *skills* have been identified. The first set includes visual discrimination and visual memory. These skills assist whole-word recognition as well as recognition of individual letter/symbol shapes. Gough and Hill-inger (in Garton and Pratt, 1989) found that children can usefully acquire a 40-word sight vocabulary as a basis for tackling new text. Such a vocabulary should comprise words which are frequently encountered in text, difficult to predict from context and phonically irregular, thus hard to decode.

The ease with which words can be recognized may depend on a number of factors;

- distinctiveness of the word shape (whether long or short);
- variation in terms of letters which have ascenders (b,d,f,h,k,l,t) or descenders (g,j,p,q,y);
- whether the word is familiar or not in the child's oral vocabulary.

Thus a text which has many short words with little to distinguish them visually may be 'harder' to read in terms of visual discrimination than a text with long words, although the latter are often believed to be 'harder'. Hence, 'the man ran to the van' could be more problematic than 'the robber fled to the truck'!

Further skills, such as auditory discrimination and auditory memory, have been identified as helping towards building up knowledge about sound–symbol match, or the relationship between letter shapes and phonic sounds. The practice of these skills is complicated by the fact that English is less regular in its sound–symbol match than most other languages. Weaver (1980) estimates that there are 211 different sounds represented by 26 letters and their combinations! Despite this wide range, at least 70 per cent are regular (Albrow, quoted in Peters, 1975). With more sophisticated phonic rules the percentage of regularities can be greatly increased. The number of phonic sounds is approximately 44, but it is the number of alternative spellings available to convey these sounds that can be so confusing. English contains thousands of homophones (words which sound alike but do not look alike, e.g. sight and site). The numbers of homographs (words which look but do not sound alike, e.g. bow of a boat and of a ribbon) are merely numbered in hundreds. Another difficulty is provided by homonyms (where the words look alike and sound alike but have different meanings, e.g. TSB bank and river bank).

Apart from the diversity of spelling in written language, there is also diversity in regional pronunciation. This is particularly evident in the length of the vowel sounds, which varies markedly between the northern regions and the home counties: for example, the pronunciation of the 'u' in bus or the 'a' in bath.

The practice of visual–auditory skills depends on two prerequisite skills: analysis (identifying each sound, symbol or segment of a word) and synthesis (being able to integrate each sound into a word). For some children, it is a major step to move from identifying isolated sounds to merging the sounds to form a word. So a child who confidently identifies initial sounds for the purposes of playing games like I-Spy (c for cat) may fail to hear how to merge the sounds together (c-a-t 'makes' cat).

Other kinds of merging are required in 'blending' two consonants, for example, pl, gr, st. This is distinct from combining consonants to create a new sound, as in digraphs like sh, th, ch. Further combinations are of vowels, to create diphthongs (au, aw, ay, ea, ew, ey, ie, oa, oi, ou, ow, oy, ui), or of vowels and consonants (ar, er, ir, or, ur). More extensive merging is needed to integrate 'consonant clusters' of more than two consonants (e.g. str, spl, scr) or deal with letter 'strings' (e.g. -ing, -ong, -ank, -unk, -and, -ent).

In addition to this form of analysis and synthesis, there are skills of a different order relating to analysis and synthesis in terms of meaning. Their operation enables us to recognize that parts of a word (sometimes very small, as in the case of morphemes) bear meaning. There are, for example:

- common inflectional endings, such as -ed indicating the past tense (crashed);
- s indicating plural or third person singular verb-ending (horrors, he runs);
- 's indicating possession (Pat's).
- prefixes (e.g. un-, de-, re-, il-, im-, in-)
- suffixes (e.g. -ness, -ous, -ive, -ity, -able, -ible, -ly).

Knowing about these meaningful parts may help in breaking a new word into recognizable bits, which could help in pronouncing and understanding it (e.g. un-break-able). Knowledge of morphemes can also help in breaking down and building words, (e.g. farm-er, detect/detector/detective, even anti-dis-establish-ment-arian-ism) or in playing with them, as when we invent new words (e.g. blueish-ness). Our understanding of a range of words is increased, e.g. compounds (door+step=doorstep), portmanteau words (break-fast+lunch=brunch, situation+comedy=sitcom) and acronyms (radar=radio detecting and ranging).

There are also skills relating to aspects of reading which focus on larger units than letters or words. Very detailed work has been carried out to examine physical aspects of reading, in terms of 'eye-movements' as the reader processes the print on a page (Smith, 1978). Readers vary in the proportion of time spent in 'bouncing' along a line of print, 'fixing' on focal points and 'regressing' over past sections. An important aspect is the perceptual span of a reader, which is normally 2 degrees and may cover eight characters of conventional adult size print (Mitchell, 1982).

However, print intended for young children is usually much larger. Therefore children are forced into viewing fewer letters at a time. This may hinder the synthesis of individual sound-symbols and make it harder to make sense of what they are reading. Glinkoff (1976, in Beech, 1985) found that children's ability to process print was related to their capacity to scan larger units of text: as they moved from letters/words to whole phrases so it was easier to 'make sense'. This also related to the speed with which a child reads: Hogaboam and Perfetti (1978, in Beech, 1985) found that increased speed can facilitate comprehension.

Not only do whole words and parts of words (morphemes) carry meanings, but the parts of the sentence and their relationships also carry meaning (syntax). Ruddell (in Goodman and Flemming, 1969) argues that the 'word' is not a natural psychological unit for communication; rather it is the phrase, sentence and group of interlinked sentences which are the key units in conveying meanings. Within such units it is the relationship between subject and verb, and the word order particular to English which help to structure meaning and convey the overall message. Meaning is also reflected in the way sentences are joined – by connectives and conjunctions (and, but, so) or by cohesive linking (see Chapter 5 (p. 195) for more detail).

Whilst the above skills may contribute to 'decoding', those which contribute to 'responsive reading' have been much less clearly identified. The skills of recognizing large units and links are often instinctively used by a reader because the motivation to 'make sense' of language is strong. Because language is highly predictable Paris *et al.* (in Garton and Pratt, 1989) suggest that simple comprehension strategies based on the 'expectancy principle' should be taught. At a general level, readers should be encouraged to consider the title and characters and to talk about the kind of text that might follow. This will encourage the oral rehearsal of words they might find in the text. They should also decide their reading goals and appropriate strategies (e.g. skim for the gist or close read for detailed appreciation) before beginning to read. During the reading, they should paraphrase and check their understanding of the text using illustrations to confirm where appropriate. This form of 'top down' processing is a key factor in the psycho-linguistic approach to reading (Smith 1975; Rumelhart, 1977).

A further way by which a reader can make sense of a text is by 'chunking' it and integrating groups of words or sentences into sections which are meaningful units. These units, together, convey a key idea, or contribute to a main theme (Durkin, 1979). The reader can be encouraged to stop and 'see' the text by 'imagizing' or 'picturing' the meanings which can be created from the text (Beech, 1985). Older children can make cartoon strips, maps or diagrams of events so that they can check their interpretations against each other and provide a visual record of the text so far. Such images do not only relate to literal understandings from the text, but can also be developed to convey inferential or projected understandings which emerge between the author, the text and the reader.

All of the above *skills* contribute to the reading process, mostly at a word or phrase level. But they are not yet adequate in explaining how we read. A further set of variables can be added in terms of broader *strategies* used by readers when making sense of the whole text. These particular ways of reading have been found to increase the efficiency of more fluent intermediate readers when they adjust their strategies to read for a particular purpose.

Work begun by Harri-Augstein *et al.* (1982) identified a range of strategies used by readers when tackling a whole text. These strategies were found to vary considerably in the case of 'good' readers who were efficient at responding, understanding and, where necessary, decoding print. The strategies were found to relate to particular purposes set by the reader.

For example, when 'reading for pleasure' the reader would

adopt a 'steady' strategy of continuous progress through the text. If reading for the purposes of studying (fiction or non-fiction) the reader might adopt an interrupted strategy, using stop–start tactics of reading interspersed with pauses for reflection or with passages taken at a slower pace for closer attention to detail.

Reading for information (associated with non-fiction, though not exclusively) may require additional strategies. For example, the index might be skimmed to find an appropriate 'key' word; the selected section might also be skimmed to see if it is, after all, suitable; the page might be scanned for particular names, dates or times before perhaps being read closely; further pages may be skipped, other skimmed, the reader might then return to read or re-read prior sections. The whole 'reading' activity would be anything but 'steady'.

Apart from the increased efficiency of adjusting reading strategies to suit specific purposes of reading, 'good' readers also adjust their reading habits depending on their mode of reading. They might, for example, read aloud (oral reading) to share with others, or read 'in performance' (dramatic presentation) or read silently and alone. Silent reading allows a wider range of strategies to suit the changes within a text.

'Good' readers will skim sections of a fast action story to get the gist of what is happening, but they will slow down and savour each word in other sections where the tension subsides and the reader can relax a little with the characters in the story. There comes a time when a devoted parent is reading aloud a bed time story and is told (politely) that 'It's boring'. This is because reading aloud slows down the action too much and the child is at the stage of being able to read it silently faster and keep up with the action. Such a declaration should be welcomed by the parent for it shows that the child has learnt to adapt reading strategies and can now skim read when reading silently. This should greatly increase the speed and also the pleasure of reading.

Goodman (1965) and Pugh (1978) identified three *stages* in reading modes: oral (where the reader voices each word aloud), aural (where the reader 'says' each word in their head silently) and silent (where the reader skims without vocalizing and without noting every word). It is important to realize that readers adapt their mode of reading to suit the particular text. When adults pick up a textbook in a specialist area which is unfamiliar to them, it is likely that they, too, will revert to aural reading, mouthing the words or actually saying them out loud.

Many children reach a plateau around the age of 9 years. By this time they are competent readers but may not derive pleasure from their reading because it is not yet effortless. This process of 'how to read' still detracts from focusing on 'what is being read'. It is important to discuss and make explicit the wider range of reading strategies for these readers so that they become aware of the differences between oral, aural and silent reading. These intermediate skills also need to be taught.

Pugh (1978) suggests that children can be encouraged to 'speed' read through games. For example, this could include scanning for specific words (e.g. place names, identifiable by initial capital letters, or dates, times or prices, identifiable by numerals). An alternative suggestion is to cover some of the print to the left and right of a page and ask a child to read the middle section (in imitation of the eye movements of fast readers).

Learning to read, therefore, does not end when a child can read sufficiently fluently to experience understanding and some enjoyment. Start and Wells (1972) estimated that 15 per cent of 11-year-olds are only semi-literate (i.e. have a reading age of between 7 and 9 years) and are likely to remain so. The act of reading for these children is still sufficiently arduous for them not to read for 'profit and delight', as HMI noted (DES, 1978).

Neville and Pugh (1982) also suggest that fluency is an aspect of reading that needs to be taught. It may develop 'naturally' if children are allowed to read plenty of books which are 'easy'. Constant pressure to move on to 'harder' books often results in children always reading books which are a challenge, where they cannot relax and skim for the gist or until they reach their favourite part. The development of fluency also requires sufficient opportunities for regular prolonged silent reading. Such periods are known as USSR (Uninterrupted Sustained Silent Reading) or ERIC (Everyone Reading in Class, including the teacher). It can also be developed by encouraging children to listen to their own reading (possibly a tape of their own 'performance'). They also need models of expressive reading, so as to note the use of intonation and expression.

This form of critical listening to one's own reading, followed by further rehearsal, allows the reader to give more effective consideration to expression and meaning. For any but the most fluent, one-off reading does not allow enough time to think ahead and anticipate the story. Another very real incentive for this kind of rehearsal and performance occurs in group play readings, an activity suggested in the Programmes of Study and which is now being increasingly supported by published classroom materials.

A further suggested way of developing fluency is the use of the 'cloze' procedure. A short extract is provided in which some words have been deleted. The reader then has to read ahead (or back) to get the sense of the passage and be able to guess the missing word. The reason for lack of fluency is often that a reader is reluctant to continue when they meet a 'difficult' word. A cloze passage which encourages 'reading on' in order to discover meaning can help to promote fluency and, eventually, silent skimming.

There are many ways of using 'cloze' (Rye, 1982). Some would argue that noting the appropriateness of children's suggestions for 'filling the gaps' is a much better way of assessing readability and understanding than using traditional readability formulae. Hence, for assessing general comprehension of a passage a regular deletion procedure is recommended (e.g. deleting every 9th, 7th, or 5th word). Sometimes for diagnostic purposes, a particular kind of word may be deleted, e.g. pronouns, to check children's understandings of their role in linking the meanings without repeating the same key word, or to delete adjectives or adverbs to check vocabulary development. In non-fiction texts key words can be deleted to check whether the specialist terminology has been acquired.

(ii) Pedagogic principles

The previous section described some of the variables which are part of being able to read but there is no one fixed link between such descriptive features and how they are translated into a prescription for teaching. The many skills that contribute to reading could be arranged in a hierarchy of complexity based on a logical ordering and a programme of activities devised based on this analysis.

This graduated 'bottom-up' approach, however, may not actually relate to what children do as they become readers.

If we assume that children are active meaning-makers, who look for patterns and purposes in their experiences, then we must also assume that they are looking for patterns and purposes in their attempt to make sense of print. In fact, based on their experiences of watching others read, children expect that print makes sense. Becoming a reader is unlikely to be motivated by the desire to acquire proficiency in a logical sequence of skills. It is more likely that a child will want to become a reader to be able to make sense of print and because they want to experience the satisfaction of becoming more confident as a reader. Such confidence can be gained by increasing the proficient use of 'expectancy', context, visual and phonic clues that will facilitate even more refined guesses about what print says. This approach is characterized as 'top down' and emphasizes that learning to read stems from a psychological desire to create whole meanings from the linguistic parts.

Clearly reading *is* a complex behaviour and the skills and strategies identified above are important contributory factors. How then does a child acquire these? Alternative approaches have been offered by competing protagonists who have advocated their method as the key to solving the problem of teaching children to read. Sometimes it seems that the method of teaching itself may have created difficulties for learner readers by being so distant from what we now know about how children learn. The Great Debate of the 1960s about the methods of teaching reading was reviewed by Chall (1967) and reviewed again in the light of new research (1983). The first review sought to identify 'the best method' and to distinguish the merits of the prevailing alternatives. The second was a much more cautious appraisal of how each of the methods might play a role at different stages in a mixed-methods approach. The main current approaches are:

Word recognition. This recognizes the need for children to be able to achieve some early success in reading and to make sense of text. The method therefore encourages the idea of developing a 'sight' vocabulary by rote learning 'key words'. These are selected in terms of the frequency with which they occur in children's books. Hence, the method emphasizes visual recognition and memory. It often results in early texts using a high percentage of these words in the text, which therefore tends to become rather

repetitive and not always inviting to read. The method is sometimes referred to as 'look and say'.

Phonic method. This recognizes the need to support children in
acquiring skills to help them tackle new words which are not in
their 'sight' vocabulary. The method emphasizes auditory discrimination and memory and also the ability to match phonic sounds
with their letter symbols. This also results in texts being devised to
'help' the reader by being phonically regular and 'easy' to decode.
Such restrictions on vocabulary make it difficult for writers to
produce interesting stories written in flowing language. It often
results in stilted texts which, again, do not provide much of an
incentive to learn to read.

Language experience approach. This approach aims to make
greater use of children's existing knowledge concerning oral language, its structures and predictability, to guess meaning from
context. It relies on children's cognitive processing of the text and
thus assumes that children already have a rich experience of both
the spoken and the written word. In a classroom context this
experience cannot always be assumed. It often needs to be
provided.

Data on how teachers actually operate in the classroom is rare.
However, a Schools Council project (Southgate *et al.*, 1981) did
collect and examine such data as part of a major research programme. They found that teachers teaching 9-year-olds to read
spent the *highest* proportion of the time on 'hearing children read'
(14 per cent). Teachers spent, on average, 20 to 30 minutes a day
hearing children read and 'testing' their performance. They only
spent between 2 and 3 minutes with any one child and approximately only 30 seconds without some interruption. A further 13
per cent of their time was spent on organizing literacy activities
and 11 per cent on commenting on and evaluating children's work.
    The *lowest* percentage of time spent on any of the literacy be-
haviours being researched was 4 per cent on direct teaching of
reading (usually sight vocabulary, phonic analysis, comprehension
and grammar). A further 4 per cent was spent on 'higher-order
activities', i.e. the teacher attempted to expand the content of a
book and discuss it with the child. It would seem from this picture

that children were largely left to teach themselves and that constant practice, or letting the materials do the teaching, was the dominant strategy.

The teaching of reading often reflects a narrow conception of the subject. Work done by Hodgson and Pryle (1985) found that the majority of teachers had a limited and instructional view of reading. Their classroom practice was dominated by the use of phonic-based and word recognition exercises and graded books which gave repeated practice in word-building.

Recent HMI reports (DES, 1978, 1982) found over-preoccupation with the 'basics'. In the majority of schools the children spent a good deal of time decoding print with the result that they read mechanically with little understanding of, or interest in, content. Whilst there is still fierce debate about the best method of teaching reading, McNaughton (1987) found that it was not the *method* of teaching which was the significant factor in children's success but the extent to which they had a clear grasp of the teacher's goals. A further significant factor was the agreement between parents and teachers on 'what counts as reading' and on appropriate support strategies and experiences (see p. 130).

To extend children's interest in books teachers relied on reading stories aloud, on average four times a week for about 15 minutes. Teachers also encouraged the use of the library to extend reading habits. Only three teachers interviewed suggested personal example, or the use of parents as a way of encouraging enthusiasm for reading (Southgate *et al.*, 1981).

FURTHER READING

The following titles are excellent books about the reading debate in general. The first emphasizes an interactive approach to reading and has a number of helpful practical applications. The second adopts a mixed-methods approach, and the next two are wide-ranging reviews of reading research for practising teachers.

Wade, B. (ed.) (1990) *Reading for Real*. Milton Keynes: Open University Press.

Roberts, G. (1989) *Teaching Children to Read and Write*. Oxford: Basil Blackwell.

Beard, R. (1987) *Developing Reading 3–13*. London: Hodder & Stoughton.

ACTIVITY

Observation of the Teaching of Reading

Observation tells us a great deal about how we actually teach, what we actually do.

Arrange for a colleague and yourself to observe each other.

Negotiate what you want to have observed,
i.e. the indices (behaviours) you want a colleague to note so you can evaluate what you do when you are 'teaching' reading.

Decide what you mean by 'teaching reading'.

What would you expect to see? e.g.

Teacher modelling:
  (i)   oral reading
       reading aloud (story, brochure, letter, etc.)
       reading along with child (shadowing child)
       reading for child (highlighting instructions)
  (ii) silent reading
       reading book, memo, child's story
 (iii) responsive reading
       leading discussion of a shared story
 (iv) using reading
       using catalogue, book index
       making notes

Teacher monitoring:
  (i)   hearing oral reading
  (ii) supplying word/phrase
 (iii) explaining sound/meaning of word or phrase

Teacher managing:
  (i)   directing book choice, interest/content or level/difficulty
  (ii) allocating associated reading activity
       e.g. game, worksheet

Chapman, L. J. (1987) *Reading from 5–11*. Milton Keynes: Open University Press.

The next two titles focus on the neglected aspects: the reading/writing link and developing response to both factual and literary texts.

Smith, J. and Alcock, A. (1990) *Revisiting Literacy*. Milton Keynes: Open University Press.

Cairney, T. H. (1990) *Teaching Reading Comprehension*. Milton Keynes: Open University Press.

The title below provides examples of teacher behaviour relating to the teaching of reading. The method of data collection is through systematic observation using schedules. Criteria for observing children are also suggested:

Southgate, V. *et al.* (1981) *Extending Beginning Reading*. London: Heinemann for the Schools Council.

The following titles all offer different ways to monitor children's reading, the first two covering all language areas:

Jagger, A. and Smith-Burke, M. T. (eds) (1985) *Observing the Language Learner*. Newark, Delaware: I.R.A.

Neville, M. (1988) *Assessing and Teaching Language*. London: Macmillan for Scottish Education Dept.

Strang, R. (1972) 'Observation in the classroom' and 'Informal reading inventories' in Melnik, A. and Merritt, J. (eds) *The Reading Curriculum*. London: University of London Press for Open University.

The following is recommended by the English Working Party (Cox Committee):

Barrs, M. *et al.* (1988) *Primary Language Record*. Harcourt Brace Jovanovich (for CLPE, ex-ILEA).

3.2.   MANAGING THE BOOK ENVIRONMENT

(i)   Structure and reading schemes

The debate on teaching methods is inseparable from the debate on reading materials. Here the main issue is often reduced to the simple dichotomy: 'structured reading schemes' *v.* 'real books'. However, in practice the choice is not always so clear-cut.

Books specially written for the purpose of teaching reading have existed for many decades. All such schemes have been based on an implicit theory of 'what counts as reading' and 'how reading should be taught'. This in turn involved assumptions on how children learn to read based on contemporary research. An overview of the advantages and disadvantages of reading schemes can be seen in the table below.

Advantages for the teacher	*Disadvantages for the teacher*
Structured and graded, with in-built monitoring.	Constrains and undermines individual decision-making.
Advantages for the child Familiar, secure	*Disadvantages for the child* Repetitive, boring, stilted 'readerese' language, unrelated to existing knowledge of stories.

Because of the wide variety of materials now available it is crucially important to match the theory of reading that underlies any materials with the prevailing reading policy of the school. Management implications, ease of monitoring, supplementary and extension materials, variety and attractiveness as well as cost will all be additional considerations.

In any scheme progression is measured in terms of levels of difficulty. These levels are based on readability formulae which attempt to determine numerically the difficulty of a particular text for a 'typical' reader. The variables used for this measurement are the length of sentences, number of words with more than 3/4/5 syllables, or the proportion of substantive 'concept' words to 'function' words (e.g. in, to, and, there) in each sentence. These mathematical formulae are calculated to produce a 'reading age' i.e. the expected age of a child who would be able to read and understand the text unaided.

The notion of readability has been much explored (Harrison, 1980) and heavily criticized. Critics point to the disparity between readability levels due to the disagreement about what makes a text difficult. Moreover the concept of a text being difficult ignores the notion that reading is an interactive process between author–reader–text. It also disregards evidence that the difficulty of a text depends partly on the experience of the particular reader as regards content and familiarity with how texts work, and partly on subjective features such as interest in the text. Further, readability formulae only measure the 'text' itself yet, particularly in younger children's books, the pictures carry much of the storyline. Hence the relationship between text and illustration could be very important in terms of the kinds of clues provided for the reader.

A further issue relating to readability is that of distinguishing between the child who can read the text accurately and the child who understands it, and at what level. Harrison suggests three levels of accuracy in reading aloud: independent, instructional and frustration. These levels are determined by the accuracy rate of a child when reading aloud. A child who achieves 99–100 per cent accuracy is said to be independent: 95–98 per cent accuracy is classified as instructional, and less than 95 per cent as frustration. More important, the degree of comprehension for each level is put at 90–100 per cent, 70–90 per cent and less than 70 per cent respectively.

However, this raises two problems: some 'mistakes' will be 'worse' than others (i.e. there will be a bigger discrepancy between what is in the text and what the child reads), and the physical and social act of reading aloud itself may pose particular problems for some children, who would read the text comfortably to themselves in a silent capacity.

In addition to the content of the text itself, which is the author's responsibility, there are also factors in the way the text is presented that have been found to affect children's handling of it. These are the responsibility of the publisher, who needs to ensure that the layout of the text on the page, the timing of the page-breaks and positioning of the illustrations all support the reader. Line-breaks, in particular, can sometimes hinder the sense of the text. For example, if the end of the line coincides with the end of a phrase a reader can sometimes begin the new line as though it is a new sentence, thus destroying the flow of the text (Raban, in Bentley, 1985). The arrangement of dialogue can also be a hindrance. For example, if a section of dialogue begins with the name of the person who is speaking (i.e. Tom said, ' ...' rather than ' ...,' said Tom) then the reader is cued in and is more likely to read with appropriate expression (Crystal, 1976). Some texts try to assist the reader by printing the dialogue in a different colour to distinguish it from the narrative text.

Design and typography thus play a part in readability but it is the quality of the story that is the most significant factor in enticing a child into reading. It is precisely the quality of reading scheme stories (particularly the early ones) which have acquired such a poor reputation. The power of 'story' to inspire a child to read has been more carefully considered in current schemes, which often use more natural language and better quality illustrations than in the past. The social context for reading is also now being recognized by publishers through the relatively recent production of 'big books'. These are large-size formats which are big enough for the whole class to see the pictures and words and read the text aloud together or follow the teacher's finger-pointing as she reads. Other attempts by publishers to encourage a social context for reading are through books which provide two versions of the text: a simplified one for the child to read, and a fuller one (on the facing page, or in a teacher's edition) that fills out the storyline.

The alternative to using schemes is to use 'real' books. This means using as wide a selection as possible from the rich stock of children's books now available. There is no restriction to one particular scheme or set of schemes. The books can be chosen for their literary merit, the quality of their storyline, the interest level of the illustrations and their popularity with children rather than because of their 'readability' as defined by mathematical formulae.

A third possibility is a compromise arrangement which lies between these two positions. For example, a mixture is provided using a number of different reading schemes, based on alternative theories of reading (on the 'something for everyone' principle) together with 'real' books. This is sometimes referred to as the Individualized Reading approach. Such an approach offers a wider range of books yet they are still structured and graded. A further possibility is to use selected 'real' books, grouped for approximate 'difficulty', based on readability criteria and classroom experience.

(ii)   Content and the power of story

If a 'real' book approach is adopted, important decisions have to be made over which books to choose. Which books do children like? To what extent should their preferences be paramount? Are there any children's choices we would not allow and on which grounds? What weight should an adult's conception of 'good' books be given? What part is played by attractiveness, interactiveness and accessibility?

A Schools Council study of the reading habits of 8,000 10- to 14-year-olds (Whitehead, 1977) showed that Enid Blyton was the most popular author for 20 per cent of the sample, particularly the girls. The Blyton phenomenon has been much analysed. Tucker (1981) believes that her appeal is especially strong with the 7–11 age group, who prefer simple novels with limited vocabularies, short sentences, clear concrete plots, stereotyped characters and constant adventure in which good always triumphs over evil. The Blyton 'formula' works for many children. It is in a similar mould to certain imported children's television series that are very visual, action-packed, explicit in plot and character and highly moral.

A more recent popular children's author is Roald Dahl. His books have a different kind of appeal. He believes that 'children are tougher, coarser and they laugh at things that make us squirm'. Dahl adapts his style and writes for a wide age range of children: *The Enormous Crocodile* is aimed at 5-year-olds; *Danny the Champion of the World* at 10–12-year-olds. He also writes books for teenagers and adults.

Whilst surveys have shown which books are most popular it is also instructive to try and identify why. Aitkin (1982) suggests that pre-school children relate well to books about things that are familiar to them (e.g. going shopping, having birthdays). They also respond to stories that have a single focal character, who often 'stars' in a series of stories. Meek (1982) reports that children often like stories about animals and toys, which allow them to feel superior and in control. Using animals and toys is sometimes one way around the problem of gender and race stereotyping.

For most children of primary school age, plot is all-important. For younger children a straightforward, chronological narration is easiest to follow. Flashbacks, dreams and other devices work with older children. An attention-getting beginning, exciting middle and satisfying ending are always popular: so too, are stories which are comfortingly familiar and provide security and warmth, especially for children who need reassurance rather than suspense. Nevertheless, Bettelheim (1977) found that some children can be helped to resolve their fears through exploring frightening and gruesome aspects, as in many traditional tales.

For children in junior school, whose stamina is greater, stories can be much more fully developed: in terms of setting, mood, characters, motives, circumstances, events, problem and final resolution. However, Chambers (1985) suggests that stories that are too explicit can dampen the reader's response. He suggests that it is important 'to leave a gap' by which the reader is drawn into the story and contributes to it, for if nothing is left to the imagination, the result could be passive, uninvolved (or 'rejective') readers.

It is important for children to have the opportunity to discuss their book preferences: not just which they prefer but why. In this way they begin to acquire a vocabulary for talking about books and a framework in which to analyse and judge them. Cambourne and Brown (in Andrews, 1989) demonstrate this as an important way of helping children get to grips with a range of genres, which once recognized can be incorporated into their own writing. This awareness of how authors write, the way stories are structured, and the language used in order to achieve their impact are aspects of writing with which children can interact.

Children's tastes, like adults', will vary enormously, according to mood and needs, so it is important to provide as wide a range of books as possible. The challenge of encountering unfamiliar genres will be less threatening if children have discussed their likes and dislikes and been helped to appreciate variety. Yet we must also remember that continual challenge is not always constructive. Readers must be encouraged to luxuriate in 'easier' books in between the challenges!

However, libraries are stocked by adults rather than children. Books ordered by librarians with the 'average' child in mind or books bought as presents by relatives are often chosen on the basis of some abstract notion of a 'good' book, or what constitutes 'quality literature'. But what is 'children's' literature? Is it, as Beard (1987) poses, writing which is exclusively for children (audience), or written about children (content), or something presented simply so that children can understand it (level)? If it is for children can it seriously be considered 'literature'? Or, if it is so good, why is it exclusively 'children's' literature? Beard suggests that fiction written for children should be judged by the same standards as that written for adults: stories of quality.

Many concepts of 'literature' exist. Dixon (1967) suggested that literature can fulfil a key role by promoting personal development and transmitting cultural heritage. Hardy (1968) suggested that literature 'develops our knowledge of the (often stubborn) conditions in the outer world and also our inner world of beliefs and values'. Rosen and Rosen (1973) argued that 'fiction allows us to speak of what has been and what might be . . . it sets the imagination free to explore possibilities'. The Bullock Report (DES, 1975) went further when it claimed

> that it helps to shape our personality, refine the sensibility, sharpen critical intelligence; that it is a powerful instrument for empathy, a medium through which the child can acquire its values. (p. 124)

This implies that the definition of literature relies not only on the structure of the text but also on its effect on the reader, and on the nature of the 'imaginative response' that it engenders.

Tucker (in Beard, 1987) suggests that what differentiates children's from adults' fiction is the degree of moral complexity. In children's fiction there is 'a firmer hand on the tiller, guiding the reader through complexities and setting sail towards a resolution that is broadly going to make moral sense'. This was certainly true of the 18th- and 19th-century children's book. This was followed by the so-called Golden Age of children's literature in the pre-1914 period, characterized by a child's eye view of the world. For the first time, children were the focus of the stories and their feelings, outlook, adventures and values were explored as they made sense of the world around them – a world peopled by all generations, though still essentially a middle-class, educated or genteel people.

The post-war emphasis seemed to be 'escapism' – either through romantic fantasy or by creating a sense of security through historical settings. By the 1970s there was a new mood of 'realism' in children's books. The focus shifted to include as yet under-represented people and settings: minority groups, working-class and urban environments. At first this was often tokenistic but as more writers from these groups began to get published such fiction began to show a truer sense of other realities.

A further role of 'literature' is outlined by Chambers (1985). He suggests that books play a crucial role in the socialization of the pre-school and school-aged child. An environment with experience of books can encourage an enthusiasm for books, rather than an emphasis on using and plundering books. Moreover, the content of the books can play an important part in the development of the child's thinking. Chambers quotes Schucking (1923) on the various types of books that children need both to confirm and extend their lives: books about familiar events, imaginative fairy stories, adventure, dreamy or sentimental books, satirical and challenging books and autobiographical literature.

If we accept that reading takes children beyond firsthand experiences, enables them to project themselves into unfamiliar places, times and cultures, then books can play an important part in their personal and moral development. We therefore need to identify what kinds of needs children might have which books might possibly help them to meet.

Kellmer-Pringle (1975) emphasized the importance of security, appreciation and love together with the importance of new experiences, praise, recognition and responsibility. Children need to feel that they belong and that they are loved. Maslow (1954) proposed different levels of universal need:

- physical needs, for food, drink, warmth and safety;
- emotional needs for love and security;
- social needs to be accepted and to belong, yet also the confidence to be an independent, autonomous, contributing member of a group.

Tucker (1981) believes that there are important stages in children's psychological development to which children's books can helpfully relate. Books which get 'inside' the mind of the child are thus likely to be successful with children.

Books for younger children, in particular, often focus on physical and emotional needs. Books can help provide a feeling of safety and normality by confirming our own kind of existence through everyday activities like getting up, going out, having tea and going to bed. The illustrations can confirm our kind of house, street, town or village. It's important, of course, to make sure that the books *do* reflect the lifestyles of children in their own classrooms. These books often feature and try to resolve common fears like getting lost, losing friends, being afraid of the dark.

Social needs, such as the need to belong, are expressed in many different ways in books, especially those dealing with situations involving change and the establishing of new relationships, such as when a member of the family is added or changed, when children move house or change school. Learning to make, keep, or break friendships may also involve change.

Being appreciated, recognized and valued is also vitally important to a person's well-being. Many books focus on grownups' inability to pay attention to children. The resulting feelings of loneliness, helplessness and inconsequentiality can be countered through make-believe and magical powers. These powers might be outside intervention (as in some fairy stories) or may involve the development of the main character's magical or superhuman powers. Alternatively, stories can show how even the youngest and smallest characters can turn situations to their advantage. This latter feature is often the theme of folk tales, where craftiness outwits strength or age (e.g. Brer Rabbit, Anansi).

The need to develop confidence and to contribute to the social group often leads to self-testing situations, dares and adventures which display courage and bravery as well as dangerous 'pranks' or even cruelty. Stories focusing on such issues range from 'schooldays' fiction and holiday adventures, to those which explore human relationships more seriously. Developing courage and independence is also the theme of many legends and traditional tales using a 'journey of discovery' as a device to demonstrate 'true' values.

Many children's stories provide role models. It is important that these heroes and heroines should not represent gender and race stereotypes or be merely tokenistic substitutes. An alternative is the 'unlikely hero' (the wimp with spots and glasses, instead of the tall guy with muscle and manliness). It is also important to encourage children to appreciate others' viewpoints and values. This could involve the need for understanding and belonging in situations of transition, e.g. between different generations, religions, races, classes. Books can help children to extend their understandings beyond their own world and to encompass a wider perspective.

Yet however helpful books may be, teachers' capacity to handle such issues will depend on their own maturity and experience. Maturity is a complex concept and one which relates to our intellectual capacity for grasping the issues, our ability and willingness to empathize with different perspectives, as well as our level of moral development and personal and social understandings. Researchers such as Kohlberg (in Fontana, 1981) and Bull (1969) have attempted to define stages of moral development, which could provide a useful guide to children's capacity for coping with many of the complex facets of real and fictional life. The following table, based on Kohlberg, and Bull, outlines possible stages of moral development.

Pre-moral (2–4 yrs)	Children highly 'ego-centric' and see the world from their point of view only. Children 'centrized' (see one aspect at a time). They note action and consequence, not always the agent or cause, and rarely grasp motive.
4–7 yrs	Children appreciate the need for co-operation, though still have difficulty distinguishing:– animate/inanimate: 'poor book' (animism); use/purpose: 'sand is to play in' (finalism); self/ other as agent: 'I pull my shadow' (dynamism).
Conformity, Socionomy (7–9 yrs)	Children de-centrize – can handle a number of issues simultaneously. Also more 'socio-centric' and understand mutual reciprocity. Know 'rules' can be made for convenience (not immutable or only an adult's preserve); create clubs, games.
9–11 yrs	Children may subscribe to 'equity justice' and create fairness by positive discrimination and handicapping. 'Justice' and 'wrongs' also no longer considered absolute. Notion of motives and mitigating circumstances emerges.

Conscience, Autonomy (12–18 yrs)	Young people can reason, hypothesize, manipulate multiple concepts and integrate others' views. Adolescents often become 'centralized' – at a conceptual rather than a concrete level (e.g. believe their views are universal, or should be, and are self-evidently 'right'; also, the distinction between ideal and reality is blurred).

The pressures and tensions at each stage are identifiable in many books which could be used to help children cope with these important growth points.

(iii)   Attraction, interaction and accessibility

Visual attractiveness influences a child's choice of a particular book. Attractiveness is partly a feature of the cover design, partly to do with the layout of the book (the type, spacing, arrangement of text and illustration) and also the quality of the illustrations.

Illustrations are an important factor in encouraging children to read a book. Alderson (1973) argued for the importance of integrating text and illustration so that the illustrations enrich and extend the text. Illustrations can serve many purposes. They can be:

- scene-setting ... providing general context and background for location and mood, thus reinforcing the text
- focusing agent ... providing a clue to new words in the text (a reading aid); clarifying unfamiliar objects or events (informational input); adding detail to the text without slowing the pace of the story with wordy description (enriching device).

Some illustrations carry their own story-line, which may contrast with the story-line of the text, as in *'Come Away from the Water Shirley'* by John Burningham. Some comics and cartoon books have characters who comment upon the story – 'talk to camera', or perform visual puns (e.g. stories about Tintin). In the case of picture books, the illustrations carry the whole story.

Whatever their purpose, there are, clearly, many different styles of illustration. It can be argued that some styles are more suited to particular purposes than others, or are more suited to particular age groups because of the amount of skill needed to 'read' the picture itself. For example, Cass (1984) asserts that children under the age of 7 tend to see illustrations as 'wholes', so need illustrations which have clear key items with strong outlines. Illustrations with a complex perspective, or from unusual angles, are more difficult to follow. Composite illustrations with multiple activities apparently occurring simultaneously can confuse young children in their attempts to identify sequence, or establish cause and effect, motive and intention. However, detailed drawings can provide a wealth of opportunity for discussion.

Two additional types of book have been receiving great attention in recent years because of their interactive nature. The first type is the picture book intended for very young children (also enjoyed by children from six to sixty). Jill Bennett's work (1982) is a major influence in helping people to view picture books with greater seriousness, for readers at many ages and stages. Their importance lies in the open-endedness and in the prediction and anticipation skills that are thereby encouraged. Such books also provide opportunities for readers to interpret and comment, engage in divergent thinking and share ideas. Thus they engender high levels of interaction between text and reader and between readers themselves.

A second type of book is the make-your-own adventure books and game/fantasy books. This type of book relies on active participation by the readers in the creation of the story. Books of such genre are no longer a passive, individual experience, but rather a responsive, interactive and often group activity. This social context in itself is an important motivating factor for many readers.

A further development in children's literature is the increased emphasis given to poems and plays. This has been a major growth area for classroom publishing. The majority of new children's poems are specially written for their audience. This is in contrast with the 'traditional' classic poems which some children find difficult. These 'children's poems' are often humorous and zany and about familiar incidents to which children can easily relate. They don't always rhyme! Michael Rosen, Charles Causley and the Ahlbergs are particularly popular writers of such poems.

Plays for children range from adaptations of traditional tales to new dramas specially written for the classroom. Plays are particularly favoured as they encourage group reading and allow children of different reading abilities to work together, as the parts are often deliberately unequal in 'difficulty'. (See *Signal* guides by Bennett, Chambers, and favourite authors from British Library, Southgate *et al.* (1981) and the Cox Report (DES, 1989).)

Promoting a greater understanding of how authors write books and how publishers produce them also encourages children to become involved with the writing–reading process. This moves children beyond the belief that 'books are written by typewriters'. It also helps them to appreciate an author's perspective. This aspect can include the writing processes (the different habits and approaches of authors). It can also extend to the publishing processes (how a book starts as the germ of an idea in someone's mind and develops, with the input from author, illustrator, editor, printer and binder, etc., into something which is registered in the British Library and assigned an ISBN number, before being distributed to wholesaler and retailer so that the book can be bought or borrowed, read and enjoyed).

Children can be fascinated by individual approaches to both writing and illustrating. Biographies of children's writers can provide valuable insights to share with a class. Also, the existing programme of artists-, poets- and writers-in-school gives some children the opportunity to work alongside a professional. By such initiatives, the link between author, text and reader is made more explicit and the interactive nature of reading heightened.

Finally, accessibility of books is an important factor in encouraging the reading habit. This can be considered with the following aspects in mind:

- location: central/classroom/corridor library
- cataloguing: use of modified Dewey system, with colour and picture symbols to help
- storage: spines visible, and/or book fronts shown, with suitable height of shelving; low-box-dividers for picture books
- furnishings: carpeted area, floor cushions and/or soft chairs to encourage browsing

- issues: how many books allowed and for how long
- staffing: unstaffed, or staffed by children, adult helpers, teacher, librarian

---

ACTIVITY

Book Choice

Which books have had an impact on you? Can you remember your age when you read/heard them? What was memorable about each one?

(Some may be memorable for negative reasons, or, for reasons to do with *when* or *where* you read the book rather than for any reason to do with the book itself.)

How have different books affected you?

Have some entertained, been humorous . . .

enthralled, induced awe . . .

excited or even scared you . . .

been escapist . . .

served to inculcate cultural beliefs/traditions (whether folk culture/high culture . . .

examined issues/events . . . (whether factually/fictitiously – through myth/legend . . .

explained matters, informed you . . .

encouraged you to reflect upon thoughts/feelings

Can you think of any other categories?

Can you think of some titles for each of your categories?

What about the content and characters in books?

How do books portray different gender roles and races?

Are both genders allowed to be tough as well as tender?

Are all races given a chance to lead as well as support?

How do books portray the world of work, the environment, domestic life in a variety of countries and cultures?

The ideal arrangement is not cheap to come by. Financial constraints may be offset by the use of such services as the Schools Library and Museum services – though these are variable in their quality, quantity and availability. Children can sometimes extend the resources by forming 'swop circles', family reading groups or through second-hand book clubs. Inevitably, the book stock in any school is crucial to developing and sustaining an environment in which children are hungry for books and become eager readers, or even bookworms.

FURTHER READING

The following books offer practical suggestions for classroom practice as well as a background rationale for learning with story:

Benton, M. and Fox, G. (1985) *Teaching Literature 9–14*. Oxford: Oxford University Press.
Butler, D. (1986) *Five to Eight*. London: Bodley Head.
Hayhoe, M. and Parker, S. (1984) *Working with Fiction*. London: Arnold.
Meek, M. (1982) *Learning to Read (0–15)*. London: Bodley Head.

The three titles below focus on the images of race and gender in children's books:

Klein, G. (1985) *Reading into Racism*. London: Hutchinson.
Stinton, J. (ed.) (1979) *Racism and Sexism in Children's Books*, London: Writers and Readers Co-operative.
Zimet, S. (1976) *Print and Prejudice*. London: Hodder & Stoughton.

The following review a wide range of issues relating to children's literature:

Bator, R. (ed.) (1983) *Signposts to Criticism of Children's Literature*. Chicago: American Library Association.
Bettelheim, B. (1977) *The Uses of Enchantment*. London: Thames & Hudson.
Cass, J. (1984) *Literature and the Young Child* (2nd edn). London: Longman.
Cook, E. (ed.) (1976) *The Ordinary and the Fabulous: Myths, Legends, Fairy Tales* (2nd edn). Cambridge: Cambridge University Press.
Grugeon, E. and Waldon, P. (eds) (1978) *Literature and Learning*. London: Ward Lock Educational.

Finally, these two books are collections of articles about specific writers of children's books:

Fox, G. (1976) *Writers, Critics, Children*. London: Heinemann.
Rees, D. (ed.) (1984) *Painted Desert, Green Shade*. Boston: The Horn Book.

3.3.   MODELLING READING

(i)   Teacher's role

There are many opportunities for modelling the reading process within the primary context. These are important so that children can be initiated into what it means 'to be a reader', and what the reader 'does' in order to be able to make sense of print.

The most common context for modelling is during 'story-time'. This is often the main way in which reading is institutionalized into the structure of the school day. It often generates a particular ritual associated with *where* it takes place (the relaxed atmosphere of a book corner, or the cosiness – or crush – of being 'on the carpet'), or *when* it takes place (at the end of the day or morning). However, *why* it takes place may not be so obvious to the children. Nevertheless, it is an occasion which is often imbibed with the air of being a treat well earned, of being special, and therefore conveys a notion that books are special and to be enjoyed.

Another practice that is becoming increasingly common in primary schools is the period of *sustained* silent reading, which is shared by everyone in the class simultaneously. This provides a private opportunity for an individual reader to really 'get into' a book rather than only dip into it briefly. It is most important that this reading period should include the teacher and any other adults who happen to be in the classroom at that time – so that reading is seen to be something which everyone does, for their own pleasure. If this sustained reading period is to promote reading successfully as a pleasurable activity, then it must be flexible enough to remain pleasurable.

The extended time for being with books is important in providing both time and space for children to behave 'like a reader'. It also provides an opportunity to browse and choose, to try out books and experiment. Sometimes the pleasure is in *sharing* the book with someone else, or, at the end of the session in sharing the book with the rest of the class by revealing a favourite picture, reading an extract, reviewing it and recommending it to others. In such a shared situation the 'naturalness' of reading becomes 'a function of social experiences where literacy is a means to a variety of ends' (Hall, 1987).

A third context for reading which the teacher can support is the social one where children are paired as *support* tutors. These pairs are sometimes made up of 'good' and 'poor' readers in the same class, and sometimes of 'poor' readers in older classes with 'poor' readers in younger classes. In either situation there are advantages for both members of the pair (see Smith, 1987). The advantages appear to derive from the regular contacts, extra time, and social context of the support. It also allows opportunities to talk about the text and about reading, which helps to generate a 'metalanguage' whereby issues can be explored, made implicit and tackled.

In addition to books and support tutors, another important classroom resource is a tape-recorder. It can serve as a listening library, where children can listen to a story and follow the text in the accompanying book. Such a tape library provides another source of well-read stories, to which children can listen and use as models for expression and intonation. It also offers opportunities for children to listen to stories repeatedly, to allow time to build up their sight and sound recognition skills, without being dependent on the teacher's time.

Tape-recorders also allow children to listen to themselves, on playback. This offers a unique opportunity for self-evaluation, in privacy. Further, children can add to the stock of tapes in the listening library, by reading their own favourites on to short tapes so that others can listen to the story too. This provides a very real stimulus for 'getting it right' and a real need for fluency and expressiveness in order to develop their skills as performance readers.

While there is no research evidence that conclusively supports the superiority of any one method of teaching reading (Corder quoted in Samuels, 1978), it would seem that the most important facilitating factor is the teacher's enthusiasm and attitudes, as well as the atmosphere within the school itself (Samuels in Smith, 1987).

(ii) Parents' role

A major development of the last decade is the increasing opportunities for partnership between schools and homes, so that the role of parents as primary educators in the earliest years of a child's life is given recognition. The value of developing parent–teacher partnerships in a professional context is that the children receive joint support. Although many such initiatives have been instigated throughout the country, this approach still has a very long way to go before it is fully implemented.

Research by Wells (1981) and Tizard and Hughes (1984) showed that the nature of book experiences which children enjoyed before coming to school was of definite significance in determining their reading progress after reaching school age. Further projects have demonstrated the positive effects which continuing parental involvement has on the reading achievement of children during their primary years. Examples of these projects include ones in the London borough of Haringey (Hewison and Tizard, 1980, 1982), Belfield in Rochdale (Hannon and Jackson, 1987) and Coventry (Widlake and MacLeod, 1984). These are all urban areas where reading achievements were generally low and parental involvement limited before the onset of the projects. The greater parent–teacher collaboration was in terms of regular support of the child, usually in terms of agreeing to read with the child daily.

However, whether it is the encouragement to read, the attraction of the new books brought in to support the experiment, or the greater amount of practice, or a combination of all three which helped to raise reading levels is difficult to determine (Bald in Smith, 1987). The results of such projects must be treated cautiously until the follow-up can show the long-term effectiveness of a change of attitudes, rather than just a temporary lifting of reading scores.

One of the difficulties in establishing conclusive evidence on the impact of parental involvement is the variety of the kinds of support which parents may offer and the range of teaching methods employed in schools. For example, a 'parental involvement' scheme is frequently but not always associated with a 'language experience' or 'holistic' approach to the teaching and learning of reading. The effects of the approach and the impact of parental support are not easy to separate.

Burman (in Wade, 1990) reports on the cumulative experiences of such initiatives and offers detailed suggestions for setting up the necessary support structures. Parents wanting to be effective partners in their child's reading development need to understand:

- the school's approach to reading
- how and when to read along with their child
- how to support and intervene
- how to talk about the book with their child
- how to monitor and record the child's strengths and difficulties.

In a two-year study by Bridge (in Wade, 1990) an attempt was made to assess the impact of a 'language experience' approach to reading in comparison with the 'traditional' method using graded reading schemes, flash cards and phonic training. The differences were particularly significant in terms of positive attitudes which the holistic approach engendered; there was an increase in quantity and quality of pupil–pupil, teacher–pupil and parent–pupil inter-action about books. Much to the teachers' initial distress, children seemed to delay in establishing their own reading strategies.

However, after a latent period, the children showed accelerated progress. They also demonstrated a wider range of strategies e.g. greater use of picture cues, reading ahead for context clues, self-correction to improve meaning, and initial phonic cues. By the end of the two-year period, although reading scores between the two groups were not significantly different, there was a markedly more positive attitude to books and a more positive self-image amongst the experimental group. They also had superior storying abilities and read more expressively. Hence, it would seem that with such an approach, in which parents can easily participate, children not only learn to read, but become real readers who want to read.

Another way in which parents are encouraged to get involved with children's reading is through Family Reading Groups. This initiative is designed for a slightly different purpose. Thorpe (in Smith, 1987) describes a project which focused on monthly meet-ings of families and teachers in a local library. Members were free to choose any numbers of books for prolonged periods of borrow-ing. These two factors were important in establishing reading as a leisure activity. The wide choice meant that there was a book for every mood. It also meant that some choices could be 'risks', which could widen the range of book experiences. The children were interviewed about their choices. It became clear that personal recommendation from the other members of the group was the most influential factor (86 per cent). Familiarity through having seen the book on TV or having read others by the same author was also influential (75 per cent). These books were 'safe' and were chosen because children could predict story and style with a high degree of certainty. This safety was derived from either a trusted author or a trusted friend.

It was also found that the context within which this choosing took place needed to be a relaxed one. It needed to be a social one, where books could be discussed and responses exchanged, so that the criteria of choosing became articulated and clarified. By such means readers became discerning and grew more confident in making decisions.

Parents also become involved in their children's reading through sharing a book with them, reading with their child, or 'hearing them read'. A number of schools have instigated projects to encourage reading at home. Some of these are very informal arrangements whereby a child chooses a book to take home each day, perhaps with a card to indicate whether it is most suitable for the parent to read the book to the child, to read with the child or for the child to read to the parent.

Other schools establish a contract between parent and child by which they agree to read together for a specified number of times per week, according to the opportunities available at home. Some schools formalize reading in a 'paired' scheme. This may involve a parent reading along and shadowing children until they seem confident enough to read on their own.

Such schemes are important in that they confirm parents as educators and encourage cooperation between teacher and parent. This helps children learn.

ACTIVITY

Preparing for Parents

Make a list of the anxieties and opportunities relating to working with parents, at home and/or school, from the viewpoints of the teacher, parents, child.

Use this as a basis for deciding what information, advice, support and help might be needed for any of the parties involved, in order to establish positive partnerships.

FURTHER READING

The first title explains a holistic approach to reading, in which parents can participate:

Waterland, L. (1985) *Read with Me: An Apprenticeship Approach to Reading*. Stroud: Thimble Press.

This title below outlines the earliest stages of reading and, drawing on American research, identifies how parents lay the foundations for literacy in the home upon which school can then build:

Gibson, L. (1989) *Through Children's Eyes*. London: Cassell.

The following titles review the British scene, involving parents:

Smith, P. (ed.) (1987) *Parents and Teachers*. Basingstoke: Macmillan.
Topping, K. and Wolfendale, S. (eds) (1985) *Parental Involvement in Children's Reading*. London: Croom Helm.

Chapter 4

Children as Readers

INTRODUCTION

This chapter focuses on the practices of developing reading in the primary classroom. As with all aspects of learning, it is essential to recognize what children already bring to the classroom. It is also important to remember that in trying to develop interactive readers it is necessary to encourage interaction between reading and writing, and between oracy and literacy.

The first section outlines the main targets for reading development; the second explores four strands of reading and examines evidence as to how this might be implemented; and the third suggests ways of monitoring provision and progress in the classroom.

4.1. TARGETS FOR READING

The National Curriculum outlines what is expected in terms of individual attainment by each child in all aspects of English. 'Attainment Target Two: Reading' comprises a single target which covers both reading for 'pleasure' as well as reading for 'information'. The aim is:

> The development of the ability to read, understand and respond to all types of writing, as well as the development of information-retrieval strategies for the purposes of study.

The Report from the Working Party (DES, 1989) makes explicit its assumptions about what counts as reading, based on current research evidence about how children learn in general and how children learn to read in particular. It emphasizes that reading is 'more than the decoding of black marks on the page: it is a quest for meaning and one which requires that the reader is an active participant' (16.2). It encourages a view which places high value on the benefits of 'being a reader' in personal as well as cultural terms. It states that the value of reading is due in part to the fact that it enables children to project themselves into unfamiliar environments, times and cultures while also providing examples of different kinds of language use (16.3).

The target for reading is very broad in its scope and refers to a range of modes, purposes and materials. Amongst the different suggested modes of reading are the following:

- reading aloud
- reading silently
- and 'performance readings'

Different purposes for reading involve:

- reading for fun
- reading for information
- reading to develop knowledge about language

Different materials for reading include:

- books, newspapers, periodicals
- lists, notices, instructions
- forms, labels, calendars, slogans

Perhaps most important, the Cox Report recognizes different ways of learning to read, quoting Bullock (1975) and stating that

> There is no one method, medium, approach, device or philosophy that holds the key to the process of learning to read (16.9).

The Report goes on to suggest that children need to be able to recognize, on sight, a large proportion of the words they encounter. They should also be able to predict meaning on the basis of phonic, idiomatic and grammatical regularities, and recognize what makes sense in context. However, once 'adequate' fluency is achieved, the emphasis is on developing children's understanding and response to reading. Further, the Report encourages the interrelation of all four language modes by promoting listening to stories, discussion about books and the reading of each other's written stories. All four language modes are seen to interrelate, for there are many different ways in which oracy and literacy, or reading and writing, might affect each other.

In terms of the relationship between spoken and written language, many have argued that children's oral vocabulary and prior experience of hearing stories relate positively to their progress as readers in school (Holdaway, 1979; Wade, 1985; Wells 1981, 1986; Tizard and Hughes, 1984). As regards the relationship between reading and writing there are three main models. First, there is a 'reading–writing' model where reading is seen to be the key to developing children's writing. Conversely, the 'writing–reading' model emphasizes writing as the stimulus for reading, whereas an interactive 'reading and writing' model assumes the influence is mutual (Shanahan and Lomax, 1986). In trying to identify the relationship more precisely Shanahan and Lomax suggest that the component variables of each model need to be identified, for the relationship may vary between different variables and may also vary at different stages in a child's literacy development.

For example, a good oral vocabulary and knowledge of word analysis was found to relate positively to reading comprehension. However, in the early years, knowledge of oral vocabulary did not clearly relate to written vocabulary because children limited their writing to words they believed they could spell. By the end of the primary years the phonic knowledge applied to reading (initial decoding) was no longer reflected in the children's spelling of written words. This is because the use of this kind of knowledge for reading declines as children develop greater fluency and rely on (faster) visual information. Being an avid reader, therefore, does not necessarily result in good spelling: good readers don't look at individual words.

At a later developmental stage, Perera (1984) found that children try out in their writing some of the more complex language forms which they have met in their reading. This occurs before they use such forms in their spoken language. In this instance, written language is more advanced than spoken language. Hence reading and writing do not always correlate positively; oral vocabulary aids vocabulary recognition in reading; and syntax experienced through reading encourages children to experiment in their writing, and only later in their speech.

In trying to explore relationships between different language modes is it important to distinguish between the structuring of the text and the style in which it is written. Bennett (1982) claims that children write the way they read. It is therefore important to enable children to experience a wide range of styles of writing. This will help them to experiment, whilst they find a 'voice' of their own.

Many teachers will be all too familiar with children's storying where the content and style is highly imitative (often TV-based). Yet, if 'gossiping is the most basic form of story-telling' (Chambers, 1985) and we all have stories within us, then it is important to validate the children's own experiences – their own stories – and encourage them to use these. The invitation to 'use their imaginations' is often not helpful, and using real-life experience may help to avoid the TV imitations.

Applebee (1978) has demonstrated that children very quickly pick up the main features of story structure and recognize that there must be a beginning, middle, and a happy ending. The Attainment Targets and Programmes of Study require that children should talk about the content of stories (level 1), describe and predict (level 2), use inference and deduction to demonstrate their understandings beyond the literal (level 3), recognize that authors provide clues (level 4), and talk about characters, motivation, action and intention using appropriate passages to support their opinions (level 5).

The main strands in the Attainment Target for reading are:

- interest in and response to written materials
- ability to read and understand
- strategies for information-retrieval
- awareness of books, their structure and language

Each of these strands will be examined in turn.

4.2. PROGRAMMES FOR ACTION

(i) Interest in and response to the written materials

Before coming to school children have already experienced considerable amounts of print in their environment, in the street and in the home. They have also witnessed the print being used by adults and they have seen it employed to convey messages which can then result in action. They have been able to see that print makes sense because they have seen people making use of it. In this way print has been heavily contextualized. Clark (1976) suggests that boys are more aware than girls of print in their environment and that they recognize its functional role where it serves their active needs.

In contrast to environmental print, the transition to book-based print is sometimes seen as being relatively de-contextualized. However, it would seem more appropriate to consider it to be re-contextualized, for book print is within the context of the story-line or information content and is often supported by illustrations or diagrams and, therefore, has its own context.

Anderson, in a review of current research concerning initial reading strategies (in Smith, 1987) suggests that the teaching of reading should rest upon the following principles:

- demonstrating the role of print in the environment
- reading to children and talking about books
- answering children's questions about language
- developing a language with which to discuss language
- encouraging a child's confidence and self-esteem in him/herself
- valuing the child's miscues when hearing a child read

These principles are confirmed by many other researchers. For example, in terms of reading and discussing books and of introducing print in story books, there is a great deal of parental activity which helps to provide a context in which children come to understand what print does and how text works. Beard (1987) indicates three crucial functions for parental involvement: 'demonstration' about what print does and what books do by reading the print and using the books, 'collaboration' through discussing and extending the story, and 'facilitation' of the reading process by talking about it and making it explicit.

Book reading, whether with a parent, sibling or teacher, is an important and pleasurable learning experience. Snow (1983) found three features which made it so. The first was 'semantic contingency' where the support partner followed up the child's initiation and answered questions about the story, picture, word or letter. The second was 'scaffolding' where the partner limited the task by guiding the child's discussion and helping him or her select the salient points so that they could answer their own questions, whether about the story content or about necessary word attack skills. The third strategy of the support partner was termed 'accountability' where the child was urged to take responsibility for the task of reading by 'having a go' for themselves, continuing until the task was completed, or reflecting, explaining and making explicit the particular knowledge or strategy that had been used in order to read and understand the text.

The features mentioned by Beard and Snow are easily transferable to a classroom context and can underpin classroom practice during whole-class discussion about a shared book, or in individual conferencing sessions between child and teacher. Parents also can be advised to adopt similar practices at home so that the approach is consistent.

One of the most common features of the primary classroom is 'story-time', where whole-class 'booktalk' can develop in response to the book being read – whether story, poem or information book. This activity can be a very positive occasion and encourage children to enjoy books, although it can also be misused and become just an infill which takes place if there is some spare time before break, lunch or home time. At such times, children are often tired and fidgety and it is difficult to hold their attention. If the story is only read in snippets at irregular times it is hard to remember the thread of the plot and to feel much involvement in it. In such circumstances story-time can become a chore for everyone, remembered only as a time when you sit uncomfortably squashed up on a hard floor and get told off if you distract/are distracted.

But well used, story-time can be an integral part of the classroom learning programme, with the story linked to the theme of the class topic and extending the children's understanding of some aspects of that topic. In particular it might add an affective dimension which encourages the children to empathize with the characters or situation related to the topic work. It can also serve as inspiration for further activities. So used, the children's growing knowledge about the context can be brought to bear on the story. They can be encouraged to predict events, project themselves into the action, and to create meanings and understandings between

author, text and readers. This collective pooling of individual perspectives may provide an important forum for discussion and
reflection, on the fictional situation as well as on each other's
viewpoints.

Children can also be encouraged to identify their preferences
and to give reasons for their likes and dislikes. This may be in
terms of process factors (whether the books are easy/hard, use
short/long words, big/little writing, few/many pictures, are thick/
thin) or content (such as interest or familiarity/difference, e.g. 'I
like animal books 'cos I want to be a vet', 'It's just like my baby
brother', 'I don't do naughty things like that'). Shared knowledge
about such story types can help to provide some 'scaffolding'
which can guide children in their choices.

In discussing book preferences, children very soon begin to
distinguish that there are many different genres of books. These
can be recognized as categories of stories which have distinctive
content, structure and style (see pp. 161–3 for example of children's understandings). Such knowledge of stories is constantly
growing and developing. It is used by children to guide their choice
of book as they become able to anticipate the type of story from
the front cover, title or pictures and, later, from the 'blurb' on the
back cover or the name of the author. This knowledge can also
assist readers in their search for clues, which will help them to
predict the story-line at a global level, as well as help them construct the context to support their word attack skills.

We have also noted the view of 'reading as thinking' where the
reader plays an important part in creating meanings with the text.
Southgate (1981) quotes an early writer, Kerfoot (1916), who
draws the conclusion that 'No story is ever told by the author of
the book; the telling is done by the reader who takes the text for
his scenario and produces it on the stage of his own imagination
with resources provided by his own experiences of life'.

Attempts have been made to identify children's level of understanding while they read as a variable likely to affect response.
Barrett (in Melnik and Merritt, 1972) identified five levels of
understanding, which are often reduced to the distinctions of:

- 'reading the lines' (literal understanding)
- 'reading between the lines' (inferential understanding)
- 'reading beyond the lines' (critical, responsive understanding)

It is the discussion following the reading which is of great significance in assessing a child's comprehension of a text. It is important in this discussion to avoid an over-reliance on literal questions that merely require the child to recall the associated part of the text. Rather, it is more helpful to ask the child to try to infer something which is left implicit or to respond personally from their own experience and thus go 'beyond the lines'.

In developing the interactive approach to 'responsive' reading, teachers need to consider carefully the nature of the questions they employ to provide the 'scaffolding' to guide children into books and to support them in their own views. Readers need to be encouraged to respond in a personal and divergent way – relating to the structure, style and content – rather than in a convergent way – relating to the accuracy of reproducing the text.

Chambers (1985) offers a framework of questions to help children 'get the story bug'. He suggests avoiding the 'why' questions as they are 'too big', but rather to ask questions which encourage the child to refer back to the text to corroborate their impressions and understandings (e.g. 'What makes you think ...?' 'How do you know ...?') and to go beyond the text to explore their own responses (e.g. 'How did you feel when ...?' 'Which parts did you like best/worst ...?' 'What puzzled you . . .?') Further questions can encourage children to look for contrast of good/evil, young/old, or patterns of sounds, shapes, colours, pace, locations and for patterns or links of events within the story or between one story and another, even a story and 'life'. Chambers also identifies a range of purposes of 'booktalk' in terms of different areas of sharing (enthusiasms, puzzlement and connections) and different ways of talking about books: with oneself or with others, and talking to recreate, recall the story or to seek new revelations and insights.

An alternative framework is offered by Benton and Fox (1985). They suggest that children should be encouraged to focus on four aspects of the story content and structure, in developing their responses:

- *Picturing*
  Which parts can you 'picture' most clearly?
  Do you see yourself in the picture?
  (i.e. which character's viewpoint do they adopt?

is it a consistent or 'wandering' viewpoint
which enables the reader to empathize with different charac-
ters, and 'live' the book?)
Do you 'fill in' details which are not in the text?
- *Anticipation/retrospection*
What will happen next?
How will it end?
Why is X significant?
How do you know?
- *Evaluation*
Which characters are good/bad, helpful/unhelpful, etc.?
Who or what did you like best/least, and why?
Would you have liked to be there?
- *Interaction*
What other books are about the same ideas/theme?
Does it remind you of anything that happened to you?

This extension of booktalk can be used to challenge readers to interact with the text at a level which is deeper than merely recalling the main events and characters. Children can be encouraged to examine the underlying theme – 'the idea that holds the story together', or the dimension of a story which 'goes beyond the action of the plot' (Lehr, 1987). Such themes are often abstractions which can link other stories and encourage children to take a broader view of storying. They can help readers explore what the book may be trying to make us think about, trying to tell us or teach us.

The attempt to identify a theme provides a considerable challenge, for it requires more than the ability to recall the story-line at a literal level. It requires the ability to infer meanings, to search for internal motivations, and then to select and summarize. Furthermore, it requires children to analyse, abstract and generalize. Yet very young children can begin to do this with stories about incidents with which they are familiar, with which they can identify, and to which they can bring their own understandings and experiences. Stories about daily routines – getting up, going out, going to bed, or stories about family visits – are ones which they can recognize and compare with other similar books, as well as with their own lives.

The teacher's role is to provide a rich book environment, in terms of both quantity and quality. This can be encouraged by arranging displays and by giving the time and opportunity for children to browse and choose books for their own reading. The books need to be used and shared by the children.

In this kind of sharing adults, children and books all help to create an environment of reading and Value Added Text results from the interchange between the participants. The joy of books can be developed through relay from one reader to another, reciprocation by sharing with each other, reflection by an individual and by refraction between a group of readers (Harding, 1990). It is important that all these opportunities are made available.

ACTIVITY

Developing Booktalk

Devise a set of questions and starting points – using a framework like 'booktalk' outlined above – to stimulate a discussion about books to encourage children to go beyond retelling the story-line, towards an awareness of story types, structure, style and themes.

FURTHER READING

A useful collection of articles on parental involvement projects can be found in the following conference proceedings:

Smith, P. (ed.) (1987) *Parents and Teachers Together*. Basingstoke: Macmillan Education.

In addition to suggestions in Chapter 3 (p. 115), the following two titles indicate ways of helping children interact with text:

Chambers, A. (1985) *Booktalk*. London: Bodley Head.
Lehr, S. (1988) 'The child's sense of theme as a response to literature' in Anderson, C. (ed.) *Reading: The abc and Beyond*. Basingstoke: Macmillan Education.

(ii) Developing reading and understanding

We have already noted some of the relevant variables in connection with books, but we also need to focus on the reader and on how children become readers. This involves being aware of what children already know about language, print and about books so that we can build on their existing knowledge rather than undermine, ignore or contradict it.

Children will already know language is for communication. Most children will also have acquired a considerable receptive vocabulary, probably over 25,000 words before the age of 5 years, none of which has been 'taught'. They have also absorbed many key features of language structure relating to syntax (or grammar) in terms of word order and word agreement.

Children's experiences of print will also be considerable. Print, as was noted in the preceding chapter, surrounds us. In the home, many children will have had experience of printed advertising on their breakfast tables from the earliest age. They have also watched advertisements on the television, seen the *Radio Times* or the telephone directory being consulted as well as magazines, comics, recipe books, instruction manuals, newspapers and books. In the streets they have seen shop signs, hoardings, road signs, bus stops and timetables.

Tizard and Hughes (1984) and Wells (1981) have both found that children who have had stories read to them at home have a considerable advantage over those who have not. Children with a book-rich background have already acquired many basic concepts about print and have developed positive attitudes and motivation towards reading.

For example, they understand that books tell stories. They have begun to become familiar with story structure and the way stories have beginnings, middles and ends. They recognize chronological development and how this can be used to predict the sense of the story. Such children have also come to realize that it is the writing on the page (rather than the spaces between the words, or the pictures, or even the 'reader') that tells the story. They have also observed (whilst reading books in English) that the story-line goes from left to right and from top to bottom. They have probably acquired such vocabulary as 'book', 'cover', 'page', 'picture', 'word', 'letter', 'beginning', 'end'. All of this builds up positive expectations about the print and the expectancy that reading is a worthwhile activity.

We also need to consider what teachers do in the classroom to build upon this knowledge or, for those children who have not had a book-rich experience, how teachers can help provide this. Classroom practice is likely to relate both to teacher beliefs about the reading process as well as to the human resources and book materials available.

The previous chapter noted some of the main issues involved in the 'patterning of complex behaviour' which we call reading (p. 110). The debate surrounding the nature of the reading process and how this relates to the various procedures for teaching reading can be summarized in a series of simplified dichotomies:

	Closely structured	Loosely structured
Nature	multi-faceted behaviour composed of sets of isolatable, related skills	singular though complex process both perceptual+cognitive
Direction	Bottom up – gradual building up of discrete skills to tackle print	Top down – gradual refinement of making meanings with print
Progression	Serial and linear	Spiral or lattice

Such differing beliefs about the reading process have led to widely divergent practices in the classroom. Teachers favouring a closely structured approach, who believe that reading is comprised of sets of skills which can be practised in isolation, may encourage the use of games based on visual matching skills, e.g. dominoes, snap, pairing or sorting games relating to visual and/or aural activities. Also 'flash cards' may be used to develop a sight vocabulary.

Classrooms where the teaching of reading is strongly influenced by phonic approaches are often characterized by a carefully graded sequence of activities, starting with tracing a letter (initial consonants, single vowels, initial consonant blends, vowel digraphs, etc.)

and progressing through drawing three pictures of items which begin with the selected sound(s) to writing a sentence containing each of these chosen words. Again, many published games are produced to add variety to what are essentially auditory matching games or sound–symbol matching games. Some games include a generative principle through substituting letters in 'paradigmatic relationships' (e.g. n/l/r/ + -ice), or by combining letters in 'syntagmatic relationships' (e.g. pa-, pe-, pi-, po-, pu-t). Progression through the 'stages' of reading is often guided by a scheme, or mixture of schemes, which are graded in carefully small steps with demands on the learner increased only gradually.

The teacher's role in such a classroom is clearly defined. It involves detailed knowledge of available materials and close monitoring of the children. In any graded scheme it is easy for the teacher to feel undermined by the 'experts' who produced the scheme and to rely on it wholeheartedly. However, no scheme can be 'tailor-made' for every child and mismatches are bound to occur. Hence the teacher will need to make supplementary materials to meet individual needs. For the child, reading becomes a series of tasks: 'Reading is doing sounds', 'We have to do a card each day to teach us reading'. 'Teaching' takes place largely through published materials. The teacher's role is to match an appropriate activity to the child's need, to introduce and explain the activity, and ensure that the child gets plenty of practice at it.

In classrooms where the emphasis is on teaching reading in a more loosely structured context, the reading environment may be very different. For example, the emphasis will be on immersion in a flood of 'real book' experiences (i.e. books which are predominantly not ones from graded schemes intended to teach children to read, but books which are written because an author has a story to tell). There may be a wide selection of books, which is frequently changed by, for instance, swapping with parallel classes or through the Schools Library service. Children may be allowed to borrow books at any time and to keep them for lengthy periods unless they are wanted by another reader. The book stock may be augmented by stories written by the children, teachers and other adults in the school.

Opportunities for using reading books may absorb a significant amount of time each day, for not only would the children be reading them, but talking about them, using them as a stimulus for investigatory activities, and responding to them in a variety of ways (written, practical, dramatic). Children may spend considerable time in 'reading-like behaviours' on their own, with other children, with an adult, or their own teacher. The social context in which the books are used would therefore vary. A book could be listened to whilst another reader (child or adult) read the text; it could be read along with a taped version of the book so that the child can follow the text and join in where possible; it could be read alone silently, with a friend, swapping extracts; it could be read aloud to other children, to an adult, to the class.

This 'real books' approach to reading has resulted in very mixed responses and has been confused by conflicting messages. The practice is based on a clear, though not conclusive, theoretical basis. Waterland (1985) outlines some key principles. The first relates to the belief that learning to read is comparable with learning to speak. Huey (1908) asserted that both could be acquired by the 'natural method', by a process of support and imitation.

This does not necessarily mean the 'minimalist' approach associated with Smith (1978) who asserts that children learn to read by reading and that they seek help when they need it and ignore it when they do not. The 'natural method' alludes to the kind of support already outlined by Snow (1983) who refers to the adult's role of responding to the child's attempts in the same way as when the child was learning to talk. The main ingredient of the 'natural method' is that the child has a purpose in wanting to read: namely that the book is worth reading.

The second principle in such an approach is the belief that reading cannot be taught in a formal, sequenced fashion any more than talking can. Hence reading is not a process by which a child conquers a series of discrete steps, but one in which the child makes sense of the text. If purpose and sense are the predominant motivating factors in the reader then the quality of the books on offer is of paramount importance. It is the power of story which lures the child into reading, not neatly graded activities (Meek, 1988).

However, to support the child's desire to read (but without allowing frustration to set in), the final principle in this 'natural method' of reading relates to the role of the adult. The superficially 'freer' structure and atmosphere in the 'real books' classroom belies a carefully planned environment. The adult's role is to be a co-reader (Meek, 1982), and to read the words the children cannot read for themselves. It means reading a story again and again so the child can become familiar with it and recognize some of the words, so that he/she can begin to join in and act like a reader. As Huey states, 'Once a child knows a story or poem it is surprising how quickly he can locate its parts on the page and read it.' McKenzie (1979) extends this by making the point that:

> Language is learned through hearing it, being part of it, and by using it. Parents and teachers tolerate the fact that children's (spoken) language gradually grows over a period of time. They don't expect it to be right from the start.

Thus in the 'natural method' the teacher's role is perhaps more important rather than less so. But it is significantly changed. Instead of being a monitor of children, matcher of tasks, and provider of materials, the teacher takes on a more interactive role in supporting, co-reading, discussing and helping the child to search for meanings, in order to sustain the child's motivation, to make sense of the text, and respond to the content. The teacher needs to read with the child in the early stages rather than 'hear the child read'. It means that, at all stages, the teacher needs to comment on what is read and evaluate the story through discussion, rather than comment on the reader and evaluate how well the text was read. This is a more time-consuming role and requires considerable sensitivity both to the child as well as to the text. It therefore has important consequences for the choice of books their quality, quantity, turnover and accessibility, as well as important implications for classroom management to ensure that children get sufficient adult support.

However, the success of any of these practices should not be based only on a theoretical analysis of reading, but should also give attention to the individual reader. For there may be as many ways of learning to read as there are different types of learners. Tentative attempts to distinguish 'ways of learning' have focused on cognitive style, personality type and motivation to achieve.

It is not always clear how these variables of 'learning theory' relate to 'reading theory' as the two areas of investigation have not often been used in such a way as to positively inform each other. Nevertheless, some tentative suggestions have emerged which indicate the value of identifying children who are 'verbalizers' (those who predominantly use aural memory) and 'visualizers' (those who predominantly use visual memory).

This distinction was further refined by Baron (in Frith, 1980) to distinguish 'phoenicians' (predominantly analytic and sensitive to aural differences) and 'chinese' (predominantly holistic and sensitive to visual differences). Other variables which have been investigated (Kogan, 1976) include children who are 'reflective' (prefer to analyse, consider and accumulate understandings and may respond to a phonic emphasis) and those who are 'impulsive' (prefer to have a go based on more immediate, global impressions and may respond to a look–say approach).

It is important to try to use a child's strengths, but at the same time to develop a wide range of possible strategies which they can use. In talking about reading it is important to make sure that children understand the terms we are using and that our strategies are consistent with our goals, and with a child's expectations, as is illustrated in the following instance. A child who was used to matching sound and letter-shapes as a word attack strategy was encouraged to use the real-world experience instead. While tackling 'neigh' the child was asked 'What sound does a horse make?' to which the phonically-trained child replied, 'Horse says "h".'

Whichever approach to the teaching of reading is adopted, the assumptions about the nature of reading must be consistent with the classroom practice and materials. These materials also need to take account of the wide variety of approaches to learning represented by differing children in the class.

Regardless of which approach is adopted, monitoring the progress will be crucial. Children at Key Stage One are expected to be able to recognize individual letters and words in context, and to increase their range of cues when reading to include picture and context clues, sight words and phonic cues. The emphasis shifts (at Key Stage Two) to the ability to read fluently and with expression, as well as to read silently with concentration for sustained periods. Further there is considerable emphasis on the importance of responding to books in discussion and of using what is learnt through this discussion to develop a greater understanding of story structure, which can also help their writing. These understandings would derive from children's growing confidence in their ability to read closely and identify clues. These should help them to predict what might happen next, to read with understanding at an inferential and deductive level, so they can read 'between the lines' and 'beyond the lines'.

ACTIVITY

Observing Reading

Using a checklist of reading behaviours select and observe 4–6 children. For example:

Child's activity:
with teacher/child alone
listens to book read aloud
browses
reads book (how . .)
initiates talk about book
responds to question/comment about book
uses and reads book e.g. for written work (maths, science, English
    arts, humanities, 'topic')

What does this tell you about these children? How can you use the
    information to devise further support for them?

FURTHER READING

The following books have plenty of practical classroom ideas for encouraging young readers:

Gardner, K. (1986) *Reading in Today's Schools*. Edinburgh: Oliver &
    Boyd.
Moon, C. (ed.) (1985) *Practical Ways to Teach Reading*. London: Ward
    Lock Educational.

(iii)   Strategies for information-retrieval

The term 'information-retrieval strategies' is often associated with the phrase 'reading to learn' or 'higher order' reading skills. This represents a further dichotomy in the possible approaches to reading, by contrasting 'higher order' reading skills with 'lower' or initial reading skills. Some have also argued for 'intermediate' reading skills (Merritt, 1975).

The distinction confuses text types, reading purposes and strategies, and cognitive demands. 'Higher order' reading skills are usually associated with reading non-fiction texts, for the purposes of study. The reader employs strategies such as skimming, scanning and close reading, and needs to *locate*, *select*, *extract* and *use* the information thus obtained. Because they are assumed to be 'higher' up the scale of difficulty, these skills are assumed to be more relevant for older children.

Yet these 'higher order' skills can be useful in reading fiction or even picture books, which can provide challenging contexts for very young children. For instance, the demands of 'higher order' reading procedures are readily enlisted in the intense discussion which sometimes occurs in infant classes engaged in thinking through picture books by authors such as John Burningham and Anthony Browne. Essentially these skills would seem to represent a highly interactive approach to making meanings between the author, reader and text.

Nevertheless, the term information-retrieval strategies, which embraces the same areas of concern as 'higher order' reading skills and 'reading to learn', is important because it identifies a number of pertinent processes that should be articulated and encouraged.

'Information-retrieval' emphasizes the collecting and accessing of information. This presupposes the need for information-seeking and the motivation to 'find out'. It is this desire to find out and to make sense that children already bring with them when they enter school and which it is so important not to stifle. Current learning theory emphasizes the child as an active meaning-maker: classroom practice therefore needs to ensure that there are continuing opportunities for children to undertake investigations – in terms of *planning*, *carrying out*, *interpreting*, *drawing inferences* and *communicating* (as suggested in the Science Curriculum Profile Component 1, Target 1).

So far, researchers have found little evidence of teachers teaching about information-retrieval strategies. Avann (1985) found that these skills were rarely taught in primary classrooms, partly because teachers could not articulate them as they, too, had never been taught them. Issues relating to locating information is sometimes 'taught', e.g. the use of indexes and the library catalogue.

However, studies undertaken by the British Library information services have constantly revealed the poor state of many school libraries in terms of stock size, as well as organization and categorization (Heather, 1984).

Other researchers have focused on the problems children have over the comprehension of non-fiction text. Debate has centred on whether comprehension is a singular skill, based primarily on vocabulary and verbal reasoning (Thorndike, in D'Arcy, 1973) or whether it is a plural skill composed of a cluster of separate skills (Davis, in D'Arcy, 1973).

In relation to classroom practice, Durkin (1978) found that only 1 per cent of teacher time was spent on teaching comprehension (rather than just practising). The results led to the suggestion that more time needed to be spent on general orientation, preparation (e.g. specialist vocabulary) and bringing prior knowledge to bear, so that the text could be anticipated and information-search made more selective.

Given the importance of prior information, Robinson (1977) has suggested that 'comprehension' should be seen in terms of 'information gain', or the difference between what was known prior to what was understood after reading. However, whilst this emphasizes an interactive conception it does not help to define how this gain might be facilitated.

Further, prior information can play very different roles depending on how it is organized and how flexibly it can accommodate new information. Rumelhart's work (1977) on cognitive schemata has highlighted this need for flexible networks of information. Flexibility allows linkages to be forged more easily and avoids forming exclusive categories of information, which may be restrictive in a hypothesis-testing situation where readers are searching for meanings and ways of extending understandings.

The issue of teacher questioning also emerged as a critical factor. Ruddell and Williams (in Samuels, 1978) found that 70 per cent of teacher questions were of a literal nature. Ruddell argued that the range and type of teacher questions could play a crucial role in influencing children's expectations and understandings of the text being read. They could also affect the processes of reading for information. Strategies suggested were:

- searching for detail – identifying, comparing, classifying

- searching for sequences – temporal, causal
- distinguishing main idea and argument
- distinguishing fact, opinion, value.

The use of such information-retrieval strategies is closely identified with the practice of 'topic work' in primary schools. A number of reports have levied criticism about the way this is undertaken. It is frequently characterized as being mundane, unchallenging and consisting of verbatim copying of chunks of text from an ad hoc collection of library books (Galton, Simon and Croll, 1980).

Further concerns were raised by HMI (1978, 1982) who reported that few children confidently used books as a source of information and that children had difficulty in extracting information from book sources. The concern was sufficient to mount a Schools Council project to investigate ways of improving current practices (Marland, 1981; Kerry and Eggleston, 1988).

Other researchers have distinguished a number of problems. For instance, children are taught to read almost exclusively by using fiction books. Story-time is also predominantly a period of fiction. Hence children often have very few opportunities to see information books, little guidance in how to use them and little experience of the different demands they make in terms of purpose, reading strategy, understanding and response. It is not surprising that many readers of books are not good users of books.

The problems in using information books can be related to a number of factors. First, lack of motivation by the readers, who may not be sure what they are trying to find out or what they are going to do with the information when they find any. Secondly, there may be a mismatch between the child and the book, for early information books have been notoriously poorly written, especially for less experienced readers (Tann, 1988). Frequently the information is so banal that the child gains nothing from it; or it has been simplified by shortening the sentences, at the expense of the connectives. However, it is these connectives which indicate the logical relationships and thereby explain and clarify the text. Conversely, it is so complex that they cannot read and understand it (Chapman, 1983).

In order to extract information effectively from texts it is necessary to undertake steps before, during and after reading. Before reading begins, it is important for the reader to have clarified the following *planning* and *carrying out* issues (using the Science P.C.1 terminology):

- What do I already know about this topic? (preparation, orientation)
- What more do I want to find out? (identification, selection)
- How can I find out? (observation, experimentation, book-sources)
- Where can I find out? (location and accessing – library skills)

With specific questions in mind, the reading will be focused and time more efficiently used. (There is a place, of course, for a more general read if the child is unfamiliar with the topic and needs to get an overview first.) Where the investigation is following on from personal experiences, readers already know something of the topic and this enables them to be selective in their reading.

Children also need to be flexible in their reading strategies in relation to the particular purpose in reading that section of text (i.e. they need to know when to skim, scan or read steadily). They also need to adopt an interactive approach to reading, and be ready to question what they read during the reading and *interpreting* process:

- Have I got what I need? (collection, checking)
- Have I understood what I've found? (comprehension)
- How can I note what I've found? (recording, storing)

They also need to be able to take notes either during or after reading. In order to discourage 'verbatim copying' it is useful to suggest that a read–cover–note–check approach should be used. In addition note-taking could involve translating the information from one medium to another (e.g. from verbal to visual/graphic form).

Meyer (in Flood, 1984) and Sheldon (in Root, 1986) suggest that different kinds of text can be represented in different forms. For example:

- narrative/sequential   picture series, list, time-line
- descriptive: characteristics   attribute web, diagram
  - spatial, location   map, plan
  - interrelational   graph, scattergram
- comparative   table, pie-chart, matrix

- classificatory: inclusive   Venn diagram
              hierarchical   tree diagram
- causal, problem-solution   flow-chart, network

This graphic approach to representing information links in with the Mathematics curriculum attainment targets on handling data. It also relates to the development of the DARTS (Directed Activities for Reading Text) approach disseminated by Schools Council research (Lunzer and Gardner, 1984).

Having collected the information, it is necessary to use it to answer the original questions. Frequently the questions will change due to the information gained, or some more will arise while others are dropped. Often, using the information involves some form of categorization, sorting or setting, which involves identifying criteria and deciding how many items to group and what they will demonstrate. Children can be encouraged to consider *inference* and *communication*:

- How can I use what I've got? (sorting)
- What does it add up to? (significance, results, conclusions)
- How can I share it? (presentation)

Using the information requires sifting, comparing and evaluating what has been collected. This means some information will be rejected, which is often the hardest decision to take, for once information has been found and noted it is very difficult to throw it away. Some practical ways of helping children become familiar with many of these procedures have been suggested by de Bono (see p. 80).

The final stage, having collected and used the information, is to present it. The audience and purpose of the presentation must be considered, so that an appropriate choice is made. Presentations can include visual as well as verbal approaches in a wide range of formats, for instance:

- tape recordings or video
- poster, pictures, cartoon strips
- models, pop-up books, zig-zag books
- plays, mime, dance
- quiz cards, make-your-own-adventures
- loose-leaf folder, booklet

ACTIVITY

Interrogating the Text

Choose a DARTS activity to appraise children's comprehension or, a recording activity to extend graphic representation skills.

(a) DARTS activities are designed to help children 'interrogate' the text in a critical, interactive manner. They are of two main types: unmodified and modified text.
Unmodified text is that which is in a book, or on a sheet, which can be photocopied. Children can then be encouraged to
- underline key points
- give a label to each paragraph indicating the main idea
Modified text is that which has been altered by the teacher e.g. to make a 'cloze' exercise by
- deleting key content words,
- regular deletions every *n*th word

(b) Recording activities are designed to extend children's skills in extracting and presenting information.
They depend on graphic representation and encourage children to translate information from a verbal to a visual format. It also serves as a check on their understanding.

Alternative text types and information formats include:

- narrative/sequential   picture series, list, time-line
- descriptive: characteristics attribute web, diagram
                spatial, location map, plan
                interrelational   graph, scattergram
- comparative   table, pie-chart, matrix
- classificatory: inclusive   Venn diagram
                hierarchical   tree diagram
- causal, problem-solution   flow-chart, network

With fiction, children are encouraged to respond to the text content and also to reflect upon their own reading process. The same should apply with non-fiction. Discussion should take place at each stage of topic work and focus on both the content (what information is being gained) and on the process (how it is being gained). These discussions allow the whole class to jointly draw out what they have learned about information gathering. Through such discussions, children acquire a 'metalanguage' to use when discussing their 'learning to learn' strategies.

FURTHER READING

The first book contains a collection of excellent and practical examples of developing children's interest and competence in reading and writing information books in a wide range of genres.

Stewart-Dore, N. (ed.) (1986) *Writing and Reading to Learn*. NSW, Australia: Primary English Teaching Association.

The following titles provide ideas for developing ways of using information books in the primary classroom.

Avann, P. (ed.) (1985) *Teaching Information Skills in the Primary School*. London: Edward Arnold.

Tann, C. S. (ed.) (1988) *Developing Topic Work in the Primary School*. Basingstoke: Falmer Press.

Wray, D. (1985) *Teaching Information Skills Through Topic Work*. London: Hodder & Stoughton (for UKRA)

These articles are useful in identifying text types and ways of graphically representing them:

Meyer, R. (1984) 'Organizational aspects of text' in Flood, J. (ed.) *Promoting Reading Comprehension*. Newark, DE: International Reading Association.

Sheldon, S. (1986) 'Representing comprehension' in Root, B. (ed.) *Resources for Reading*. Basingstoke: Macmillan (for UKRA).

(iv)   Awareness of books: their structures and language

(a)   Non-fiction

Southgate *et al.* (1981) reported that most children learn to read with fiction books. They may also encounter 'faction' – books which are written like fiction in a narrative style but conveying factual information. Faction may or may not promote children's desire to read alternatives to fiction or their ability to extract information from texts. It certainly offers yet another possible model for writing, but not one that will assist children to use the non-chronological forms (e.g. description, explanation, argumentation) that are characteristic of most writing intended to convey information.

These difficulties were evident in a 7-year-old's efforts to write about dinosaurs. The class had been encouraged to 'brainstorm' by making a 'web' of facts/issues with the key word in the centre of the page and lines radiating from it to each separate item. The next step was to imagine what the potential reader would need to know so that the author could decide how to group and order these facts. This would serve as a plan for writing up the facts in the information book.

However, this child was unclear as to the characteristics of information books. She knew that she must write a 'true' and not a 'made-up' story so she began a 'true story' about megalosaurus and tyrannosaurus who met in a wood. The story was true ... 'because my Daddy told me so'. Her flow of ideas was deliberately checked to help her identify 'facts' and information that she might give so that her readers should learn more about dinosaurs. But there was a constant reversion to the 'true story'.

After this, an attempt was made to look at an existing 'faction' book (about two children watching a new road being built when, suddenly, the workmen noticed a huge skeleton) and compare this with a non-fiction book about dinosaurs. The child noted the following differences:

	Faction	*Non-fiction*
illustrations	drawings	real photos/diagrams
punctuation	speech marks	no speech marks
source	author	typewriter
language	friendly high tunes 　(fluctuating 　intonation due to 　dialogue)	stern low tunes 　(unmelodic as 　there were no 　dialogue patterns)

| structures | introduced the children on holiday, story unfolded | indicated time scale, described environment, described each dinosaur, its dimensions, foods, unique attributes, etc. |

The differences listed are not consistent between these two categories of books but the exercise indicates how children can be encouraged to notice the distinctive features. It was the structure that provided the clearest indication of what was unique to non-fiction. By reading and discussing the structure and style of the books an understanding of the fiction, faction and non-fiction categories began to develop. Later, the child showed the teacher a comprehensive draft with a contents page and chapter titles such as 'How big were the dinosaurs?', 'How heavy are dinosaurs?', 'What do dinosaurs like to eat?', 'When did dinosaurs live?', 'What did they look like?', 'Why did they all die?' and 'Which ones were dangerous?'. The question format appeared to have arisen in an attempt to consider 'What questions do you think the readers will ask?'.

This instance of a child's unfamiliarity with non-fiction writing is typical. Reading non-fiction books in class at 'story-time' and discussing their features would help to change the situation.

(b) Fiction

Greater awareness of fiction is also important. Children do not often need to be encouraged to indicate their preferences, but they may well need help in developing a more critical and discerning approach to different kinds of stories.

Young readers, interviewed in a reception class, were able to articulate clear ideas about different kinds of story. These differences were identified in terms of, for example:

• subject matter: naughty children, animals, babies, grown ups

- emotions: funny/silly, cross, sad, happy
- presentation: flip-ups, feely books
- publisher/symbol: Ladybird, Puffin, Lion

Older children made finer distinctions, such as:

subject matter: witches, ghosts, magic, animals, funny, scarey, detective and mystery stories, fantasy, romance, also myths, legends, fairytales

adventure (stories set in school, home, space, different worlds, different countries, travel books, journeys, quests)

'character books' ('where there is an adventure but it is really about someone who is lonely, or dying, or handicapped or something, and it's about feelings')

Whereas younger children depend almost exclusively upon the pictures as a clue to the type of book, older children employ a wider range of clues to help to confirm or challenge their original first impressions about a book. For example, the picture on the front cover will be checked against the 'blurb' on the back. The title may attract, particularly if it is unusual, ambiguous, intriguing or funny. Older children are also more likely to start to read the text to test expectations. The 'shelfwise' kid doesn't begin at the beginning 'because the beginnings just tell you the people's names ... you should read a bit from the middle where it ought to be exciting and things start happening'.

Other aspects which children identify as clues to guessing what a book will be like are the names of the characters. For example,

'This one's got a Jake in it ... it's got to be a pirate story. Yes, definitely ... look there's even a parrot in it!'

'Lugsey. Hm ... sounds like a nickname. It could be a robber or a schoolboy. Ah, here's Miss Chalk. It's a school story.'

The actual language of the text is also used as a clue in determining the genre of books, as in the following instances,

'This says "He sneaked round the back of the building". Well it sounds like someone's up to no good. It's an adventure and the children get into trouble.'

'This is full of "thee" and "thou". It's old-fashioned, so it must be a fairytale, or a myth perhaps.'

Opportunities for exchanging such insights about books are an important part of classroom life. One such opportunity is when the teacher reads to the whole class, using stories, poems and non-fiction books. The session can also be used for reading short extracts from the beginning, middle or end of books. This can stimulate discussion about what kind of a book it might be, what might happen, how can we tell. Or a number of books could be presented which are about the same theme, content or topic but written (and illustrated) in very different ways. The contrasting styles could be compared and their effect commented upon.

Further, after a period of individual silent reading, children can be encouraged to read out a special passage and say why they like it, or read out a new word which they've not met before or is particularly interesting in some way. This too can lead to fruitful discussion, for example, about description and how an author makes something seem spooky, scarey, soothing, smelly, scrumptious. Or passages can be picked because they don't seem to make sense, possibly because of unfamiliar vocabulary and/or the structuring of the sentences. In addition, individual words may be chosen because they are difficult to pronounce or to understand. Subsequent discussions can lead to strategies for tackling new words in terms of phonetic or semantic components, e.g. roots, affixes.

ACTIVITY

Book Bank

Try building up a data-base which identifies books in terms of theme, content or topic.

Try building up a collection of titles which illustrate structural and stylistic features. These can be used when appropriate to draw attention to such aspects and develop this kind of awareness.

Clearly, much of this kind of discussion will arise naturally from the books which the class reads. Teacher input can, however, extend this further.

FURTHER READING

A useful book which discusses the characteristics of different genres is:

Andrews, R. (1989) *Narrative and Argument*. Milton Keynes: Open University Press.

A more complex analysis of information texts can be found in:

Davies, F. and Greene, T. (1984) *Reading for Learning in the Sciences*. Edinburgh: Oliver & Boyd.
Friedman, M. I. and Rowls, M. D. (1980) *Teaching Reading and Thinking*. New York: Longman.

4.3.   MONITORING CHILDREN'S READING PROGRESS

The amount of detail concerning individual children on their entry to school at the age of five years varies considerably. Sometimes information is passed on from a previously attended nursery class. In any event, most schools like to record their own information about a new child, whatever their age. It may only be basic information about name, address, telephone numbers for emergency contacts and medical information, or it may be fuller information compiled by teacher, parent, child and all teachers or other support staff involved with the child.

The Primary Language Record, published by ILEA (see Barrs *et al.*, 1988) and recommended by the Cox Report (1988), provides a threefold structure. It begins with a summary of a conference between parent and teacher at the beginning of each year. The conference would normally include exchanging information about the languages used at home, attitudes to oracy and literacy and about experiences in both these areas. There is then a conference between child and teacher, which might include discussion of favourite books, what language activities the child likes best and the activities with which they think they need more help and practice. Part 2 includes observations made of the child whilst engaged in language activities so that a more detailed picture of how the child works can be established. Part 3 provides a summary of the child's achievements and recommendations for future action.

This procedure is lengthy, complex and very demanding in terms of teacher time. Nevertheless, it marks an important breakthrough, in that parents and children are both actively involved in commenting on the progress. This is consistent with the declared aims of the Educational Reform Act 1988 which include the intention of clarifying what schools and teachers do and why, so that each child's entitlement is made more explicit. This in turn is intended to create greater consistency between schools and, by demystifying the schooling process, to strengthen the partnership between home and school.

Such records are not totally new. Teachers have been encouraged to incorporate views of children and parents in other ways. For example, Strang (1972) advocated the Information Reading Inventory, which was compiled by teacher and child. It gave information on many items: favourite books, whether the child read at home, when, where, how often, to whom, also what were their interests/hobbies/out of school pursuits, favourite TV programme and any other data the teacher felt important, in order to help them understand the language experiences of the child and the place of reading in a child's life.

Reading records or diaries have also been used in some schools for many years. These take different forms, but are likely to include when the child reads, whether at home or at school, which book was read, whether by the child or an adult, what the child's response to the book was, and (if they read it themselves) how they read it. Parents, teacher and child are encouraged to contribute to the comments. Entries vary from a brief recording of the title and date, to more lengthy entries indicating how the child is making sense of the text in terms of decoding and comprehension skills.

Details concerning the child's reading behaviour may involve the use of many of the component attitudes, skills and knowledge outlined above, including prerequisites, purposes, processes, product and response outcomes. Process variables very often relate to whether the child 'had a go', 'waited to be prompted' or 'missed it out'. Further features which may be noted are whether the child self-corrected and which words they may have used as substitutes for those actually printed but which they couldn't decipher. These substitutions show how a child is tackling text. It is relevant to note whether the child substituted another word which was

- graphically similar (i.e. looked like the original but didn't make sense, e.g. 'head' for 'hard);

- syntactically similar (i.e. grammatically appropriate but not good sense, e.g. 'house' for 'head');
- semantically similar (i.e. makes sense but is different from text, e.g. 'home' for 'house').

Clearly substitutions can fall into more than one category. Those which are semantically appropriate show that the child is reading for meaning, whereas the other categories may indicate that the child is merely struggling with decoding.

This process of analysing substitution is based on a procedure known as 'miscue analysis' (Arnold, 1982), which offers a method of using a child's reading 'errors' to provide a 'window' on their approach to reading. For these 'errors' give important clues as to how the child tackles the process of reading.

A formal miscue analysis involves asking the child to read a text which is slightly 'harder' than one currently being read (the miscues that emerge will demonstrate how the child approaches text). A teacher can either take note of miscues, categorizing them for subsequent analysis, or can 'mark up' the miscues on a photocopy of what the child is reading.

After 'hearing the child read' the next step is to ask the child to retell the story and then to discuss it, so that the level of comprehension can be appraised (for grasp of main idea, details, character, plot, events, at a literal, inferential or response level). Such retell and response could even be scored (Weaver, 1980; Mitchell, 1983).

The information gathered on the child's strengths, the various strategies used and how well the child makes sense of the text can then be used to direct future steps to develop the child's reading. Possibly if the child is overdependent on one strategy (e.g. phonic) then they need encouragement to try other strategies (e.g. reading on or re-reading and guessing from context to look for meanings and make sense of the text). Or, if the child is only comprehending at a literal level then discussion strategies, such as those outlined in 'booktalk' (see p. 143), could lead the child to expect to explore deeper responses to the text.

'Hearing a child read' is the category of teacher behaviour related to literacy teaching which is predominant in primary classrooms. Yet if it merely consists of listening to a child with one ear for a few minutes (whilst keeping a watchful eye on the rest of the class and tuning in to potential trouble spots or areas of need), then it is not an experience that will encourage a child to believe that reading is a valued, much less an enjoyable, activity.

Southgate *et al.* (1981) suggested that the aim of many teachers to 'hear children read' daily, especially in the infant classes, was not only impractical and unnecessary but also ineffectual. They suggested that it was more important to allow children to enjoy books, share them with each other, be left to 'get into' a good book and experience 'being a reader'. Less frequent contact with each child but longer sessions with subsequent discussion about the book, to ascertain whether it had been enjoyed, understood, or returned unread was probably more profitable. Further, too much emphasis on oral reading could hinder the development of the development of aural and silent reading strategies (Pugh, 1978).

These discussions about books can also take place in a whole-class situation, where it is still possible to identify and note particular contributions by individual children that may confirm or challenge a previous assessment of their achievements. In addition to such discussions and 'conferencing', there is also value in observing children's behaviour with books as an important supplement to hearing them read aloud. However, rather than just vaguely scanning the room to see what the children are doing, it is important to be highly systematic in observation in order to gain maximum benefit from the time invested in such activities. Chapter 1 mentioned some key principles in observation and recommended that it was important to clarify in advance, questions of

- who
- why
- what
- how
- when
- what will be done with the information afterwards.

Observations can take two main forms: structured or unstructured. The structured observations could be in the form of a number of listed behaviours to look out for (on a checklist, which can be ticked off when the behaviour is noted), or it could be a mental 'framework' of items of which a teacher might wish to take note in order to guide and select particular aspects for field note or diary recording purposes.

It is important, especially with emergent readers, to observe a wide range of reading-like behaviours of children with books, and not only when they are just reading them. Much can be gained concerning children's attitudes to books as well as their knowledge of how they work by watching them browsing and choosing books, as well as reading, sharing and using them.

- *Attitudes*
  Do they appear enthusiastic, confident?
  Do they choose, or use, the book(s) on their own?
  Do they share with others, become distracted by others?
- *Knowledge*
  Do they make use of the front cover?
    (to gain information from title, author, pictures)
  Do they make use of the back cover?
    (to gain information from the 'blurb')
  Do they flick through the pictures, sample the text,
    find out whether the book is fiction or non-fiction?
  And, if the book is non-fiction,
  do they use the catalogue, contents, index?
- *Skills and strategies*:
  Do they read orally, aurally?
  Do their eyes move between picture and print?
  Do they scan the print in a random or regular way?
  Do they read the pictures and tell a story,
    or read the print?
  Do they appear to be reading 'steadily', 'skimming and scan-ning', 'using stop–go strategies'?
  If they seem to get 'stuck', what do they do then?
- *Response*:
  Do they frown with concentration and effort or appear relaxed and comfortable with the book?
  Do they react to the text – sigh, gasp, smile, laugh?
    (perhaps we should measure comprehension by using the 'chuckle factor' as a response index ...)

This type of 'mental framework' is soon internalized and can inform observations. Many teachers seem to use it instinctively.

An alternative way of observing children, is through 'kidwatch-

---

ACTIVITY

Miscue Analysis

Select individual children and undertake a miscue analysis.
First, choose a text which is challenging for the child.
Make a photocopy of the page(s) so that you can 'mark up' the text.
Then, ask the child to read the text.
While the child reads, 'mark up' the text so that the following features are noted:

hesitation	/
repetition	the wolf
reversal	said Dad
insertion	⋋
omission	we both ran
self-correction	✓
substitution	the next time (day)
Note whether the substituted word	
looks similar	(garden for garter)
sounds similar	(when for then)
similar meaning	(Nana for Gran)

Finally, ask the reader to re-tell the story. Ask follow-up questions relating to given details as well as to gauge possible inferential understanding and personal response (i.e. full comprehension).

Use this information to identify the reader's strengths, any limitations in range of strategies and, therefore, the nature of possible future help.

---

ing' (Goodman, 1965). This is a more open approach to observation, more impressionistic, more anecdotal. It is, though, very hard to be 'open' in our observations of children whom we already believe we know. Such snapshot pictures are essentially descriptive: interpretation comes later. But beware, it is easy to collect great quantities of such data of which it is then difficult to make sense. Often it is useful to invite the child to help in the interpretation.

Finally, tape-recorders can be an especially useful additional tool in monitoring reading. They can be used in a number of ways. Children can read into a tape, play it back and assess themselves. This can lead to self-correction in an unthreatening environment. Children can use it for rehearsal and the final product can be assessed by the teacher, and, with the reader's consent, used to supplement the tape library of class favourites.

The tape-recorder can also be used to tape children's reviews of books, which can then be used by other children as a guide when choosing their own books. From these assessments a class 'Top Ten' can be compiled. Group or class discussions about books can also be taped, listened to by others in order to compare notes, and listened to by the teacher for further insights into children's understanding and response to stories, poems, and non-fiction books.

Further sources of data can be derived from the methods suggested in Chapter 1, such as children's logs, child–parent–teacher conferencing. However, these may need to be summarized for transfer purposes at the end of each year, 'key stage' or level of schooling. We need to remind ourselves before embarking on devising elaborate schedules that time is limited, and that we should not collect more data than we can use for improving our support for each individual.

FURTHER READING

Arnold, H. (1982) *Listening to Children Reading*. London: Hodder & Stoughton.
Mitchell, I. (1983) 'A procedure for assessing richness of retelling'. *Journal of Reading*, **26** (5).
Strang, R. (1972) 'Observation in the classroom' and 'Informal reading inventories' both in Melnik, A. and Merritt, J. (eds) *The Reading Curriculum*. London: University of London Press for Open University.

Part III

Writing

Chapter 5

Teachers and Writing

INTRODUCTION

Written language is a dominant feature of our environment: in the street, in shops, on the television and in the home. Children coming from such a print-rich background will already have ideas about 'writing', what it is and what it does. These ideas will vary considerably according to the nature of such experiences and, in particular, their experiences of seeing writing in action, modelled by people around them, who can demonstrate its value and purposes.

Written language is also a dominant feature of the classroom. It is found in published books, official notices, displayed posters and brochures, and is produced by the adults and children during activities in the classroom. The term itself, however, is ambiguous as it refers not only to the *physical* processes of writing (letter formation and spacing, whether handwriting, typing, wordprocessing), and its final product (requiring secretarial skills including spelling and punctuation). It also includes *psychological* processes (composing the content, identifying intent, anticipating impact), and the *linguistic* processes (structuring and organizing the text to convey meaning).

This chapter will begin by examining some characteristics of written language: the differences between the spoken and written word and the impact of purpose, audience, genre and style. The second section will briefly review current practice relating to writing in the classroom and the teacher's role in managing space and time for modelling the process of writing. The third section will present a framework for analysing progression in children's writing. This comprises structural organization at text level, syntactic structures at sentence level, vocabulary and punctuation. How this might be developed and monitored in the classroom will be the focus of the following chapter.

5.1.   THE NATURE OF WRITTEN LANGUAGE

The Attainment Target for writing, defined in the Orders for English, states that the goal for 'writing' should be to develop:

> a growing ability to construct and convey meaning in written language matching style to audience and purpose.

We need therefore to identify the purpose(s), audience(s) and style(s).

At the societal level, the Working Party's Report (DES, 1989) suggests that written language serves the general 'purposes' of record-keeping and storing both information and literary works. It can, therefore, support and transmit culture. At the individual level it serves a cognitive function in that it helps to clarify and support thought by enabling detached reflection upon what has been written and how it has been written. Thus it has a communicative, cognitive, and aesthetic function.

The range of types of writing will vary according to the audience and the particular purpose. What may be even more important is the relationship of writers to their audience. For example, the teacher is often the sole audience for classroom writing and his/her role is often that of assessor. The National Writing Project, which has collected and disseminated current 'good practice', has consistently demonstrated the key, and varied, role that 'a sense of audience' has on writers and their writing.

To appreciate this role of 'audience', it is necessary to examine more closely the range of purposes, and the alternative genres and styles which might be appropriate to them. Above all, it is necessary to clarify the key differences between the child's use of the spoken word and his use of the written word, and what makes writing different.

(i)   Differences between the spoken and the written word

The relationship between the spoken and written word is a very subtle and complex one, and much debated. Any analysis needs to take into account the age of the writer/speaker, and above all, her intention. There are some obvious distinctions, with significant implications.

	Speech	Writing
physical mode	aural oral	visual motor
stability	transient	fixed
speed	what can be said in 1 minute . . .	. . . takes 6 minutes to write

context
and
audience
	situational
	context-bound
	makes use of:−
	   surrounding clues
	   immediate feedback
	often implicit − unless
	listener interrupts
		independent
		context-free
		makes no use of:−
		   non-linguistic clues
		   para-linguistic clues
		needs to be explicit − to
		help unknown audience

unit markers	prosodic indicators:−
	   intonation, stress
	   rhythm, accents
		no such features, so
		'punctuation' used instead

style	more often informal, less attention to formal grammar	usually more formal, more attention to structural conventions
structure	looser organization more redundancy	tighter organization often complex and condensed

Although these distinctions are not firm they do represent tendencies, of which children need to become aware so that they can adopt the appropriate style and structure to achieve their purpose. Awareness of range allows children to become effective communicators in a variety of situations. Knowledge of the different demands made on the writer (or speaker) and on the reader (or listener) can also help the teacher support the child appropriately. For instance, the slow and physically tiring nature of writing can reduce a five-minute oral recount to a single written sentence − unless the child is allowed to dictate to an adult or into a tape recorder.

In shifting from an oral to a written mode, the Working Party Report (DES, 1989) suggests that there is a tendency to move from casual to formal, from spontaneous to planned forms, and from known to unknown audience. In addition some children will need to add a change from non-Standard to Standard English. Such simplistic dichotomies are crude. For example, it is easy to identify occasions where the same form can be used for different purposes/audiences and are therefore very different in style: a formal letter to a known Headteacher, an informal letter to an unknown pen-friend. In addition, the same (oral) mode could be used for a prepared speech to explain absence, or a casual conversation to a friend's parent, or to leave a (non-interactive) enquiry on a shop answerphone. Further, written modes can also be informal (taking notes) and spontaneous (sending notes).

These are differences between the oral and the written mode in terms of communicative function, in relation to purpose and audience. There are also differences in terms of cognitive function, which are of considerable significance in the classroom context. Kress (1982) argues that different modes of language indicate different modes of thinking. For example, in speech, topics are typically developed by sentences in a sequential relationship (or chaining) whereas, in writing, topics are also likely to be developed through subordination and embedding. Further, different forms of writing show different ways of thinking: 'storying' is typically serial whereas 'transactional' writing is typically analytical, causal and hierarchical. Hence, talking and writing have distinct structural and syntactical organization.

Furthermore, it is important to remember the effect that such different demands may make on a young writer. Neither talking nor writing can necessarily be regarded as 'windows' on the child's cognitive abilities, for they entail additional specific abilities related to the particular mode. Kress suggests that the implicitness of young children's context-bound writing has sometimes been interpreted as indicative of their egocentricity. But, it could also be indicative of the lack of an interactive context. In an oral context there is always a partner who can challenge any ambiguity and demand clarification.

Bereiter and Scardamalia (1987) go further in identifying distinctions between an oral and written mode. They agree that the transition from oral to graphic communication is both a physical and social difference, for instance using a manual writing tool rather than voice, and being autonomous rather than interactive. They also suggest that writing demands additional, specialized knowledge about language in terms of syntax and style. In the more formal kinds of writing the text is usually shaped more than it would be in spontaneous speech. Sentences are more complete, vocabulary more precise, and connectives between sentences (e.g. so, but, because) more explicit. The writer will use clearer pronoun referencing (e.g. it, they, she), so that the 'thread' is easier to follow.

Finally, writing demands different 'knowledge structures' – an ability to shift from using 'knowledge-telling' to using 'knowledge-transforming'. 'Knowledge-telling' is a less crafted 'tell it like it is' discourse structure, whilst 'knowledge-transforming' is characterized by 'signs of wrestling with words, indications of revisions, or self-reported changes in thinking and attitudes' (Bereiter and Scardamalia, 1987). Changes will have taken place in terms of reworking the text, so that the content is refined and its expression is reformulated: reflection and self-regulation are involved.

Such reflection includes the need to identify the purpose of writing in terms of the cognitive operations (e.g. describe/compare/analyse). There is also the need to define the communicative goals in terms of how the message is to be presented and therefore the kind of language that will be needed. These kind of decisions are performed by more experienced writers as part of an 'internal dialogue'. However, precisely because it is internal, it is often mysterious to inexperienced writers. Bereiter and Scardamalia found that generating conversational protocols to guide reflection released writers from the mystery. Such protocols helped them to practise in the social context of a partnership between a writer and a reader (response partners). Later they internalized the dialogue and found they could operate more easily as autonomous writers.

Whilst writing clearly has a cognitive function, it is the relation between this and the communicative competence of the writer which is crucial. A writer has to learn to construct and convey a message that is understood in the way it is intended.

As indicated above, there are particular syntactic and textual features associated with a written mode which children need to acquire. Hunt (1970) and Perera (1984) both suggest that children often try out such new linguistic devices in writing before they use them in speech. However, in general it has been found that the writing of 6-year-olds is like the speech of 3-year-olds and not until the ages of 10 or 11 do the speaking and writing competencies become more equal. Initially then, writing does not enhance cognitive processes: rather cognitive competencies are constrained and linguistically curtailed.

(ii)   Effect of audience, purpose, genre and style

Work stimulated by Graves (1983) has suggested the need to extend the range of audiences and purposes, so that writing does not remain a formal mode of transmitting information or conveying ideas to the teacher for appraisal. Conversely, writing should not be an essentially private activity, as in a diary. Instead, writing can be developed as an interactive mode for constructing meanings between the writer and the reader. This can happen through using a set of protocols (see p. 215) to guide an 'internal dialogue', such as Bereiter and Scardamalia, Graves and others have encouraged.

Alternatively, a 'writers' workshop' approach can be used in which writers read each other's work, comment and share opinions. In this way the 'audience' becomes real to the writer. By asking questions and making suggestions, the reader is able to help the writer understand what he – the reader – needs to know. It also helps the reader understand the clues which the writer might have inserted. In this context 'audience' implies an informal relationship, with the reader playing a responsive, responsible and often evaluative role (see p. 76).

One outcome of writing could be to 'publish' a final polished version of the story. This not only confirms status on the author and gives a real incentive to write, but also provides the opportunity for a much wider audience to read the story. (Responses are often invited in the form of comments inside the back cover.) Other initiatives include older children writing for younger children. Sometimes this means that an opportunity is provided for writers to read their stories to younger children. Sometimes older children write a story 'to order' after discussion with a younger partner. Many schools are now experimenting with extending the range of audiences to parents and members of the community, so as to heighten a real sense of purpose in their writing which in turn enhances the self-esteem of the writers.

Additional 'audiences' can be addressed where different formats are appropriate. For example, children can write letters seeking information about museum opening hours for a class excursion, invitations to friends to attend a birthday party, or menus for school dinners. The daily life of the child, in school as well as out of school, provides a wide variety of different opportunities. In these instances the role of the reader and the nature of the interaction is different.

In addition to 'audience', a second variable which affects writing is 'purpose'. Wilkinson (1986) lists a 2,000-year-old distinction of narrative (chronological), description (information), argument (logical) and explanation (relational). Kinneavy (1971) identified writing with both purpose and audience in mind: expressive (personal, diaries), literary (story, drama), referential (factual) and persuasive (argument, analysis). Britton (1975) suggested a continuum with three identifiable points representing alternative purposes or functions: transactional, expressive and poetic. A further, vertical dimension was added to represent the relationship of the writer to the writing, as either spectator (commentator, often affective) or participant (instrumental, often impersonal). However, as Williams (1977) points out, these models lack specific linguistic differentiators. They display a 'logical skid' by inferring the author's intentions from descriptors of the end product.

Subsequent work has attempted to remedy this by identifying indices relating to the type of language being used and how it is organized in terms of text and syntactic structures. Research undertaken in Australia offers a way of identifying linguistic criteria associated with different forms. Kress (1982) identifies non-fiction text in terms of linguistic features such as:

- the use of the 'universal present tense':
  'The milk bottles pass through the sterilizer.'
- the dominance of the verb to be/have:
  'They have to be completely clean to be safe.'
- the effect of objectivity: (i) avoiding author's voice
  e.g. using agentless passive (subject of sentence not given):
  'The bottles are washed.'
  e.g. unspecified 'it' or impersonal 'you':
  'It is vital that you have good hygiene.'
  (ii) objectifying

e.g. nominalizing, using noun form, instead of verb:
'The controls regulate the throttle ...'
(instead of 'The pilot controls the throttle by ...')
'The discovery and exploration of the New World by
Columbus ...'
(instead of 'Columbus discovered and explored the New
World ...')

Martin and Rothery (1986) suggest a framework to distinguish particular characteristics of factual genres.

Focus Item	Specific	General	Explain, reason	Debate, judgement
'event'	recount [investigation]	procedure [instruction]	explanation [problem–resolve]	exploration [argument]
'thing'	description	report	exposition	discussion

Recount and procedure are likely to be chronological and share features with narrative: temporal connectives (first, then), simple present tense or imperative (is, put, get, goes), generalized human agent (you, they, or use of passive to avoid specifying the agent, e.g. It is made from ...). Whereas recount primarily employs temporal sequence, procedure is based on goal-method sequence.

Reports are similar to descriptions: both feature identification of attributes and their relationships, possibly comparison and even classification. They also contain many 'timeless' verbs in the continuous present tense (e.g. eats, lives, hunts, climbs).

Explanations and expositions are likely to relate to empirical items, and are characterized by both temporal and causal connectives (then, after, so, because) and also use simple present tense as well as the passive. In Martin and Rothery's schema both genres identify and indicate relationships: explanations are mostly material (e.g. what something does, how it works); expositions are more likely to include mental processes and value-based reasons as well (e.g. believe, feel, ought). Debates and discussion relate to issues and therefore present evidence for and against in order to make a judgement.

The term 'expository' is more commonly applied to all 'transactional' writing, i.e. with a non-fiction content. The use of the term, as given by Martin and Rothery, may well cause confusion. The form of writing to which they refer with this term is more often called 'positional' or 'persuasive' writing.

There appears to be no clear reason why these genres could not apply to both 'events' and 'things'. Kress (in Andrews, 1989) suggests that the degree of openness and closedness, the conclusiveness of the evidence, and the purpose of the text (to explore, present alternative arguments, or persuade) are also important influences on the style of language and structure of the text.

A less-linguistic alternative is offered by Perera (1984), who draws a clear distinction between chronological and non-chronological writing structures and their characteristics:

	Type	
Characteristic	Chronological	Non-chronological
Structure	Temporal sequence	Logical sequence
Style	Personal	Impersonal
	Narrative/story	Description, explanation
Subject	Familiar experiences with which reader can identify	Factual input Additional information to what is already known
	Feelings, fantasy	Authenticity, problematics
	Engages the affective	Engages the cognitive

The Working Party Report (DES, 1989), drawing heavily upon Perera's work, identified a wide range of forms which were divided into two main categories: chronological and non-chronological. This related to discourse structure rather than function, and hence to how the content is organized rather than to how the particular function might affect the nature of the language used (register, syntax and style).

- Examples of chronological writing include:
  diaries, stories, letters, accounts of tasks completed, personal experiences, records of observations, and instructions (e.g. recipes).
- Non-chronological writing includes:
  lists, captions, labels, invitations, greetings cards, notices, posters, plans and diagrams, descriptions, notes.
- Finally, children should be encouraged to play with language, by making up:

jingles, poems, word games, riddles and games that involve word and spelling patterns.

Work by Davies and Greene (1984) focused particularly on non-fiction writing (mostly non-chronological, though with some important exceptions regarding procedures and processes):

Category	Label	Constituents
Activities	Recipe/instruction manual	Action-orientated, steps/procedures, ingredients/materials, equipment, conditions/cautions, results
Phenomena	Process	State/form, agent of change, stage/sequence, transformation/reaction
	Structure	Name of structure/substance, location, property, function
	Mechanism	Name of mechanism, location, property, function, action, object acted upon
	Classification	Groups, property/feature
	Categorization	Comparisons, dimensions of groupings
Ideas	Concept–principle	Definition, law/principle, measure, restrictions/conditions, applications
	Hypothesis–theory	Question/problem, tests/methods, results, interpretations.

Adapted from Davies and Greene (1984), p. 81.

This theoretical breakdown of writing activities cuts across what has become the traditional divide of 'creative writing', i.e. personal, expressive and poetic writing (stories, poems and plays), and 'information writing', i.e. transactional writing (reports, newspapers, essays, topic folders). It also highlights the cognitive functions identified with these categories, namely, a sequential ordering in contrast to a hierarchical arrangement.

A final component in distinguishing types of language is 'style'. This is commonly used in a colloquial fashion without clear definition. Something may be described as having a certain style relating to its 'character'; romantic, lyrical, journalistic, aggressive, conversational, officious and many more. However, Joos (1962) distinguishes style on a five-point scale: frozen, formal, consultative, casual and intimate. An alternative representation is offered by Leech (1966), who suggests four 'polarities' which influence choice of linguistic elements: colloquial–formal structure, casual–ceremonial situation, personal–impersonal relationship and simple–complex content. Hence style relates not just to text organization and syntactical structures but also to register.

ACTIVITY

Identifying Genres

The characteristics of each of these genres need identification, in terms of audience, purpose, language features:

Make a table to record the distinguishing characteristics of children's chronological, and non-chronological writing, which you believe will be useful in your classroom.

How would you provide opportunities for each of these in a classroom?

FURTHER READING

The following titles give important details on different kinds of writing, the differences in oral and written language and strategies for developing writing:

Bereiter, C. and Scardamalia, M.(1987) *The Psychology of Written Composition*. Hillsdale, NJ: Lawrence Erlbaum.
Kress, G. (1982) *Learning to Write*. London: Routledge & Kegan Paul.
Perera, K. (1984) *Children's Writing and Reading*. Oxford: Basil Blackwell.

5.2. THE PRACTICE OF WRITING IN THE CLASSROOM

Research reports in the last decade have consistently shown the continuing dominance of writing as a feature of classroom life. In

1980 the ORACLE research (Galton, Simon and Croll), based on observations in upper junior classrooms, showed that 33 per cent of class time was spent on language activities, of which the vast majority was 'writing' but only 8 per cent of which was described as 'creative' writing. Hence, 'language exercises' and writing associated with topic work predominated. The following year a Schools Council report (Southgate *et al.*, 1981) produced similar findings but discovered interesting differences between lower and upper juniors. Southgate found that 7- to 9-year olds spent 20 per cent of writing time on 'creative' or 'free' writing and 7 per cent on topic-associated work, but with 9- to 11-year-olds these percentages were reversed. Subsequent reports from HMI (1978, 1982) have also highlighted the dominance of writing and commented on the repetitive and dull nature of the tasks.

Despite these reports of narrow product-orientated practice, there seems to have been change in two areas. First, children are being encouraged to view writing in a broader context with the aim of developing a wider repertoire of purposes and audiences. This change is accompanied by an emphasis on appropriateness (matching style) rather than mere accuracy. This has resulted in a wider range of written forms and contexts being considered. Children write for themselves, in journals/diaries. They write for each other and share in a collaborative process of revision and development. They may write to a commission from a younger child. They may write for school publication, where the book joins the library shelves for future generations. Such different audiences and purposes influence form and style and heighten the writers' understandings of the relationship between author, text and reader. This encourages the need for reflection and the kind of 'knowledge-transforming' to which Bereiter and Scardamalia refer.

Secondly, a classroom of writers needs to be encouraged to discuss the crafting of writing and to focus on the writing process. The Cox Report (DES, 1989) identified these processes as decision-making with regard to the audience, purpose and context; planning and organizing thoughts and ideas; drafting and revising. However, it is important that the process of drafting does not become a new straitjacket. After all, not every draft is worthy of re-drafting. The child must be encouraged to select those which they wish to develop, otherwise drafting merely leads to 'copying into best'. The drafting process, on the other hand, requires a great deal of time and emotional effort to prune, re-structure, clarify or develop an original draft into a final script.

The different contexts of writing suggest different foci for crafting. In addition to storying, a typical range of writing activities and some associated characteristics upon which children could focus might include the following:

personal/diary	reflective, introspective
letters	both formal and informal
description	detail, vividness
instructional	sequence, precision
information/report	factual accuracy, synthesis
explanation	explicit reasoning
'empathy'	relating to others' feelings
argument/persuasion	clarity of values/goal, coherent argument

In addition, there should also be opportunities for poetry and plays. Further, these activities mentioned so far rely solely on written verbal modes, but could include visual/verbal combinations. The final medium in which the 'composition' might be presented could be extended into other media such as audio- and videotape, 3D modelling or mime and movement.

Somehow the teacher, as manager in the classroom, has to keep track of what opportunities there are in the classroom so that each child experiences as wide a range as possible. There is a concomitant need to manage and monitor the opportunities at three different levels: a) longer-term records (which monitor the nature of the provision); b) short-term records (which monitor what each child is doing and which demands the activity is making); and c) ongoing records to monitor how well the child is achieving over the series of situations.

(i)   Managing space and resources for writing

Supporting opportunities for writing is important for all ages. In reception and infant classes many alternative contexts have been successfully tried: a home corner with a telephone message pad, a restaurant where children take orders and provide bills, health

centres which give prescriptions, a travel shop which devises desti-
nation plans and maps. All such contexts offer a chance for 'writing
behaviours' to be employed in 'real' play situations (Hall, 1989).

Many classrooms also make provision for a 'writer's corner' or
'writer's den', as a separate area of the classroom (often a quiet and
secluded area) where children can go in order to write without
disturbance. It is important that the necessary resources are also on
hand, so that practical constraints are reduced. Hence, rough paper,
'best' paper, pencils, rubbers, pens, dictionary and thesaurus should
all be accessible. Further, it is important that there should be space
for displaying a whole range of different kinds of writing, thus
valuing a wide spectrum of written products. For example, a notice
board could be used for notes and memos, a shelf could display
'published' stories, and a letterbox could hold correspondence.

(ii) Managing time to model writing processes

It is important for children to witness adults writing, not just the
physical act but to have access to the composition processes by
hearing an adult 'think aloud'. This can be achieved in a number of
ways. For example, the class (or group) may wish to compose a
notice, a message for parents, or a summary of an investigation
which they want to display. The teacher can act as scribe and talk
the group through the process of identifying what is going to be
written and how it is going to be written.

Alternatively, just as the children are frequently asked to write
their news so too can the teacher. This can be modelled on a wall
board or sheets of paper clipped to an easel. The teacher's 'thinking aloud' about what to say (where, when, what, how, so), and
how to say it (choosing words, adding details which the children
request for clarification, changing items) can help children to
understand the reflection that is needed to change knowledge-
telling into knowledge-transforming.

Another form of modelling, which can be done with a whole
class or a group, is the initial brainstorming for ideas followed by
selecting items and deciding the order in which to present them.
This can be done at the start of a class project or in connection
with individual pieces of writing, with children being encouraged
to share their own brainstorms and help each other to select and

order. Such public sessions can help to make explicit the process which the individual writer would otherwise struggle to achieve alone – or might omit. It also provides the interpersonal support that, for the inexperienced writer, is a helpful substitute for the 'internal dialogue' conducted by experienced writers.

Apart from initially stimulating writing through preliminary discussion and subsequently modelling and supporting the processes, the teacher needs time to 'conference' with individual children and provide feedback on their drafts or final products. Finally, it is important that teachers should be developing their own writing, with the children. If the teacher is also writing, it gives value to the activity. This can be a salutory experience, providing valuable insights into the writing process and its challenges.

In addition to the teacher's own writing, the teacher can also highlight particular features of structure and style in the work of different authors. The way in which a teacher presents and discusses writings (by children's authors and by children) can play an important part in raising awareness of the author–text–reader relationship. During these discussions children will generate their own labels for features of the story, in their own words. Such (home-grown) terms will be more meaningful and helpful than any that may be introduced by an adult.

ACTIVITY

Managing Writing

Review your own classroom, in terms of:–

(i)   the management of writing space and resources
who uses the facilities
for how long
what do they actually do
what are they learning

(ii) the management of time for modelling
when and where do you model writing processes
to whom and why in particular
what strategies/protocols do you use
what kinds of prompts might be helpful in class

FURTHER READING

The books listed below, in chronological order, show some of the major findings concerning writing as it is practised in primary schools:

Harpin, W. (1976) *The Second 'R'*. London: Allen & Unwin.
Southgate, V. *et al.* (1981) *Extending Beginning Reading*. London: Heinemann for the Schools Council.
Beard, R. (1984) *Children's Writing in the Primary School*. London: Hodder & Stoughton/UKRA.
Wilkinson, A. (ed.) (1986) *The Writing of Writing*. Milton Keynes: Open University Press. (See especially Medway, P., Perera, K., Kress, G.)

The following booklets (published by Nelson, for the National Curriculum Council) aim to disseminate good practice and are produced by the National Writing Project, out of their three-year research work: *Perceptions of Writing; Audiences for Writing; Writing Partnerships*.

5.3.   ASPECTS OF WRITING PROGRESSION

The Working Party documents (1988, 1989) outlined detailed principles upon which their targets are based. The overall aim was to develop the composing and secretarial aspects of writing so that children can construct and convey meaning in written language. This is admitted to be a complex process and children 'cannot be expected to learn everything at once' (17.7) as development is 'recursive' and 'language competence is dependent on task' (17.25).

We have already noted how development of range is seen in terms of audience, purposes, genres and style. Additionally, in order to 'construct and convey' meaning appropriately pupils should be encouraged to 'craft' their writing. This crafting (17.32) is seen as being marked by:

- increasing control over the structure and organization of different types of text;
- a widening range of syntactic structures and an expanding vocabulary;
- using punctuation to help the reader identify the units of structure and meaning that the writer has constructed;
- increasing proficiency in revising text, and an ability to reflect on and talk about the writing processes;

- using the conventions of spelling patterns and a legible hand.

The first three 'strands' will be examined in more detail in this chapter. In each case it is important to consider what metalanguage the teacher or the children might need when talking about the writing process. The fourth strand will be the focus of the following chapter.

(i) Text structures

Kroll and Wells (1983) have identified a number of stages through which children appear to progress. These relate not just to the structure of the writing but also to the child's attitude to writing. The first is described as 'preparatory', when the child is acquiring the basic mechanisms of handwriting and spelling. By the age of 7 these have begun to become automatic for many children, so that writing is no longer such a physical strain.

Children at this point have reached the second stage, 'consolidation', where writing is still personal, colloquial, situational and context-bound. Children are willing to rub out and alter letter shapes or spellings, but are rarely willing to revise or edit.

Between 7 and 9, children are becoming fluent story writers. Graves (1983) and Calkins (1981) suggest that at about 9 years, children become more aware of audience. This raises awareness that the success of writing depends on its communicative effectiveness with others, rather than the feeling of satisfaction for self. This leads to a much greater willingness to draft and edit in order to fulfil the communicative function of writing. At the same time there is a need to provide continuing opportunities for the personal style of writing, through logs and diaries.

The 'differentiation' stage at around 9 or 10 years shows evidence of structures of writing and speech becoming more distinct. The structure of the story text becomes more shaped and organized, and the sentence structures become more formal, less colloquial.

The final stage, 'integration', is reached when the writer shows a wider range of writing styles and an awareness of audience, purpose and appropriateness. Many children do not reach this stage till 12 or 13. However, the speed with which children progress is linked not only to their rate of maturation, but also to the classroom climate, the range of demands made upon them, and the nature of positive support from the teacher and peers.

(a)   Story structure

The characteristics of story structure are recognized by children from an early age. For instance, Applebee (1978) found that young children recognized the adult model of story structure: they judged that a proper introduction and conclusion (satisfying ending) were essential. An ambiguous ending was often regarded as 'unfinished' and disliked if it left the reader feeling insecure. Whilst some understanding of the components of story structure can be useful to teachers, to help in diagnosing the strengths and weaknesses of a child's work over a period of time, it is equally important to have some understanding of the stages of children's growth as writers.

Recent research (Christie in Stewart-Dore, 1986) has identified a number of different genres of children's writing within the 'preparatory' style which suggests developmental progression, though not a smooth or continuous one. The very first writings are often in the form of 'labelling' usually alongside a drawing: 'This is my house'. The second genre which emerges is perhaps an 'observation/comment' – 'We went for a picnic on Sunday it was lovely.' – in which persons and things are described and personal responses included. Observations are often about 'material processes/ actions' and comments about 'relational processes/feelings/being'. As confidence increases, writers often begin a 'reconstruction' genre. This is often a list of actions or events based on real time sequence, describing, for instance, what happened on a trip to a circus or how a science investigation took place. This is often linked by 'and', 'and', 'and' (chaining), though later more sophisticated linkages may emerge.

Writers may then develop a 'narrative genre' such as a piece of fictional writing/storying, featuring a simplified form of story grammar such as setting, characters, problem, resolution. This type of storying has a strong chronological basis and is easily transferred to the kind of narrative non-fiction reportage that is associated, for example, with write-ups about the life-cycle of

mini-beasts. Such narrative non-fiction is used in many information books for young children, as it is believed to be easier to
understand than formal expository writing, which develops later.

Other researchers have elaborated a more detailed analysis of
story structure, often referred to as story grammar (see Mandler
and Johnson, 1977; Stein and Glenn, in Freedle, 1977; Kroll and
Anson, in Cowie, 1984). The components are variously described
as:

beginning/opening
  setting, mood
  characters, motives
middle
  action
  problem
  events
ending
  resolution
  conclusion

Infant children can be expected to move towards shaping the three
main categories of a beginning, middle and ending whilst junior
children can begin to work on the sub-categories within each main
category (see p. 218). The terminology, here, seems to be relatively self-explanatory and could also be used with children
throughout the primary stages.

(b)   Non-chronological structures

Non-chronological writing, as identified by the Orders for English,
embraces what is sometimes referred to as an 'expository' or 'transactional' genre. This includes descriptions, explanations, opinion,
argumentation and persuasion. However, these terms relate to
purposes rather than to the structures which may help to communicate those purposes or be conventionally associated with them.

The 'expository' genre is usually the last to develop, or the last
to be demanded, and is also the genre of which young writers
usually have least experience through their reading. Further, the
distinction of chronological and non-chronological, and of fiction
and non-fiction are not co-terminous. The boundaries are still

more confused by the genre of 'faction' writing. This genre has arisen partly because of the difficulties of non-fiction text which are experienced by young readers.

Faction is written in a chronological format but with the intention of conveying information – for example a story about a family of animals, or the daily life of postmen, or of a child living in Chile. Reading such texts may be 'easier' to understand. However, whether it is easier to extract the information is not clear. It may well relate to how the information is presented in relation to the illustrations, which could help to focus on specific items or merely provide a background scene-setting function to help the reader 'imagize' the contents to aid general recall.

Different types of expository text have already been identified (see p. 178). Needless to say, exposition is rarely found in a single, 'pure' form, but is usually mixed in any one book, chapter or section. One of the critical factors in understanding expository text structure is the different nature of the cognitive demand which is likely to be made of the children, as well as the different levels of complexity. For example, narrative text is temporally sequential, whereas 'explanatory' text is causally sequential. More complex explanatory text (characterized by exploring issues, identifying problems, offering a solution and explaining its appropriateness) may involve both temporal and causal sequencing which is then followed by interpretation of the information, selecting, sorting and applying it. Further, whilst simple 'description' may focus on a singular item (e.g. 'my puppy') more complex descriptions, involving comparison and classification, (e.g. 'pets') focus on more items therefore requiring more analysis.

Furthermore, the degree of difficulty in interacting with the text depends very much on the type of task and on whether the child is alert to facts, opinions, to the question of accuracy and the nature of the evidence provided. The text may not be inherently difficult. Difficulty may reside in the amount of preparation required before reading the text, the need for clarity of purpose and for knowledge about what to do with the results of interacting with the text.

By the junior age children will be expected to be learn that:

> non-chronological types of writing can be organized in a variety of ways and so, generally, require more planning. By reading good examples of descriptions, explanations, opinions and by being given purposeful opportunities to write their own, they should be helped

to plan and produce these more demanding types of writing. (DES, 1989, para. 17.41 iii)

Lack of clear purpose may well contribute to the problem of 'verbatim copying' which many observers point out should be avoided, though few suggest how. It could also be argued that the division between reading and recording/writing is artificial. The division neglects the support which children often need to understand the structures of the non-fiction texts they read. It also discourages using such structures for ways of recording, handling and presenting information in the children's own writing.

At present graphicacy, as a way of recording and communicating ideas, is only referred to in the Writing Target, although it is mentioned in the Programmes of Study. If we turn to the Maths Attainment Targets on Handling Data (11,12) there are more helpful suggestions offered on how children could be encouraged to translate information from the verbal text to the visual or vice versa (see p. 156).

(ii)   Sentence structures and word structures

Children's language continues to develop throughout the primary years. Their oral language experience is critical in the earliest years but, later, as they acquire literacy skills their language changes. This change is twofold: children gradually learn to differentiate between the informal oral language structures and the more formal written counterparts, and they also acquire more complex, hierarchical structures which they find particularly in non-fiction texts.

(a)   Acquisition of further sentence structures

Six- and seven-year-old children are often inconsistent with their use of the conditional tense (e.g. would or could). When talking or writing about conjectural situations, rather than from direct experience, Romaine (1984) noticed some confusions, e.g.:

Adult: 'Why *would* you like to be an air hostess?'
Child: ''Cos I *will* go all over the world.'

> *Child:* If I was a dragon I *would* breathe lots
> of fire and I *will* scare people.

> *Child:* To make my kite fly I *could* throw it high
> and I *can* throw it straight.

Eight-year-old children are beginning to get to grips with the passive. It is a form of verb which they are more likely to find in their topic work reading than in story books: 8 per cent of verbs in fiction books are passives compared to 18 per cent in non-fiction books (Keenan and Comrie in Romaine, 1984).

In the following examples children are often not sure who got hurt:

> The lion was wounded by the hunter.
> The boy was hit by the girl.
> The Legions were defeated by barbarian hordes.

In such sentences there may be the false expectation that the first mentioned item (topic) in the sentence is the active agent (subject) which does something to someone else. If the information is familiar children can work out the meaning from context by using internal psychosemantic rules, but not from external linguistic–syntactic rules.

As well as tenses, complex sentence structures also pose difficulties. By nine years of age children will often write embedded phrases or clauses:

> The boy, with the football, went to the park.

Younger children are more likely to place the detail regarding the football at the end of the sentence. Greater difficulties are encountered by children trying to imitate the relative clauses they have met in their reading. Perera (1987) found that 11- and 12-year-olds often make mistakes like the following:

> We have many clubs *of* which I belong.
> My favourite possession is my bicycle *in* which I received three months ago.

Further problems arise from the fact that children fail to distinguish between a spoken and a written form. The use of the double negative is common in some dialects, e.g.:

> I *don't* need *no*body.

Don't use *no* double negatives.

Similarly, the repetition of the focus of the sentence is common, e.g.

It was really good *that* film.
The woman on the cheese counter, *she* said, 'No'.

Confusion about the differences in register and style appropriate for different modes and different purposes is still evident even at the ages of 11 to 12 years, and beyond. There is, however, still considerable debate as to the relationship between speech and writing: between those who argue that it is a continuum (Greenfield, 1968, in Romaine, 1984, and Luria, 1976) and those who argue that it develops separately (Whiteman, 1981).

It may well be in the initial stages, before Kroll and Wells's 'differentiation' stage, that children do not regard speech and writing as having distinct structures and style. However, in the late primary/early secondary stage their writing and speech often demonstrate different features, with their writing showing more Standard English features: a higher proportion of verb agreements and tense endings, and more use of plural *s* and possessive *'s* (Whiteman, 1981). Perera (1984) also found children experimenting in writing with constructions that they did not use orally. Romaine (1984) suggests that familiarity with the written and printed mode is an important factor in developing metalinguistic awareness. Perhaps the written mode offers time for reflection and an opportunity for children consciously to try out new forms.

(b)   Sentence linkages: connectives and cohesive ties

Another feature of language development, apart from vocabulary and sentence structure, is the development of linkages between sentences. These have come to be known as connectives and cohesive ties. Recent findings have helped us to understand the nature of children's difficulties, particularly when reading non-fiction texts. Such information is invaluable when trying to plan effective support strategies, or when devising workcards or giving a set of instructions. Research has identified different types of ties and also provided some evidence for a developmental trend in the way children acquire a working understanding of both connectives and cohesive ties.

Hart, Walker and Gray (1977) have identified a developmental trend relating to the acquisition of connectives. For example, 6-year-old children typically overuse the additive connective 'and':

We got a tadpole *and* we put it in a jar *and* we put weed *and* . . .

More mature language users of a similar age will also use a temporal connective 'then':

We cleaned out the jar *then* we put a water snail in.

The causal connective is also one which children of this age use easily, such as 'because':

We think he died *because* he was homesick.

Adversative connectives such as 'but' were found to develop a little later:

We did feed it properly, *but* it was too sad to eat.

Although these examples of common connectives occur in children's speech and writing, they are likely to meet many others in written texts which may need explanation and discussion, e.g.:

after, later, thirdly	(temporal)
so, consequently, hence, thus	(causal)
however, nevertheless, conversely	(adversative)

Connectives join phrases and clauses, linking them together so that the text 'flows' well. Cohesive ties serve a similar function but are more varied and complex in how they achieve this linking. Much of the evidence relating to cohesive ties is to be found in Anderson (1983) and Chapman (1987). All of the following ties can be found in children's oral language even in 5-year-olds (Garber, in Perera, 1984). However their use in writing emerges later.

Five- and six-year-old children often link their ideas by adding information and repeating the key word. They soon learn to develop the idea by using associated words to extend it:

lexical cohesion
e.g.   reiteration (repeating the same word)
       We saw a *baby bird*. The *baby bird* flew away.

collocation (associated words)
It was a big *fire*. There was lots of *smoke* and *flames*.

When children introduce characters and develop a story line over several sentences, the thread of the story can be sustained by using pronouns to refer to the characters, or objects:

referential cohesion
e.g.   personal (she, it, they, etc.)
        We saw the *mummy bird*. *She* fed the babies.
        demonstrative (this, that, these, those)
        We saw the *huge valves*. *These* let out the steam.

The young story-teller with three characters of the same gender, who uses 'she' too liberally, can cause great confusion as to which character the pronoun refers. Demonstrative pronouns can also cause difficulty They are a conspicuous feature of early information books, for example, where the demonstrative pronoun refers to the picture or diagram. Unless the child reads the text with the picture (assuming they are on the same page) it may be hard to follow the text.

The last two categories of cohesive ties are called 'substitution' (using an alternative word to avoid repetition) or 'ellipsis' (where the word(s) is omitted but the sense carried over). These are likely to be used confidently in the upper junior age range.

substitution
e.g.   nominal
        They are building lots of *houses*. The *ones* near us . . .
        verbal
        Parent birds *feed* their babies worms. They *do* this . . .
        clausal
        I hope *I can join soon*. I expect *so* . . .

ellipsis
e.g.   nominal
        Put all the *pencils* in the box. Some * can go here.
        verbal
        We tried *measuring* the beans. Peter tried * with string . . .
        clausal
        We had to find out *which was the biggest*.
        How can you tell * ?

Finally, Chapman (1987) distinguished two general categories: any of the above types of cohesive tie could be either 'backward acting' or 'forward acting' – the latter still posing problems amongst many nine-year-olds. For example,

backward acting (anaphoric)
Our teacher is very kind. *She* often . . .

forward acting (cataphoric)
They used to scare us. The *old couple* . . .

The National Curriculum urges the mastering of connectives and cohesive links so that grammatical constructions 'can be chosen to ensure the intended meaning is expressed with precision and clarity' (para 4.51). These grammatical constructions include:

- the ways in which sentences can be linked together e.g. use of connectives and some cohesion devices;
- the ways that references to a number of different people can be kept clear throughout a passage e.g. use of pronouns;
- the ways of avoiding repetition in passages e.g. use of the passive thus avoiding the subject/agent, use of ellipsis.

Understanding these terms may help a teacher to make judgements about a child's writing or a book they are reading. However, children would find them confusing at the primary stage.

(c)   Word structures

Apart from the obvious implicit knowledge about many sentence structures which children of junior age display in their writing, children also acquire considerable knowledge about word structures. In the period before children come to school, most have already deduced a wide number of language rules. The capacity of young children to deduce such rules, without being explicitly taught, continues to amaze parents, professionals and anyone else in contact with young children. From the mass of language which they hear around them they are able to sort the data, make hypotheses as to its rule-based nature and test out and modify their hypotheses (Crystal, 1976; Romaine, 1984). Throughout the infant years and beyond, this process continues. 'Miscues' are frequently made where there are exceptions to the rule, a typical one being the extension of the '-ed' rule to verbs which are exceptions, e.g. 'goed' or 'swimmed'.

Parts of word, such as '-ed', are examples of morphemes, the smallest language units with grammatical meaning. Others are plural *s*, possessive *'s*, verb ending -ing, etc. Any miscues made over these often have more significance in terms of social status than in terms of communicative competence, i.e. you are thought to say more about who you are than what you are saying.

Some of the first rules which children acquire are those relating to inflectional features, such as the '-ed' that indicates the past tense and the final 's' which can distinguish the match between subject and verb in the case of third person singular. Miscues continue to be made but are gradually ironed out. There are, however, significant regional and dialect differences which can be a source of interference between home or playground language and the Standard English which may be required as a means of formal written communication in school and at work.

It can be difficult for primary children to stand back from their own writing and reflect upon what they instinctively do with language. For example, 8-year-old children were given verb forms, as suggested by Doughty (1971) – walk, walks, walking and walked – and asked to put each into a sentence. They were then encouraged to try to explain how they knew when to use each word and what difference it made to the meaning of the sentence. They had considerable difficulty. Some identified that 'She walks to the car' tells you she is doing it now, but 'She walked to the car' tells you she did it a while ago: 'It shows when she went.' But the children could not articulate any reason to distinguish 'I walk to school', 'She walks to the park' or 'They are walking past the shops'. 'Time' was clearly easier to note than 'number of people'. Further difficulties arose when many of the children used 'walks' as in 'I take my dog for walks'. Some were intrigued, some bemused by the task. Many said, 'You just know 'cos it sounds right.'

Other issues arose when attention was drawn to the use of a final 's' to indicate plural status. Again, most children understood this and used it correctly without being able to articulate a rule. However, knowledge of irregular plurals depends on a wide vocabulary not on an implicit understanding of rules which have been generated intuitively. Hence, a child was puzzled when her use of 'mouses' was questioned and when asked 'Do you know the word for lots of them?' replied, 'Rats'!

Another aspect of morphemic investigation is possible through the examination of prefixes, suffixes and word roots. This is a further way of word-building in which children can engage:

> sub-, super-; ante-, post- (antonyms)
> il-, im-, in-, ir-, un-, de- (negatives)
>
> -ness, -ment, -ance, -ence, -ity (abstract nouns)
> -ly (adverbs)
> -ful, -en, -er, -est (adjectives)

During the junior stage, children begin to understand the structure of words and how their meaning and role in a sentence can be altered by adding different morphemes.

> crack, cracks, cracked, cracking, crackers (even cracker-jack)
> happy, happier, happiest [adj]; happiness [noun]; happily [adv]

Breaking down words in this fashion is a helpful strategy for tackling new words. Such syllabification may not only be achieved through morphemic analysis, e.g. toast-er, but also through the natural rhythm of the word, e.g. toas-ter.

Creating opportunities for children to hear stories and poetry read aloud is a valuable and pleasurable way to encourage them to listen to and become more aware of the music and magic in words, as well as the rhyme, rhythm, syllables and sounds. Even without understanding all the words children can still enjoy the overall impact of both poetry and prose. Moreover, such readings will also extend vocabulary. Unfamiliar words, or known words used in different contexts or combinations, can be discussed. These discussions also extend the technical vocabulary with which to discuss language.

An example of such discussion was noted in a class of middle juniors who were used to talking about their books after their silent reading lesson. These discussions took many different forms. Sometimes children would tell each other about their books and give a brief critical review. At other times they would read out a passage which they particularly liked: funny, tense, atmospheric or just 'nice'. Discussion might focus on particular words, images or ambiguities which the reader might be puzzled over and want to test out through others' reactions.

The focus on unknown words in particular led to the introduction of such terms as syllables, prefixes (un-, il-, dis- which gave opposite meanings) and suffixes which had specific functions (joyful, helpful, where '-ful' changed a substantive noun into an adjective; encouragement, argument, where '-ment' changed a verb into a noun), as opposed to endings which just sound alike (where the endings have no inherent meaning and are therefore just letter strings: plate, pirate).

(iii)   Presentation: punctuating units of meaning

A further difference between the oral and written mode is evident in how the speaker or writer indicates 'units of meaning' to help the listener or reader follow their meaning. In an oral mode text is communicated by a combination of factors (Gumperez in Tannen, 1984). These include 'theme' (internal links of co-ordinated meanings and understandings within the text), 'texture' (the multi-level linkages which include the external links with the reader's previous knowledge), and 'prosody' (the paralinguistic features of the actual delivery which help to convey meanings through the emphasis and expression given to the words).

However, in moving to the written mode, a number of particular problems emerge. 'Prosodic' features are no longer available and have to be expressed through punctuation and typographical variation (such as use of capital letters for emphasis). 'Texture' is more difficult to maintain, especially if the audience is unknown. Similarly, the success of 'theme' is less certain where there is no interactive feedback and the relater has to rely on the cohesive links.

Learning the 'feel' of the sentence is certainly an important aspect of writing. Yet, as Shaughnessy (1977) states, children usually compose in sentences as they move into a written rather than a spoken mode of writing. However, they tend to demarcate their text in rhetorical units which encompass what, to them, seems to be a single episode. This might be at the end of a descriptive phrase, a complete incident or action, or a series of linked actions which in fact could comprise the whole 'story'. Thus the full stop might come at the end of the text or the end of the page, when the child pauses to think or at the end of a dialogue exchange.

As the 'story' becomes more complex and the 'chunking' changes, and as the writer becomes more aware of the reader's need to pause for breath – if not for thought – then the units of punctuation become closer to the syntactic unit of the sentence. Also, speech marks begin to be used, by top infants, to distinguish who says what. Paragraphing, to indicate changes in the sequence of action, is also gradually acquired during the junior school years.

At the same time we must be aware that adult novels are not always written in conventional sentences, as authors search for ways of conveying their meanings and establishing a relationship with their readers. We must consider punctuation in terms of its function in supporting communicative competence, rather than as a fixed and unchanging set of rules. We need to recognize that conventions about punctuation change with the times and the context.

Hence, it would seem that the emphasis on 'the sentence' by the age of seven years may be premature. For, as Kress argues,

> The sentence is not the basic unit of the spoken language of young children ... A major part of learning to write is learning to master the linguistic unit we call the 'sentence'. They gradually learn the feel of the sentence. (p. 70)

Children are likely to identify a sentence in semantic terms as 'something that makes sense', or a 'complete idea' rather than use a grammatical definition such as 'it's got a verb'. Identifying parts of speech is not something which children are likely to do without prompting. Examining the whole meaning and its relationship to the real world (external validity) is likely to take precedence over examining the meanings of individual words, their interrelationship and functions (internal validity).

The Working Party report recognizes that teaching grammar in isolated exercises is unlikely to result in an improvement in children's writing competencies. Instead, the emphasis is put on the communicative function. Grammatical issues which arise from writing in the classroom need to be aired as they emerge in a relevant context. Developing the metalanguage for this is a high priority, so that awareness of the issues is shared. This does not preclude the benefit which some children may experience from reinforcing such understandings, separately, once they have grasped the communicative function of a point of grammar.

Metalanguage is important to the teacher in order to appreciate the level of linguistic skills as well as content. Knowledge of text structure, connectives and cohesive ties can offer clues about the 'flow'; variety of sentence structure and range of vocabulary can influence pace, tension and interest. Two examples of the way in which teachers can begin to use such information to inform their analysis and understanding of children's writing can be seen in the Appendix (pp. 272–3). Such knowledge can provide a guide for future action.

ACTIVITY

Criteria for Progression

Review the children's written work – across the curriculum – which you have appraised during the past week.

Which of the above criteria relating to text structure, syntactic structures, vocabulary and punctuation have you applied – either consciously or unconsciously?

Which additional criteria do you think would have been useful to apply to support your diagnosis?

Construct a bank of criteria which you could use to focus your appraisals.

Choose some of these to use, with particular children, on particular pieces of work, during the following week.

In the light of such trials, it should be possible to develop a policy for appraising work that can inform your future support for each child.

FURTHER READING

There are many books that identify these structural features of texts. For example:

Cowie, H. (ed.) (1984) *The Development of Children's Imaginative Writing*. London: Croom Helm. (See especially Kroll and Anson.)

Stewart-Dore, N. (1986) *Writing and Reading to Learn*. NSW, Australia: Primary English Teaching Association.

The following explain the linguistic features of children's text at sentence and word level:

Chapman, L.J. (1987) *Reading from 5–11*. Milton Keynes: Open University Press.

Dougill, P. (ed.) (1990) *Developing English*. Buckingham: Open University Press.

Kress, G. (1982) *Learning to Write*. London: Routledge & Kegan Paul.

Mittins, B. (1990) *Language Awareness for Teachers*. Buckingham: Open University Press.

Perera, K. (1984) *Children's Writing and Reading*. Oxford: Basil Blackwell.

Romaine, S. (1984) *The Language of Children and Adolescents*. Oxford: Basil Blackwell.

Chapter 6

Children as Writers

INTRODUCTION

The acquisition of literacy skills is a key objective of schooling. As all the language modes interrelate, developing skills in writing will depend on the 'company we keep' with respect to language – the kind of language environment we experience. This applies to each aspect of writing: the psychological (content, intention, anticipated impact), linguistic (communicative competence, structure and clarity) and physical (calligraphy). Initially oral experience will be reflected in writing, when children 'write like they speak'. Their writing will also reflect the books and stories they have experienced. Later, because writing can be 'fixed' and is easier to review and reshape, writing can also reflect children's conscious experiments with language and ideas.

In order to gain understanding of children's writing development, this chapter begins by clarifying aspects of writing and then describes examples of developing children's writing. The first section examines children's perceptions of the purposes of writing in general and the functions of writing in school in particular. The second section focuses on how children might develop their ability to structure and organize their writing in a range of genres, chronological and non-chronological. The third section highlights ways in which children 'craft' their writing processes and the next reviews aspects of presenting written work: proofreading, spelling and handwriting. Finally, the chapter ends by reviewing some of the ways teachers might monitor such developments so that they can support the children more appropriately.

6.1. TARGETS FOR WRITING

In Profile Component 3: Writing, in the National Curriculum, the
target is to promote

> a growing ability to construct and convey meaning in written lan-
> guage matching style to audience and purpose.

The Working Party report (DES, 1989) recognizes that children
will come to school having already had varying experiences of the
print-rich society in which we live. It acknowledges that it is
through

> increasing encounters with a range of examples that children make
> sense of literary experiences and it is the responsibility of the
> teacher to provide and foster that range in the classroom (para.
> 17.13).

The report also recognizes the important interrelatedness of writing, reading, speaking and listening, and the need to develop an
ear for language through reading or listening to a wide variety of
works. It also notes key problems in the attempt to devise a writing
curriculum and to diagnose its success. It quotes a comment from
the National Writing Project that 'to put ages against these expectations produces great problems' (para. 17.25). Further it states
that the best writing is characterized by qualities such as vigour,
commitment, honesty and interestingness, none of which can
easily be 'mapped' on to levels (para. 17.31).

Nevertheless, goals are defined in terms of purposes, audiences,
genres, styles and the component skills that might contribute to
the ability to construct and convey meaning and are listed develop-
mentally. The main strands in the writing attainment target (para.
17.15) are:

- write in different forms for different purposes and audiences
- write coherently ... organizing texts in ways which will help
  the reader
- craft writing which is significantly different from speech –
  control of grammatical structures, differentiated vocabulary,
  and appropriateness of style
- know when and how to plan, draft, redraft, revise and proof-
  read their work
- understand the nature and functions of written language

Within Profile Component 3, there are three Attainment Targets: Writing (3), Spelling (4) and Handwriting (5). Each of the Writing strands will be examined in turn, with Spelling and Handwriting being considered in connection with preparing work for presentation. Understanding and awareness of language will be discussed in connection with the other strands and illustrated by giving examples of children's comments on their own writing.

6.2. PROGRAMMES FOR ACTION

A major thread running through the Working Party documents is the desire to encourage children to develop more explicit knowledge about themselves, and others, as language-users. The suggestions to talk about children's own writing could appear to meet two needs: first, it could encourage awareness about language and reflection on the forms and functions of language, and secondly, it could encourage self-assessment, appraisal and the fine-tuning of how to construct and convey meanings. It again raises the question of what metalanguage children need in order to be able to talk about their writing.

(i) Perceptions about writing and purpose

Children bring varied experiences of writing to school. There is evidence of a considerable amount of writing undertaken in the home by a pre-school child which goes unnoticed. Writing of older children appears to be mostly of a forced nature: the compulsory 'Thank you letter' or greetings card (Heath, 1983). For many children, therefore, writing does not enjoy the same status or the same association with pleasurable shared experiences that reading does.

Wells and Raben (1978, in Davies, 1982) found that key variables in determining children's literacy achievements in school were quantitive (the amount of pupil interest in literacy and their experience of it in the home) and qualitative (the nature of the response and the encouragement to the child).

Most children probably have little experience of writing at home; nevertheless writing retains a very high status in school.

New entrants can often be seen engrossed in making marks on a piece of paper, pencil held in a vice-like grip, tongue slightly protruding with every sign of deep concentration. When asked what they are doing, they will proudly tell you they are writing. There is magic and power in what marks on paper seem to be able to do and to make happen. Children very soon realize this and are keen to join in.

(a)   Perceptions about writing

Research from Ferreiro and Teberosky (1983) has tried to identify children's understandings about 'written language', for example, where exactly the message lies (some children think it is the 'spaces', some think it is the 'squiggles'). We need to be aware of children's understandings of the metalanguage of writing. For instance, there may be confusions regarding terms like 'word'. Young children are rarely convinced that anything of less than three or four consecutive letters could be a word. Similarly, we need to be sure of understandings about 'letters'. On the basis of their experience of seeing writing in their environment, children often differentiate between a 'number' and a 'letter', and between something which looks like a 'letter' or 'character in their own script', and something which is not 'letter-like'.

However, there is also considerable confusion about what writing is, what it does, and how it does it. A survey in *Language Matters* (ILEA, 1985) found that children thought that:

'writing is them marks'
'writing is making letters' (or 'doing words')
'it's when you do a story'
'it's so as you can tell people things'

Understandably the descriptions relate partly to process and partly to purpose. The process seems to involve marks (or letters/words) that have a meaning (or tell something). But who or what actually does the 'telling'? The possible confusion over this is illustrated by the following incident in an infant class. Two 6-year-olds were writing in their journals at the beginning of the term. They were using their own invented script. On taking it to the teacher they were surprised to be asked 'What does it say?' In the ensuing discussion it emerged that the children thought that the teacher would give it some meaning (after all teachers know everything). When the teacher suggested that you needed to have something in your head that you wanted to say to another person, that the writing communicates this thought, it was clearly a novel idea.

Other children, also using their own invented script, had already grasped this notion that writing conveyed a message from the writer to the reader. Their teacher, having had the message 'read' to her, would often write her own message in reply (in conventional script), thus encouraging the idea that the purpose of writing could be interactive, with messages passing between writers.

(b) Understandings about purpose

Attitudes concerning why children learn to write in school can very often be conveyed through the hidden messages delivered in how we present writing. We need to consider the messages being transmitted through this 'hidden curriculum' through the classroom organization, writing tasks and teacher support.

HMI (1978) noted the large amounts of time spent on writing and commented that much of it seemed to be copying, with too many dull, boring and repetitive exercises. The Schools Council report (Southgate *et al.*, 1981) supported this finding. They found that teachers spent almost no time on the processes of writing (how to structure and organize writing, how to draft and what to review) and spent uneven amounts of time on handwriting, spelling, grammar and comprehension. There was very little time allowed for discussing the crafting and drafting processes in order to improve the quality and the satisfaction derived from the end product. It is precisely on these areas that the National Writing Project focused. It is to be expected that, with the evidence they collected concerning 'good practice', 'writing' in classrooms is now undergoing a change.

The answers children give to questions about why they learn to write in school can reveal important discrepancies between the teacher's goals and the child's. These may reflect the children's experiences and the messages they have gleaned from the activities. Such mismatch could have significant implications for children's motivation for writing. Typical responses are:

'cos the teacher tells us'
'to get better at writing'
'it makes you more educated'
'to learn you to get a better job'
'writing is very important ... you can write notes to your friend
   to tell them something, write shopping lists so you don't
   forget things, write a diary, write jokes, write rude things, write
   stories ...'

In addition, children distinguished between fiction and non-fiction
writing. Again their perceptions of the task varied. Their answers
relating to fiction can be categorized as follows:

- *purpose:*
  to learn more english
  open up your imagination and let the other bits of your brain
     rest
  you can drift into another land
  I dont like it cos I have nuthing to say
- *easiest:*
  spreading my imagination on the page
  copying from a book
  to put the fulstops in the write places
  I dont find anything easy
- *hardest:*
  finding an idea
  putting what I am thinking into logic
  doing a beginning, middle and end
  getting the punctuitions and fool stops rite
- *how a teacher can help:*
  telling you your merstaiks
  giving you some ideas
  tell you off if you dont pay atention
  give you confidence
- *how you can get better:*
  consontrate more
  make it neeter, do proper speling and punchuation
  streching my imagonasion
  read lots of stories to get good ideas

Apart from writing stories, children are also expected to write journals, poems, re-tell stories, write accounts of visits, write letters and write 'projects' or 'topics'. This latter activity has its own easy and difficult aspects:

- *purpose:*
  to find out about something that interests you
  to look things up and write them down
  cos you have to
- *easiest:*
  looking things up
  copying from the board
  doing the pictures
- *hardest:*
  finding the information
  understanding the books
  sorting it all out
- *how a teacher can help:*
  letting you choose what you want
  showing you how to find the stuff
  helping to make it make sense
- *how you can get better:*
  doing more work
  put it in your own words

Children's views on writing poetry have also been investigated in the APU survey of Language Performance (1982). The survey revealed that while 59 per cent of primary children enjoyed poetry, only 32 per cent of 15-year-olds did so. Benton (1986) investigated the teacher's misgivings about 'doing' poetry and found that 27 per cent had difficulty in finding suitable resources and a further 27 per cent found 'no time'. They also feared the 'tough guy' attitude from boys who claimed that poetry was 'pathetic'. However, very often it was the teacher's inhibitions, their lack of confidence about poetic forms and inadequate knowledge of how to help children move away from badly rhymed verse that formed the underlying reasons for not finding time.

A discussion with classes of 7-year-olds and 9-year-olds revealed very mixed reactions to poetry:

- *characteristics:*
  it has to rhyme [and] it doesn't have to rhyme always . . .

it is short [a ballad of three sides was 'not a poem']
it has to have short lines
it has to have gaps [spaces between verses]
there has to be a pattern . . . on the page
it kind of sings [rhythm]
if it doesn't rhyme it still has to sound like a poem, the words
    sound the same at the end or the beginning

- *good things:*
poems are funny
poems paint pictures in your mind
you can see poems better than stories
they are short
poems sound nice
it makes me feel tingly
you don't have to do proper sentences
you can write just how you feel

- *bad things:*
poems are silly
you can't understand them
often the words are twisted round
people read them in a funny voice

ACTIVITY

Perceptions of Writing

Ask the children in your own class:

    Why do you learn to write?
    What does writing do?
    What do you find easiest/hardest?
    How can a teacher help you?
    How can you get better?

How can you use this information to help to provide a better 'scaffolding' and support for developing the children's writing?

In classrooms where poetry was read regularly it was often regarded as 'fun' and 'enjoyable'. An important feature of the poetry experience was the variety of forms and themes of poems which were modelled. In such situations, children appreciated poems because 'they really make you think about each word'. It thus gave greater insights into using language and playing with language. It also encouraged drafting, as children were more willing to change words in a short poem where they appreciated the need for every word to 'count'. Also the intensity of poetry developed a sensitivity to words as well as the feelings they conveyed.

FURTHER READING

The titles below demonstrate children's attitudes to writing and suggest ways to develop a range of writing forms in the classroom:

Hall, N. (1989) *Writing with Reason*. London: Hodder & Stoughton.
Marsh, G. (1989) *Teaching Poetry*. London: Hodder & Stoughton.

The following titles demonstrate some children's attitudes to writing, and to language in general.

APU (1988) *Language Performance in Schools: A Review (1979–1983)*. London: HMSO.
Language Matters. London: ILEA Centre for Primary Language.
Neville, M. (1988) *Assessing and Teaching Language*. London: Macmillan for Scottish Education Department.

(ii)   Organizing and structuring texts: genre

We know very little about how children come to understand 'what makes a story'. We know that there is a close link between reading, writing and talking about story, but the nature of the relationship is complex. Certainly research from Meek (1982), Wells (1986) and Tizard and Hughes (1984) has indicated that a rich book experience in the home appears to contribute to the ease with which children learn to read and come to understand how stories work. Research distinguishing between children's composing and scribing abilities and showing how these abilities relate to the range of possible factors in their book experiences is so far incomplete.

Children can be exposed to a wide range of books with very different formats. For example, the popularity of the Dr Seuss series relies not on 'story' but on word games and typographical contrasts. Richard Scarry books consist often of a series of almost discrete cameos or verbal pictures which invite the reader to participate and provide the story, as do the wordless picture books now available. This greater role of pictures in relation to the text is evident in stories by authors such as Anthony Browne, John Burningham and David McKee, where the pictures often tell one story while the text tells another. Such a diverse experience of 'story' may well affect children's perceptions and influence their own productions.

Margaret Meek (1988) suggests that texts teach children about reading and writing, and demonstrate the way in which children create their own text in conjunction with the author, the reader and the listener. Any attempt to theorize about the relation between book experience and writing must therefore take into account the whole experience of sharing the text, the illustrations and the accompanying talk.

A further influence on children's notion of story must inevitably be their experience of 'story' on television. The story-line in cartoons aimed at the very young child is often very explicit. The characters are introduced in each episode, their special powers articulated, the action commented upon and motivation put into words. Nothing is left ambiguous, the demands on the viewer are minimal. In series for older children, where the emotions, motivation and reactions are demonstrated in action, much of the story-line is not articulated verbally. In addition, much is conveyed through the visual or aural (music) medium. Visual plot clues are given through, for example, a close-up of the 'baddie's' partially hidden gun and tension is heightened by spooky music. This verbally implicit model is very dissimilar to the written story that the teacher expects. For the details of the story are in the pictures in the child's mind and what the child actually writes is more like an action-dialogue for a film.

(a)   Developing story genre

When encouraging children as writers Cowie (1984) warns that there are three common 'blocks' which a writer may experience:

procedural (writer dries up), *psychological* (writer feels threatened) and *physical* (the task of writing is itself tiring). Solutions to each of these need to be explored. Young children can dictate a story to an adult or into a tape-recorder to reduce the physical stress. A supportive atmosphere in the classroom where a child understands clearly what the purpose of the task is and the nature of the audience, then positive feedback, sharing and openness during the writing process may help reduce the psychological stress. Brainstorming techniques using webs/flow charts/pictures to plot an outline, together with plenty of discussion in the preparation stages may help to overcome the procedural problems.

Further analysis by Bereiter and Scardamalia (1987) identified problems of *accessing* ideas and experiences, *selecting* content and setting boundaries upon what to write about, and *encoding* the selection into the written word in a particular discourse schema. They found that training children to identify stages in the writing process and to use protocols as prompts helped to de-mystify 'writing'.

The following framework, devised by children, served as a reminder to help them over the procedural difficulties of *accessing* experiences and ideas.

Where do the ideas come from?
  by looking
  by listening
  by using our experience of
    everyday things, books, films, people and places
  by talking about our ideas and feelings
  by using our dreams and imaginations
Why don't we?
  keep a diary, or journal, about ideas and feelings
    as well as the things that happen
  keep a scrapbook of postcards
  keep souvenirs of visits
  keep cuttings from comics and magazines about favourite things

Brainstorming for ideas through word association can sometimes help break a procedural block. Children could be asked to jot down anything and everything that comes to mind in association with a trigger word or phrase. They may need to be encouraged to use single words or a maximum of three-word phrases, in order to avoid the habit of drafting in full sentences rather than learning to jot.

However, brainstorming in words can sometimes be difficult for those children who find thinking in pictures much easier. Encouraging them to picture something first, to visualize it in their minds in detail, before trying to draw or describe it can help to make the writing much more vivid.

The resources in classrooms can themselves either inhibit or inspire children. For example, for young children a white, blank page is a daunting phenomenon. Young children can find it more fun to write a story about a train or a cat if the paper is cut to that shape.

Many writers find it helpful to talk about the topic or to share ideas with friends. Allowing time to let children talk first (and during, and after) their writing is an important for rehearsing ideas, selecting material and ordering their content. It may also be necessary to encourage periods of 'silence' so that concentration need not be interrupted.

Young writers, as well as older ones, need help in sorting and sequencing their ideas. To get beyond the one-line picture captions, it can be useful for some children to be encouraged to draw the story first or be given 'story-planners' in the form of a set of questions, best generated in discussion.

Story structure can more simply be presented to children as a modified form of the traditional parlour game 'Consequences'. Children can be encouraged to plan a story in terms of:

Where does the story happen?	(setting)
What is the place like?	
Who is in the story?	(characters)
What is each person like?	
What is happening/are they doing?	(action)
What goes wrong/is the problem?	(goal)
What do they want to do?	(intention)
How is it sorted out?	(episodes)
What do they do?	
What do they say?	
What do they see?	
How do they feel?	
What happens next?	

... and then?
How does it end?   (resolution)

This approach can start as a game of 'Consequences' played orally to get used to the idea of developing a story-line. It can be done collectively (by writing key words on a board or a shared sheet of paper) or individually (by dictating key words to an adult, or by using a cartoon strip approach, or a word web). Ideas generated by such brainstorming can then be selected and numbered in readiness for a first draft.

Writers later move into dialogue and later still into character portrayal. They may also comment on the action, make asides to the reader or give general reactions to the story. These show the writer being able to stand aside from the story and to see it either from the different characters' viewpoints or the reader's viewpoint. Such devices indicate shifts in the writer's perspective, from the self-centred to the other-centred, to deep-centred and, finally, de-centred.

Children need help in thinking about developing their characters, for example, by the simple act of giving them a name. This can be extended into a table, used as a planning device:

What are their names?	What are they like?	What do they look like?	What do they do?
Mrs Jones	bossy	skinny	moans
Jamie	brave	little	calls the police
Black the dog	lonely	starving	barks at the robber

Pearson (1987) suggests an extension of this by encouraging children to draw 'literary sociograms' to show the relationships between the characters: how they feel about each other, what they do with/to each other.

During the *encoding* stage, further difficulties may arise in trying to develop a narrative. Kroll and Anson (in Cowie, 1984) identified these as:

associational: where the writing is about a series of incidental events with no real coherence,
descriptional: where the writing is a catalogue of details with no development,

unanchored action: a sequence of events with no setting or context,

entanglements: where the events become overinvolved and no resolution is possible,

abandonment: where the writing just ends,

e.g. 'That's all I know . . .'

Once children begin to scribe their own stories with greater independence the structure of their story may well appear to revert to a more 'primitive' model than the one they might have been using in their 'tellings'. This is often due to constraints which the secretarial demands impose on storying stamina. Often children will compose what they believe they can scribe and spell rather than write what might be in their heads. Thus children have to balance their intent and the risk-taking it might involve against their willingness to reflect and fine-tune what they have written.

It is noticeable that young story-tellers find it difficult to conceive of 'audience needs'. Children tend to assume that the audience shares their background to the events being told. Because of this they sometimes neglect to provide a 'beginning', indicate the setting, or even to introduce the characters. Instead, the writer moves straight into the action and ends up with '. . . and then we went home to tea/bed' or later, 'and then I woke up.'

Observation of a class of 6-year-olds, some of whom were emergent independent writers, indicated a shift

from: a picture caption, or label
         additive units apparently in random sequence
         cumulative units beginning to be shaped and sequenced

to: chronological narrative
         initially concerning everyday events (temporal) or
            journeys (temporal+spatial)
         later focusing on adventures with cause-related events
         later still, with characters and goal-related behaviour

These types of writing reflected the books that the children were reading in their class library. Many of the new books did not actually provide a model of an obvious story structure, i.e. beginning (setting, characters, problem/goal), middle (actions, intentions) and end (resolution, conclusion). The books illustrated a new vogue of books which encouraged the reader to contribute to creating the text. This often resulted in the text appearing as captions or disjointed units.

Once the children had understood that writing communicates and had gained enough confidence to compose and sufficient skills to scribe they usually enjoyed writing. Their own attitudes to writing affected whether they wrote 'safe' stereotyped compositions or they risked experimenting, whether they become hesitant or fluent writers.

At this stage many of these children were demonstrating a range of different beginnings and endings. All the stories were composed 'on the run', off the tops of their heads, with no pre-planning or discussion. The stories tended to be linear, with a singular plot, were action-oriented, and 'peopled' but not with characters. For example:

instant entry (no 'setting')
  We made a cake . . . (re-tell)
  There was a house and the witch got burnt (narrative)
temporal conventions
  One day . . .
  Once there was a witch . . .
character naming
  Once there were four children K,L,D and J.
location setting
  Once there was a hill and on the hill . . .
action setting
  One day D and J were playing and . . .
then,
temporal complexity
  It was raining. The river was flooding. Meanwhile . . .
character development
  Once there was a girl called Milly and Milly was not afraid of
    ghosts . . .
location, mood setting
  One day H found a mysterious cave. It was dark and spooky . . .

Initially, stories tend to follow a strictly chronological format. Chronological, action narratives are typical of children during the primary stage. Later, children may experiment with dreams and flashbacks.

Endings also became more varied as these writers gained experience. For example:

stops, with no ending
It got bigger and bigger.
conventional
And they lived happily ever after. THE END.
refuge, security
Then we went home and the cats went up to heaven.
resolution
And so they turned the bad witch into a stone.
conclusion
And so it was time to go. 'Bye, see you tomorrow'.

Most importantly, a child must have something to say – and that doesn't always happen at a set time each week. Ideas need time to incubate, to be worked on and thought about before putting pencil to paper. Some children need much more time than others: some need to be encouraged to take more time before dashing off another ripping yarn.

Apart from having something to say it is also important to have someone to whom to say it. Ways of sharing writing are important. Ways of presenting a story in alternative ways so as to make it attractive need to be explored. Stories can be composed in a number of ways, e.g. joint stories planned and written together, a shaggy dog 'wall' story (where children add on the next section as and when they feel inspired), or a collaborative story by the whole class where the planning is done together and the writing is delegated to different individuals or pairs. Stories can also be presented in a range of formats, e.g. pictures/cartoon sequences, zig-zag folding (either horizontal or vertical), a make-your-own adventure with choices.

Finally, children need to be helped to evaluate their own work – and the stories they read – so that they begin to appreciate what makes a good story. Having *encoded* the ideas in draft form, the revision process is often hindered because, once having written something, it is hard to de-centre and think of another way of putting it through adding, modifying, deleting or reordering. The first two of these options rely on 'tactical' adjustments, whereas the latter two require 'strategic' processing. Figure 2 shows an example of a child's re-drafting which employed adding, modify-

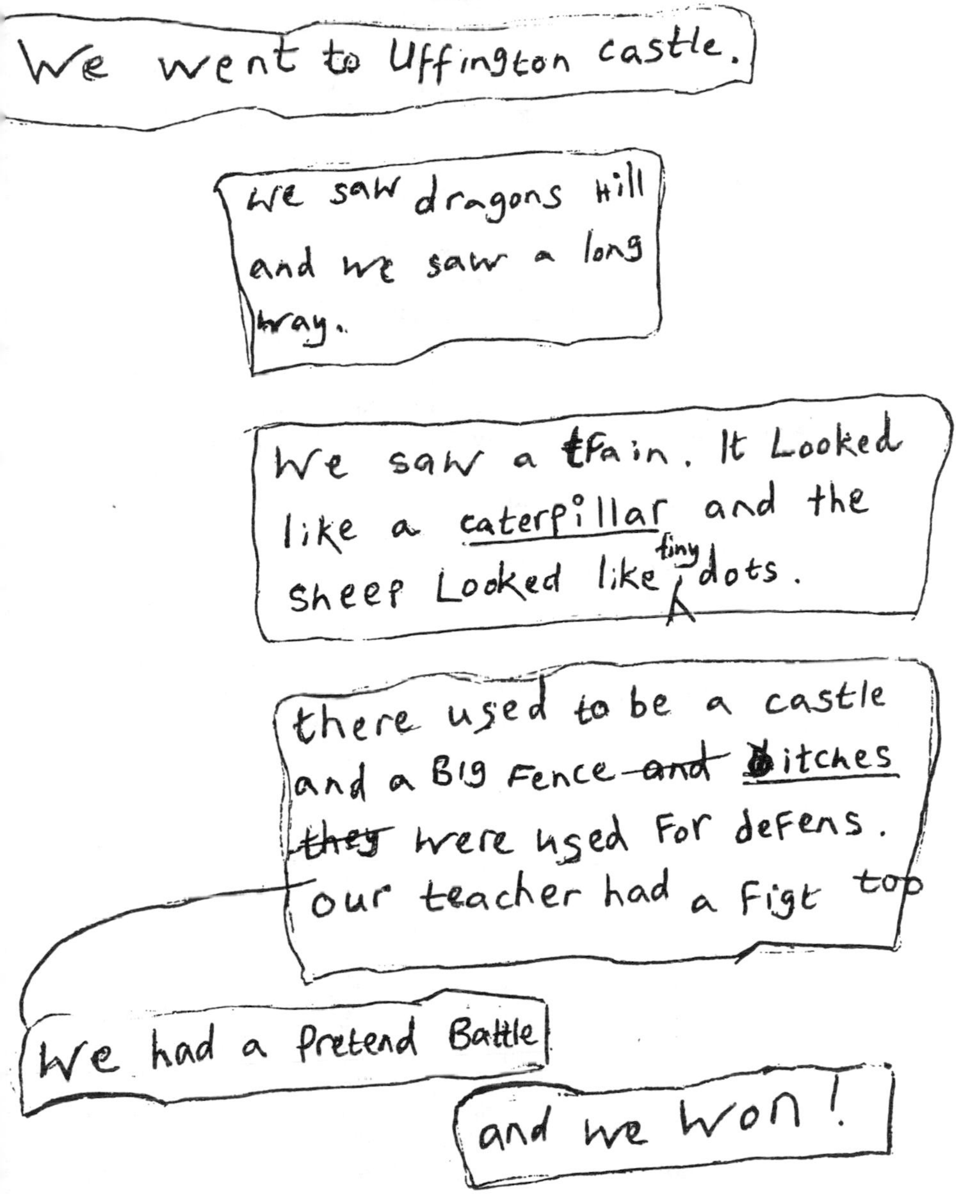

We went to Uffington castle.

We saw dragons Hill
and we saw a long
bray.

We saw a tfain. It Looked
like a caterpillar and the
sheep Looked like tiny dots.

there used to be a castle
and a BIg Fence and Ditches
they were used For deFens.
our teacher had a Figt top

We had a Pretend Battle

and we won!

Figure 2

ing, deleting and reordering. Reordering was facilitated by cutting the original draft and physically sorting and sticking the sentences.

Children rarely get better at writing stories just by writing more of them. They need to be helped to identify what they are trying to achieve and also some of the strategies for overcoming key problems: getting started, getting it down and getting it better. The processes of drafting and editing are useful, but only if they are focused and purposeful.

The above sections have focused on the content and overall structures in the children's writing. Yet already there are an enormous number of variables to consider. Newman (1984) suggests that in this plethora of indices we should remember four key factors. We must start with the writer's 'intention'. With this in mind we can reflect on the appropriateness of the 'organization' and how well the writer has 'orchestrated' the possible variables which may contribute to its effectiveness. However, development will not be continuous. Children should be encouraged to 'experiment' – in their text structures and in their sentence structures. For it is only by trying things out that they will discover their own voice and their own competence as writers.

As teachers we have a grave responsibility in encouraging this to happen. Our support for writing and our response to writing will greatly effect the warmth of the climate for writing and thus, the likelihood of children becoming writers rather than merely learning to write.

(b)   Developing non-chronological writing genres

Though children may be willing and enthusiastic story-writers, they also need help and encouragement to develop their non-chronological writing. Many different frameworks have been offered by a number of researchers on children's writing, most of which imply both text features and developmental stages. For example, in terms of genre, Moffett (1968) suggested:

what is happening	(recording/recounting)
what happened	(reporting/narrating)
what happens	(exposition/generalizing)
what may happen	(argumenting/hypothesizing)

This is based on an assumed progression of cognitive development as children move from an undifferentiated to an organized approach, from instances to generalizations. It seems that this growing intellectual maturity shows as a child moves from being a 'describer' to an 'explainer', from being implicit to explicit and when increasing the range and elaborateness of writing. This may be evidenced by a change in the content of children's writing (from people and events to processes and principles). There is also a stylistic change (from the personal to the impersonal), and linguistically (from the predominant use of I/we to greater use of it/they).

The shift from 'story' to chronological, non-fiction writing (e.g. animal life-cycle or 'A day in the life of . . .') is not particularly difficult. However, we have already noted how difficult it is for children to shift from the story genre, with which they are familiar, to an information genre which is a non-chronological collection of facts. The differences lie in how the information is organized and in the language 'register' used, e.g. use of specialist terminology and formal sentence structures.

A modified form of the scheme offered by Martin and Rothery (1986) can be used to distinguish particular characteristics of factual genres (see p. 180). Whereas recount/investigation and procedure/instructions are chronological, the remaining genres are not. Description and report are logical, but without a clear 'order' (as in the case of chronology) children may have difficulty in deciding where to begin.

With regard to a specific description (e.g. local church, musical instrument, machine/model), the type of guidance offered could include:

Where should the description begin?
    What is it and what is it for?
    What does it look like?
        e.g.   from the general to the particular;
               top to bottom; west to east;
               colour; shape; size;
               what it is made of.
    How is it made?
    How is it used?

With regard to a report (e.g. on the class hamster, which may include general information about hamsters as well as information specific to a pet) a possible framework could be:

What the animal is called?
What it looks like, the function of specific features?
How does it live/learn/adapt?
How does it behave with its own kind/other animals/humans?
What problems/issues/solutions are there?

In both instances, the original plan could be done as a list or web of ideas. These can serve as separate paragraphs or sub-headings. They can be numbered so as to record the order which has been decided. The subsequent first draft will then need revisions. A checklist for guidance could include questions relating to the content and clarity of presentation as well as the accuracy of the data:

Content
    What am I writing about ... what is the title?
    What do the readers already know?
    What background do the readers need?
    What more does the reader need to know?

Clarity
    Is the draft clear and concise?
    Which bits of information are necessary/unnecessary (to whom)?
    Are there any gaps, ambiguities?
    Is information repeated in different sections?
    Is the information adequate and accurate?
    Are there any unresolved contradictions?
    How do we weigh alternative evidence?
    Have we distinguished facts/opinions/interpretations/response?

However, a whole text is rarely written in just one genre: it is more likely to embrace a range of genre: 'description', 'explanation', and 'argumentation', etc. In order to support children's efforts in these alternative genre, we need to consider many factors. For example, when presenting feedback on a model-building technology investigation, children may need to:

describe the task
explain why a particular approach was chosen
describe the materials used

recount the procedures
explain their purposes
evaluate the outcomes and method

Alternatively, if the investigation concerned finding a snail's speed, the ethics of such tests might also involve:

expressing opinions – in a persuasive/discussion genre,

or, in arguing the pros and cons of animal experimentation:

debating propositions, alternatives, limitations, exceptions, relevance of evidence, consequences, reasons, conclusions.

Finding good models of these genres in existing information books for the primary age is not easy. Nevertheless it would seem to be an important exercise for both teachers and children to read information books critically with a view to how the information is presented, how it is written, whether it is well-written and well-presented, in an effort to try to identify what criteria we should be using which will require using appropriate metalanguage.

The final form of writing to be considered, in contrast to narrative (story) and transactional (information) writing, is poetry. As with the other genres, it does not always clearly fall into the chronological/non-chronological dichotomy. For example, ballads are sometimes referred to as 'narrative' poems (chronological). Other poems can fall into any of the other genres/categories.

Marsh (1988) argues that 'poetic discourse' is fundamentally different from 'narrative' and 'expository discourse'. Poetry is essentially lyrical, it aims to inspire (not transmit or inform). It reveals by moving the reader, it evokes feelings by presenting an experience. Marsh asserts that 'it shows, it doesn't tell': it distils, it is, it doesn't explicitly analyse or explain.

Perhaps, partly for these reasons, poetry sometimes has a reputation for being obscure and elitist. However, poetry is also entertainment, witty, satirical; it can be irreverent, lusty, comic, sensational. As its origins are in oral culture, it is composed 'for the ear' and is usually memorable in its patterns – in rhythm, rhyme, repetition. There is also poetry composed 'for the eye' that relies on visual patterning on the page. Hall (1989) emphasizes that poetry is 'a delight', it 'nourishes the imagination'. But it also exposes feelings and generates anxieties.

How does poetry achieve this impact and, in particular, what kinds of language are used to create this effect? Poetry is a form where language is 'foregrounded': it draws attention to itself by being unusual, concentrated, connotative rather than denotative. It often uses imagery and metaphor, figurative rather than literal language. It is often sonorous and even sensuous.

However, there is also the danger of poetry becoming 'precious'. Marsh refers to children who (metaphorically) take their words out of a special drawer marked 'poems' and contrive to be too decorative in their compositions. Children need to be encouraged to be original and, to counter the tendency to be clichéd, a wide range of poetry should be experienced in schools. HMI (DES, 1982) criticized first schools for offering a diet of too much comic verse. Children of this age also enjoy good rhythms and clear rhyme. Older children enjoy narrative poems, action and character poems. The variety of 'favourites' of children of primary age is evident in the poems chosen by children for Kaye Webb's book *I Like This Poem* (1979).

For children with little experience of hearing poetry, it may help to provide a 'closed' framework at first before moving on to encourage writing more open styles of poems. For example:

acrostics (where a word written vertically e.g. WINTER, PARTY, name of a friend, provides a theme and the first letter for each line)

limericks (with a marked rhythm, line lengths, rhyme pattern 'aa, bb, a', as immortalized by Edward Lear)

definitions (where each line lists a characteristic associated with the title object or event)

shape poems (associated words are arranged on the page in the shape of the title, e.g. waves, buses)

tri-poems (a three-line poem with each line telling (3-Ws)
what the poem is about, e.g. animal
where it is
what it is doing . . .

descriptions (list of characteristics using compound adjectives, e.g. flipper-digging turtle, silky-swimming swan, which could be used in conjunction with 3-Ws)

Children can also be encouraged to imitate poems with strong rhythm, e.g. 'Night Mail', or 'Hiawatha', or the rhyme pattern of well-known nursery rhymes – with updated content, or the work of any favourite writer, until they develop the confidence to try out their own 'voice'. However, initial attempts at rhyme may degenerate into doggerel, and attempts at free verse may be little more than 'chopped up prose'. The best approach is to immerse children in poetry so they develop the ear and the eye for this very particular form of writing.

ACTIVITY

Appraisal of Text Structures

What evidence (list of characteristics) would you wish to look for to enable you to make an appraisal of children's writing?

How will you decide which characteristics to select for any task or for a particular child?

How will you monitor the frequency of opportunities which you provide for these different dimensions of writing to develop?

How will you record individual progress?

FURTHER READING

The following books offer plenty of theoretical insight into current good practice:

For young writers:
Hall, N. (1987) *The Emergence of Literacy*. London: Hodder & Stoughton.
Nicholls, J. *et al.* (1989) *Beginning Writing*. Milton Keynes: Open University Press.

For a wider range of ages and genres:
Andrews, R. (ed.) (1989) *Narrative and Argument*. Milton Keynes: Open University Press.
Cowie, H. (ed.) (1984) *The Development of Children's Imaginative Writing*. London: Croom Helm.
Hadley, E. (1985) *English in the Middle Years*. London: Edward Arnold.

Newkirk, T. and Atwell, N. (ed.) (1988) *Understanding Writing: Ways of Observing, Learning and Teaching*. Portsmouth, NH: Heinemann.
Newman, J. (1984) *The Craft of Children's Writing*. Toronto: Scholastic.
Raban, B. (ed.) (1985) *Practical Ways to Teach Writing*. London: Ward Lock Educational.
Roberts, G. (1989) *Teaching Children to Read and Write*. Oxford: Basil Blackwell.
Wilkinson, A. (ed.) (1988) *The Writing of Writing*. Milton Keynes: Open University Press.

For poetry:
Brownjohn, S. (1985) *Does It Have to Rhyme?* London: Hodder & Stoughton.
Corbett, P. and Moses, B. (1986) *Catapults and Kingfishers*. Oxford: Oxford University Press.
Hall, L. (1989) *Poetry for Life*. London: Cassell.
Marsh, G. (1989) *Teaching Poetry*. London: Hodder & Stoughton.

(iii)   Crafting writing: control of grammatical structures, differentiated vocabulary, appropriate style

In addition to talking about, and coming to understand, structures at the level of the whole text, the National Curriculum also includes targets concerned with another level of structure. This is the structure of the sentence and its components. It was this aspect in particular which led to heated debate after its announcement, because of fears of a return to teaching formal grammar and sentence parsing.

The Cox Report itself stated that it was difficult or impossible 'to show any direct cause-and-effect relationship between teaching formal grammar and improved writing performance'. However, the broader approach that the Report recommended, covering larger patterns of (text) organization, sentence structures, spoken dialect and stylistic varieties, would, it was argued, help to improve children's sensitivity to their own use of language (para 6.8).

The Working Party Report states that by the age of 7 years, children are expected to have been taught, in the context of discussion about their own writing, such grammatical terms as a sentence, verb, tense, noun, pronoun, and should be able to demarcate sentences using full stops (DES, 1989, para 17.40). It is important to note that this learning is to be done in the context of 'discussion' about children's 'own writing', and not regarded as a 'separate body of knowledge to be added on to the traditional English curriculum' (para 6.2).

(a) Sentences and full stops

A class of top infants, when asked to explain how they knew where to put a full stop in the writing they were engaged in, gave a number of suggestions:

'You put a full stop at the end of the line.'

'You have to think in your head then you put it when you know you've finished saying something.'

'You can't put it after "He was hunting" ... You have to put it after "He was hunting for shells." It has to be more than three words.'

'I put my full stop after "Snails have feelers and eyes on the end of their tubes." I could have put it after "eyes" but then you can't have "On the end of their tubes" just by itself ... It doesn't sound right.'

All these children wrote in well-formed sentences, even if they were not 'demarcating' them conventionally. Whether knowledge or use of technical terminology at this point would be of benefit – or even be absorbed, much less applied – is unlikely. Three months and a lot of reading later, they were punctuating in an increasingly conventional manner but still could not articulate why.

Some 7-year-olds offered a wider range of answers concerning the purpose of full stops:

'Full stops help you to read.'

'It helps you to know who is saying something.'

'You put a full stop after things which belong together, like "Fritz was very angry and he threw the doll on the floor and it broke." '

Older children, of 9 and 10, also experienced confusion in explicitly articulating their implicit understanding of a variety of sentence structures which they were using competently. They even used adverbial fronting phrases and clauses to introduce a sentence,

'Near the football ground, we . .'
'As I was going along, I . . .'

as well as a range of conjunctions to form complex sentences. When considering whether to shorten or lengthen sentences in their draft, children picked out main clauses correctly. This often left a remaining short phrase which was sometimes extended by adding new information or content (a semantic solution) rather than by just adding a verb (a syntactic solution) in order to form a complete sentence. One child decided to divide up some lengthy sentences and described the effect of the short sentences thus:

'It makes it sound like a book – an adventure book. It's sort of exciting and breathless.'

Here sentence structure was used deliberately for stylistic effect.

(b)   Extending patterns of vocabulary

Children's acquisition of vocabulary is, as we have seen, phenomenally rapid in the pre-school years. It continues to grow, though at a much slower rate, throughout an individual's life. Certain developments often become evident in children from approximately 8 or 9 years. Two of these will be mentioned here.

Growth in types of vocabulary undergoes considerable development during the primary years (Hart, Walker and Gray, 1977): for example, between the ages of 5 and 7 the following are learned:

relative pronouns: that, which, who
prepositions: after, about, from, around, by, as
conjunctions: but, if, then, or, than
use of comparison: bigger – than
evaluation: – or –
hypothesis: if – then

'Nouns' and 'verbs' (the first categories to be acquired) are usually the categories that least need attention in terms of communicative competence. They are also two of the more difficult categories to grasp. At a simple level children make few mistakes, but at a complex level the subdivisions are conceptually difficult. The simple categories of nouns include:

nouns may be 'naming' words, for common things: boy, city
proper nouns may name people or places: Joe, Oxford
nouns can be abstract: happiness

More complex categories include:

superordinates: classificatory terms, e.g. furniture, cutlery
abstract terms: happiness, fear, bravery, sadness
irregular plurals: ox/oxen, child/children, sheep/sheep
parent/offspring terms: goose/gosling, kangeroo/joey
collective nouns: flock of birds, kindle of kittens,
paddling of ducks, parliament of owls

The concept of a 'verb' is also complex. The usual definition – that
it is a 'doing word' – doesn't help very much when some of the
verbs children use most in their sentences are 'have', 'am', 'like',
which don't obviously appear to 'do' anything. The categorizations
used in the English language are not universal. 'Verb' is a category
constructed by people to reflect a feature that they wish to highlight in a particular culture. This categorization 'verb' is not
shared, for example, by Amerindians or Australian aborigines
(Kress, 1982).

The range of verbs include:

verbs that are action, 'doing' words, e.g. she is jumping
verbs that define a 'state', e.g. I am happy
verbs that express a 'process', e.g. the city changed

Defining a verb is highly problematic to linguists: little wonder
then that the teacher might have difficulty giving a clear definition.
Many verbs can be transformed into nouns (e.g. to jump, a jump),
or nouns can be used as verbs (e.g. a video, to video). Other
confusions exist, as illustrated in the example of an 8-year-old
child who identified 'naughty' as a doing word 'because my dog
does naughty things'.

From this it follows that trying to identify grammatical terms
(e.g. sentence) by using further grammatical expressions (e.g.
'must have a verb') is not always helpful. Furthermore, a sentence
is a grammatical construction which is not necessarily appropriate
for an author's intended meaning or effect (not all modern writers
use sentences all of the time). Also, discussing style and structure
in abstract linguistic terms may be less useful than developing an

'ear' for language (does it sound right?) and a 'nose' for meaning (does it make sense?).

However, children do sometimes experience a mismatch between the demands of their spoken language and the demands of 'correctness' if using Standard English for written communication. The mismatch occurs in the relationship between noun (subject) and the verb where this is irregular, e.g. 'I were going . . .' and 'They is coming to tea'. It may be for this reason that the term 'verb' is often one of the first to be introduced to children. . . . But explanations that rely on analytic metalanguage ('parts of speech', etc.) could be abstract and meaningless for children.

To develop vocabulary, children can be encouraged to go for variety and vividness in their storying, in setting, mood, characterization and action. This can be done through introducing alternative words, using the following ways of exploring the parameters of meaning:

synonyms: words that are similar in meaning
   e.g. different ways of saying 'nice'
antonyms: words that have opposite meanings
   e.g. nice/nasty
hyponyms: words of the same set
   e.g. kind → friendly, gentle, helpful;
      said → whispered, called, shouted

Further, children learn to understand more about word relationships and their role in a sentence, according to their grammatical function. Adjectives are added to provide greater detail in story setting and mood, for effect, and for atmosphere. Adverbs are included to give greater precision to action and to character motivation. This sometimes needs encouragement from the teacher, as well as modelling through reading appropriate books.

Apart from such teacher stimulus, there is peer stimulus. Children's writing skills are encouraged through responses from an audience and through discussion and drafting which take place as children share writings. These demands encourage the author to find ways of making the story clearer and better and thereby improve the writer's communicative competence. 'Making things clearer' often requires the careful use of connectives. This draws attention to further categories of words, especially conjunctions and pronouns, which relate to sentence links discussed earlier (see p. 193).

ACTIVITY

Identifying Grammatical Development

Select three pieces of children's writing over a period of time.

Identify any incorrect grammatical structures and note any new structures
   (e.g. use of connectives when joining sentences;
   adding adverbial frontings;
   using pronouns to link sentences).

Where there appears little change and development during the period, what intervention strategies might you use to help the child use new structures?
   (E.g. talking about such features when reading books;
   encouraging a 'response partner' to comment;
   helping the child find other ways of expressing their message.)

FURTHER READING

Dixon, J. and Stratta, L. (1986) *Writing Narrative and Beyond.* Sheffield: NATE.
Harpin, W. (1976) *The Second R.* London: Allen & Unwin.
Harris, J. and Wilkinson, J. (1986) *Reading Children's Writing.* London: Allen & Unwin.
Keen, J. (1978) *Teaching English: A Linguistic Approach.* London: Methuen.
Stubbs, M. (1986) *Educational Linguistics.* Oxford: Basil Blackwell.

(iv)   Presentation: spelling, handwriting

Mention has already been made of brainstorming techniques and a 'web of ideas' as ways of stimulating a flow of possible starting points, developments and outcomes, or using story-planners and literary sociogrammes which can then be employed in a first draft (see pp. 213–28). The Programmes of Study make a clear distinction between redrafting and proof-reading. This is to discourage the use of redrafting as a process of correcting surface features such as spelling. Instead, redrafting is identified as

> shaping and structuring the raw material and making alterations which will help the reader, e.g. getting rid of ambiguity, vagueness, incoherence, or irrelevance

and proof-reading as

> checking for errors, e.g. omitted or repeated words, mistakes in spelling or punctuation (para. 17.48 viii).

It is the process of proof-reading which leads into spelling – not just in the sense of correcting individual words but by developing an alertness to generative spelling patterns that can be applied on other occasions. This leads to an understanding of word structures and word-building.

(a)   Spelling

Children develop their own strategies for tackling new words in their reading. This can be through using context to guess the meaning or by looking at the shape of the word and relying on visual memory. They may also note parts of the word which they recognize and work out the remainder by adding on the additional letter-sounds. In writing, however, the child has none of these supports. They may rely on memory, use the analogy of a similar sounding words, or build up the components 'from scratch'. Conversely they will consult their 'word banks', class wall-charts, 'word books', their neighbours or the teacher.

If they build up the word they may start with the smallest unit of sound ('phoneme'). But each letter (grapheme) may have more than one 'sound'. Also children learn early that in English combinations of letters also represent sounds. These may be

initial consonant blends (bl, br, cl, cr, fl, gl, gr, sc, sl, sm, sn, spl, squ, str);
final consonant blends (ck, nd, ng, nk);
digraphs (ch, gh, ph, sh, sch, th);

vowel diphthongs (ee, oo, ai, au, aw, ay, ie, oa, ou, oy, uy);
vowel/consonant combinations (ar, er, ir, or, ur)

What is particularly confusing in English is the fact that the same vowel or digraph does not always represent the same sound. For example:

'a' in pat, is different from that in father
'o' in pot, is different from that in woman

Barnhurst (in Lamb, 1967) calculates that there are 230 spellings for the 40 basic 'sounds' in English, and that a knowledge of 3000 basic phonemes is needed for the children to spell 80 per cent of their primary age vocabulary. However, Albrow (in Peters, 1975) suggests that 70–80 per cent of spelling is grapho-phonemically regular.

Children's own investigations into spelling patterns may lead towards discoveries such as:

sound alike but not spelt alike
   (initial consonants of celery and salt)
alternative spellings of vowel sounds
   (raw, awe, poor)
saying and sounding mis-match
   (lion, Brian, iron)
same spelling but different sound
   (read and read; tear (cry), tear (rip))
same sound but different spelling
   (bear and bare)
same spelling and sound but different meaning
   (pen: writing implement; enclosure)

Discussing these features can encourage children to try out tongue-twisters and a wide range of puns in their language play.

Other language play may develop. For example, some top infants were fascinated by the way in which words that sound alike are spelt differently. When trying to 'have a go' with their spellings, they were encouraged to think of other similar-sounding words. This produced words that follow different spelling rules, which the children enjoyed trying to fit into their own self-generated 'pattern' lists. Through discovering patterns together – finding that there is some logic to the 'irregular' words – spelling turned into a game rather than a trap. It was also a game in which everyone could join as and when they saw another word which might fit the pattern.

Older children in a class of top juniors were observed trying to establish rules for 'changing the sound a letter makes' (often different ways of changing a short vowel sound into a long one). The rules were treated as 'helpful hints' to which anyone could refer (e.g. like, tie; hope, soap, blow; Jean, Bede, green; made, rain). Similar charts were frequently extended to demonstrate different spellings of 'or', 'ir', and 'ow' sounds (for, claw, four, naughty; bird, term, nurse; town, house).

In addition to sounds, there are other patterns which help to explain phonemic/graphemic discrepancies. These relate to the numerous invasions which Britain has experienced, i.e. whether the particular word originally came into English from Anglo-Saxon, Norse, Norman-French, Latin, or familiarization with Greek during the Renaissance, or through languages of countries that were explored or colonized. The different spelling rules of such different families of languages are reflected in English today. Older juniors can enjoy searching for origins of different words and discovering 'families'. In multi-lingual classrooms, and where families visit relatives overseas or holiday abroad, children can often offer examples of 'loan' words between languages – there are certainly plenty of Americanisms and trade names worldwide. A good dictionary (e.g. *Shorter Oxford*) helps in the search for origins.

Another reason why the phoneme/grapheme relation is so varied in English is because English was one of the first languages in which spelling became stabilized, through the early introduction of the printing press by Caxton in 1476. This fixed spellings more consistently than the scribes had managed to do.

However, during the fifteenth century a Great Vowel shift is reported to have taken place (Stubbs, 1980). Although it is impossible to be sure how English used to sound (Thomas Edison's first phonograph was only demonstrated in 1877), there are clues. Most literature of the Middle English period (1199 to 1450) was composed in verse, for oral recitation in a society which was basically illiterate. It is suggested that verse was easier to learn by heart. The need for rhyme requires that words should have a similar sound pattern. But the patterns which we find in much of this literature do not rhyme in modern pronunciation. Either the words were mis-spelt when written down later or their pronunciation has changed. The consistency of the mismatches seems to indicate the latter.

A further stabilization occurred as a result of the codification of the English language by the great dictionary compilers, such as Samuel Johnson (1755). This also helped to 'fix' spellings, despite the fact that the spoken word differed in different regions, classes and also continued to change over time, until it became more standardized (in terms of social acceptability) with the spread of radio in the 1920s.

From time to time attempts have been made to reform English spelling. The philosopher Bertrand Russell and playwright George Bernard Shaw were both keen supporters of the idea. Attempts were made in 1959 by Wijk with 'regularized spelling' and by Pitman and St John in 1969 with the 'initial teaching alphabet' (i.t.a.). However, these attempts have not lasted.

The mismatch between phoneme and grapheme imposes a tremendous burden on a young reader or writer. Research has suggested that sounding the letters out (the 'phonic' approach) is only one strategy which children may find useful at particular stages in their development of reading (Dale, 1983; Biemiller, 1970). Children's attempts at storying independently may well display evidence of 'invented spellings'. These are the child's own efforts to come to grips with the English phoneme/grapheme mismatch. However, certain developmental patterns do emerge. At first efforts seem to depend on a match of letter name or consonant 'sound' and letter 'symbol' (Clay, 1988). The resulting words are often vowel-less, e.g.

KLR   LTL   later   SIYINTIFIC
colour little   scientific

and also (Bissex, 1980)

RUDF; GNYS AT WRK
(Are you deaf; genius at work)

It is an inductive method of spelling derived from the sounds of the words. An understanding of the variety of ways in which a 'sound' can be 'spelled' develops gradually, through reading and discussing unusual words, looking for regular patterns and learning irregular words which are commonly used by the particular child.

Current practice varies considerably in how best to help children tackle the difficulty of mismatch between phonemes and graphemes which results in so many children asking for 'spellings' during their writing, thus interrupting the writing flow. Strategies range from trying to encourage children to 'have a go' and use invented spellings based on the implicit rules that they have so far inferred from their reading–writing experiences, to postponing the need for help by encouraging children to 'write the first letter and leave a space'. Both of these emphasize the importance of getting the ideas down in the first draft and leaving spelling problems till the revision stage.

Researchers have identified alternative approaches that have been found to be useful to children: which one is 'best' would seem to depend on the particular child's own strengths and weaknesses. Bryant and Bradley (1985) stress the need for the children to be able to hear the word components, a focus on aural discrimination, which, they believe, can be enhanced by greater use of rhyming and attention to aural word games. Peters (1967) emphasizes the need for children to see the word and to feel how it is written, for visual discrimination and the development of an automatic motor response. Frith (1980) suggests a multi-sensory approach. A common approach to new spellings in classrooms is to encourage the child to Look–Trace–Say, then Cover–Write–Check and re-write if necessary.

Finally, in order to understand why children might have difficulty in producing certain sounds – the focus of phonetics – we need to identify how sounds are made. The following chart, adapted from Stubbs (1980, p. 38) shows the key distinctions:

	Labial (with lips)	Dental (against teeth)	Post-dental (behind teeth)	Palatal velar (roof-of-mouth) front mid	Glottal (throat)
Stops	p, b	t, d		ch, g(in) k, g(et)	
Fricatives	f, v	th	s, z	sh	h
Nasals	m	n		ng	
Approximates (liquids)	w	l	r	j(y)	

Given the diversity of research conclusions, of individual strategies and the large number of variables involved, it would seem that the most important contribution to the development of spelling is the close monitoring of individual children so that their different strengths are noted and 'miscues' analysed to see if there is any consistent patterning which may indicate the appropriate support for that child. Awareness of the various types of miscues and the range of responses available to help correct them forms the basis for professional support strategies.

(b)   Handwriting

Apart from being able to identify the sounds (phonemes) in language, children also have to match this to the appropriate letter shapes (graphemes).

By the age of four most children conceptually distinguish between their own 'writing' and 'drawing', and they soon begin to experiment with letter shapes which occur in the script of the adults around them. Ferreiro and Teberosky (1983) found that pre-school children who have learnt the word 'word' usually decide that a 'word' should have four or more letters: anything less doesn't really count.

Researchers such as Clay (1975) who have followed children's scripting development closely suggest a number of distinct stages. First comes gaining control of the pencil and being able to use this in up–down, clockwise, anti-clockwise and travelling movements. Children usually begin with:

gesture writing,
straight-line movements

scribble writing,
using anti-clockwise and
clockwise movements

streamer writing,
using travelling movements

unit isolation,
letter-like shapes

The first three stages may not include any recognizable letter-like shapes. By the age of 3.9 to 4.0 years, children often produce isolated letter shapes which are repeatedly practised. By 4.6 years children frequently experiment with these shapes and they may select their own favourites and enjoy 'repeat writing', making their own patterns. This writing, or copying, of disconnected words or letters in lists (often only four or six characters wide, though sometimes covering the width of the entire page) appeals to children as a visual pattern, not as a means of verbal communication, and is sometimes referred to as 'inventory' writing.

By 5 years, many children will be able to write their own name. They may be prolific 'writers', but in forms which do not communicate to others. Nevertheless they are behaving like writers, believing themselves to be writers and developing a confidence in writing. This 'developmental writing' stage is, it is argued, vital for the child to experience, as it contributes to a positive self-image as a writer and about writing. Laying the basis for enthusiastic attitudes could be the surest way to motivate children to develop the skills to write in more conventional orthography which others can then read.

The desire to use conventional orthographic symbols often causes great frustration, as the physical act of writing can be very tiring, and it also interrupts the cognitive and social act of composition. The development of storying may cease for a while as the attention is drawn to the act of scripting itself. A reversion to stereotype 'labelling' is common.

For this reason it is important to distinguish and separate writing in terms of the physical act of scripting from the psychological act of composing. Many children can compose (e.g. stories, procedures), but may find it very difficult to put it on paper. This may be so particularly for the very young child who is not yet at ease with a pencil, for a handicapped person, and also for those whose mind goes faster than their hand. It is useful, therefore, to separate these two very different skills of scripting and storying. As already mentioned this can be done in various ways, e.g.:

- dictation of story by child/group to adult, or to tape-recorder, for the 'listening corner' or for subsequent transcription;
- wordprocessing, where the child can compose first and correct the spellings and layout later.

Figure 3 shows examples of children's writing based on Temple's writing stages (1982).

Teaching handwriting usually begins with the child being asked to *trace over* or, later, *copy under* individual letter-shapes and learning to 'print'. But printing does not follow on from the flow of a young child's scribble and there is now some debate as to whether it might not be better to introduce the letter 'tails' to provide the basis for linking letters and developing a more flowing hand from the very beginning. Encouraging a joined hand from the start helps children become more aware of the correct formation of letters, avoids the need to relearn letter-shapes when starting a cursive hand later, and encourages awareness of the patterning of letter strings and word spacing.

The implications for classroom practice of such a viewpoint would be to allow young children plenty of opportunity to enjoy pattern-making (clockwise, anticlockwise, horizontal, vertical, diagonal and travelling action) through finger painting and tracing shapes in sand, before practising repeated letter-shapes.

Fears that the freedom associated with allowing children opportunities for 'developmental writing' may encourage children to shape letters wrongly have been articulated. It is important to remember that the two activities have different purposes and different audiences. If developmental writing is used for 'meaning-making', for communicating in a journal/diary for self or for

a 'Inventory' writing

My nameisBEN

d Mixed upper and lower case

TISqaIBonε

b Linear letter shapes

I Sed no I Wont give you them

e Word spacing and line spacing

the rockets Arep lWΩDS oM RWΛFббoe DR

c Correct letter orientation

I am a ball of wool. I am winding along the floor The cat is after me. HELP

f Consistent letter size; and discrimination of ascenders and descenders

Figure 3

teacher, then its main purpose is to encourage the child to behave like a writer, to want to communicate through the written mode, to become confident with using writing. However, if a child wants to communicate with a wider audience, they will realize that they need to use the conventional orthography and will ask for help in making an appropriate transcription – where the teacher (or helper) may write or type the message, or the child *copy out* the words dictated to the teacher and written as a model by the teacher. Until the child wants to write in conventional orthography, they can still be practising basic patterning and letter-shapes, separately, in order to acquire the appropriate motor skills. Later, when confidence increases the child will write *independently*.

There is no need, therefore, for there to be an either/or choice between 'developmental writing' and 'conventional orthography'. What is important is to choose the script which is appropriate for the purpose and audience, and to separate the function of patterning from writing. Authors such as Sassoon (1983) and Jarman (1979) have many examples of alternative patterning which can be used alongside developmental writing. However, both authors agree on the importance of establishing good motor skill habits from an early stage so that 'legibility, speed, beauty and a personal hand' develop easily (Sassoon, 1983).

Further practical aspects about encouraging a 'good hand' are such factors as pencil grip, body posture, paper position, paper surface and whether lined/unlined. Many combinations are possible – and are certainly very personal. The key criteria is whether legibility and speed are helped or hindered.

Older children trying out both left and right hands often find that they use more finger control with their natural hand whereas the pencil is pulled across the page by the whole hand and arm with their unnatural hand, reducing flexibility and dexterity (Alton and Taylor, 1987). Further, legibility and speed is helped where the direction of the gripped pencil, position of the arm and the angle of the paper are in a continuous straight line.

Finally, there is some evidence that for younger children (aged 6) unlined paper is important so that they are free to concentrate on direction and formation, whereas for older children (aged 9) lined paper is better so that they can also think about evenness of size and straightness of lines (in Pasternicki, 1986).

To help children continue to develop their awareness of letter/

word formation, one needs to find additional ways of encouraging an interest in letter shapes and word patterns rather than attending always to the communication aspect of writing. Activities that encourage older children to play with letter shapes, or words, may emphasize the way letters are formed rather than their sounds or meanings:

Calligrams: words that are written to look like their meanings.

Mirror letters: writing inverted letters using mirrors to find symmetrical and a-symmetrical letters.

Palindromes: words that can be read backwards or forwards to mean the same, e.g. dad; or to mean something different, e.g. mad/dam. Children often enjoy the latter.

Anagrams: words that can be made out of another word by rearranging letters, e.g. dear/read. One can also make words by selecting and rearranging letters, e.g. garden: are, den, red, drag, etc.

Letter ladders: changing one letter at a time, e.g. to turn a pig into a hen (pig, peg, pen, hen).

Children can also be introduced to the different type founts and styles of designing alphabets, for example, through an examination of newspapers (in particular, advertisers' scripts), different types in printed books (Helvetica, Baskerville, Times, etc.), or different styles of handwriting (italic, 'round' hand, etc.). This can be extended geographically to cover a wide variety of scripts (Chinese, Japanese, Arabic, Hindi, Cyrillic, Roman) and historically to include much older ways of recording messages (Mesopotamian cuneiform around 3500 BC, Egyptian hieroglyphs from 3000 BC, Chinese ideographs from 2000 BC and also the Phoenician script in 1000 BC, which provided the basis for the 'alphabetic principle' from which modern western scripts derive).

All of these scripts have their own conventions as to direction: top-down (Chinese), right–left (Arabic). Early Greek writing changed direction on alternate lines, known as 'boustrophedon'. This resulted in many of the original Phoenician-based letters being reversed. (Some children begin writing in this fashion.) Scripts also have their own shapes, and have traditionally been written with particular tools (brushes, pointed implements, pencils/pens, on tablets, papyrus, bamboo, bark, paper). Other forms of writing (making marks to convey words and sentences, etc.) could include more visual forms of writing (signs/symbols that could be used in music or choreography, for traffic directions, or washing instructions).

In the West, the custom of leaving spaces in between words only developed in the 11th century when 'word boundaries' emerged and crystallized (Goodman in Goodman and Flemming, 1969). However, modern advertising techniques often involve deliberately changing such boundaries – as well as the spellings. Terms such as 'lower case' and 'upper case' are even more modern inventions. They derive from the early days of printing when letters were kept in racks or cases, and the 'capital' letters were in the upper cases and the 'small' letters kept in the lower cases!

Investigations into our own writing systems and the associated conventions can lead to comparative studies in our multi-lingual society. It can also lead to investigations concerning printing and book-making and link the process of 'writing' to the objects for 'reading'.

CHECKLIST

Identifying Classroom Spelling Problems

How is spelling 'problematic'
  for the child: does it constrain writing?
    does it inhibit storying? (motivational problem)
  for the teacher: is it difficult to understand what is written?
    (appraisal and monitoring problem)
    are there constant interruptions for words?
    and long queues (management problem)

What is problematic?
  types of mis-spelling . . .
  mis-spoken . . . word literally transcribed as spoken
    e.g. I fink (think)
  missed-out letters or syllables (often, as spoken)
    e.g. Please Mr Pliceman where's the Libry?

mis-application of phonic rule on an irregular word
e.g. Thay are playing in the ruff grars.
mis-assembled letters (in the wrong order) where the general shape of the word or its components is remembered but the sequence muddled
e.g. was (saw), aeplane (aeroplane)
incomprehensible . . .

Also, is there any pattern in mistakes/miscues made . . .
i.e. are the same mistakes made, or the same kind of mistakes
how consistent are the mistakes
what percentage are incomprehensible . . .
and cause problems in understanding the written work

Why is it problematic?
child's lack of confidence to 'have a go'
child's lack of basic phonics and (therefore)
child's lack of dictionary skills
child confused over expectations of the task,
its purpose . . . relative importance of
expression/accuracy, communication/correctness
its status . . . draft or final stage

How does the child tackle the problem?
consider the child's approach (cognitive style, strengths) when reading, or looking at pictures:
(i)   does the child use a global approach
(e.g. looks at a picture for general impact before noticing details . . . notices the shape of the word but not necessarily the component letters)
(ii)   does the child respond quickly (impulsively), perhaps only glancing at the beginnings of words
(iii)   does the child use an analytic approach
(e.g. looks at tiny details before seeing it as a whole picture . . . notices the letters before seeing the whole word)
(iv)   does the child respond slowly (reflectively), works things out in his/her head before having a go

USING such information, gained through observation and discussion, to support children's spelling strategies . . .

child needs to hear the sounds, the segments (aural)
child needs to feel the shape and flow of the word (motor)
child needs to recognize the word (visual)
child needs to reinforce each component (memorization)
child needs to understand the word (semantically/morphemic-ally)

e.g. realizing that 'infant' is the root of 'infancy' could help avoid literal phonic mis-spelling – 'infuncy' (sem.) or realizing that 'to compete' is the root of 'a competition' (sem.) *and* that -tion can change a verb into a noun could help to avoid mis-spellings like 'compatishun' (morph.)

(a) adding a wider range of strategies where the child is weak
  • by encouraging a global approach moving from word to context adding an analytic check by looking at component letters
  • by encouraging self-checking, quick re-read to check meaning adding a reflective check by looking at all letters
  • by encouraging an analytic approach moving from word components to comprehension of whole text,
  adding a global approach by looking at the picture or using the part of the story already read to predict the next section
  • by encouraging the child to move from words to reflect on story-line

(b) building confidence and clarifying expectations
  • by encouraging children to guess how to spell a new word, to ask a friend, refer to wall charts or banks, or dictionary, put the first letter and leave a blank s . . . or draw a picture instead
  • by preparing the class/group/individual by discussing the intended writing and thinking about words that might be wanted and giving the spellings before beginning the work
  • by encouraging children to use phonic skills to attack the spelling challenges which will, in turn, make it easier for them to find the word in a dictionary
  • by making expectations clear for each piece of work, whether draft or final presentation
  • by ensuring that only selected (not all) mistakes are corrected

(c)   the teacher can help children overcome 'immature' strategies by reading and listening to poems and rhymes
   • by encouraging aural discrimination through listening to stories for nonsense/substituted words (e.g. Dahl's *Hairy Tales*, *BFG*) or to tapes for specific phonemes ... initial/terminal/blends
   • by forming the letters in sand, finger paints, felt shapes or tracing over the letters (motor skills)
   • snap and lotto type games to increase visual recognition
   • word analysis ... break the words into recognizable and known segments (either semantic FARM-er or morphemic play-ING)
   • learn the words which the child frequently uses and often mis-spells (write them on card and keep in envelope inside the back cover of writing book or in folder).

FURTHER READING

The following titles give a wealth of information about the development of the English language:

Burgess, A. (1975) *English Maid Plane*. London: Fontana.
Crystal, D. (1988) *The English Language*. Harmondsworth: Penguin.
Hawkins, E. (1984) *Awareness of Language*. Cambridge: Cambridge University Press.
Stubbs, M. (1986) *Educational Linguistics*. Oxford: Basil Blackwell.

The next set of titles contain considerable detail relating to the psycholinguistic processes of reading and how this affects spelling:

Gibson, E. J. and Levin, H. (1975) *The Psychology of Reading*. Cambridge, MA: MIT Press.
Goodman, K. and Flemming, J. (eds) (1969) *Psycholinguistics and the Teaching of Reading*. Newark, DE: International Reading Asociation.
Frith, U. (1980) *Cognitive Processes in Spelling*. New York: Academic Press.
Weaver, C. (1980) *Psycholinguistics and Reading*. Michigan: Little, Brown.

The following group of titles contain practical suggestions about children's spelling problems and ways of teaching spelling:

Gentry, J. (1987) *Spel is a four letter word*. Leamington Spa: Scholastic.
Peters, M. (1985) *Spelling: Caught or Taught?* (2nd edn). London: Routledge & Kegan Paul.
Radebaugh, M. R. (1985) 'Children's perceptions of their spelling strategies'. *Reading Teacher* **38** (6).
Torbe, M. (1985) *Teaching Spelling* (2nd edn). London: Ward Lock Educational.
Cripps, C. and Peters, M. (1988) *Catchwords – Ideas for Teaching Spelling*. London: Harcourt Brace Jovanovich.

The last set of books relate to handwriting. The first is theoretical, the next three have a practical bias; the last includes spelling:

Alston, J. and Taylor, J. (1987) *Handwriting: Theory, Research, Practice*. London: Croom Helm.
Jarman, C. (1979)*The Development of Handwriting Skills*. Oxford: Basil Blackwell
Jarman, C. (1989) *Teaching the Left-Hander*. Oxford: Basil Blackwell.
Sassoon, R. (1983) *A Practical Guide to Children's Handwriting*. London: Thames & Hudson.
Temple, C. A. *et al.* (1982) *The Beginnings of Writing*. Boston: Allyn & Bacon.

6.3. MONITORING PROVISION AND RESPONDING TO CHILDREN'S WRITING

(i) Pedagogy and provision

The pedagogic principles endorsed by the National Curriculum specifically reject the notion of teaching 'about English' through isolated, 'corrective' exercises. Instead, the classroom emphasis is expected to be very much on the social nature of language and its appropriateness in different contexts. The pedagogical emphasis is to be on discussion of these differences rather than on formal written exercises.

This rejection by the Kingman, Cox and NCC Reports of a return to formal exercises could lead to a similar approach to that adopted by Doughty (1971) in *Language in Use*. This Schools Council project produced materials to encourage children to adopt the 'fieldwork approach' and was later given additional confirmation in Bullock (1975). However, it became a singular failure, partly because teachers did not have the linguistic expertise to follow through the activities. The Cox Report (1989) fears that the same would be true of today's teachers (para 6.3). Nevertheless, the fieldwork approach is advocated by the Programmes of Study.

The previous chapters have each included examples of classroom practice where a fieldwork approach has been adopted. Activities arose from the children's work and were based on the richness of the children's own linguistic resources – language at home, in the playground, the environment, the media and in books which they read and write. Discussions concerning these activities helped to introduce a metalanguage which enabled the children to reflect upon their language, sharpen their understandings, and make their knowledge explicit.

Distinguishing and refining the understanding and use of the vast range of variables already mentioned necessitates a complex monitoring system. This has to be based on a sound knowledge of the components and an appreciation of their significance. A structured approach, using a set of graded materials consisting of isolated and sequenced exercises is much easier for a teacher to administer. Adopting a fieldwork approach requires the teacher to be able to spot the learning point as and when it emerges, and to judge the timing and method of intervention.

Such a pedagogy returns the responsibility for teaching to the teachers (who no longer have to remain predominantly managers).

The Cox Report recognizes some of the problems in such fieldwork:

> A problem in studying language is that it is too often too close to individual speakers to be observed dispassionately: it is either taken for granted and not seen at all, or it is too intimately involved in individual and social identity to be discussed objectively (para 6.11).

Further, awareness about language should also come in the context of discussions concerning the social significance of language and language diversity, particularly in oral language, and the differences between oral and written language. Many children already have a wide, implicit knowledge about language in terms of social variety and some have a well-practised capacity for changing their style of language according to their audience and their needs. (Evidence for this can easily be found by listening to the language used in role play in the Home Corner, or to the language for persuading and cajoling out on the playgrounds.)

However, some children either find it difficult to control their language to suit these differing occasions or are unwilling to do so. It is the role of the teacher to make such knowledge explicit and to extend the understandings of its implications, so that children increase their knowledge about language and can make more informed and conscious decisions about the language they use. This more subtle approach to developing children's awareness of language structures and encouraging the crafting of the language they use makes heavy demands on the teacher. It requires the teacher to have a very firm grasp of the necessary linguistic understandings so that they can spot the child's need as it arises and can also devise strategies to help the child meet the particular challenge.

Standard and non-standard English

The way language is talked about and explored in the classroom is very important. The documents clearly state that no one language is 'superior' to any other. The appropriateness of different kinds of English in different situations is recognized in the Orders for English and all languages used by children are appreciated as language resources. Further, teaching should bring out the social significance of language – its social uses and effects, how it varies, and its importance in relation to a person's sense of social identity (paras 6.17, 6.18).

However, given that the National Curriculum requires that the nature and function of Standard English be explicitly taught in the top years of the primary school (para 4.38) contradictions may emerge between the policy of respect for all languages and the superior social status of Standard English. It may well prove difficult to sustain the rhetoric of parity, despite the fact that the main focus is to be upon the differences between the spoken and the written word and not between Standard and non-Standard spoken English.

The Cox Report acknowledges the difficulty in 'standing back' particularly with relation to Standard and non-Standard English caused by the emotive nature of the issue. Cox suggests (para 6.21) it is usually easier to:

- give examples from local varieties of English (rather than ones which are more distant geographically, historically, socially)
- talk about language (rather than write about it)
- give examples of individual words which distinguish dialects and style, (rather than to give examples of pronunciation, grammar or textual organization)
- give relevant, but isolated examples (rather than to give more systematic, sustained analysis)

In this way discussion is related to the language which the children use and experience for themselves. It can therefore be discussed in the context of appropriateness for the communicative functions it serves rather than as an abstract exercise concerned with accuracy.

In distinguishing Standard and non-Standard English, the most common differences are in vocabulary, and also in particular constructions which are used by some children, and adults, such as:

regularization of subject–verb agreement
    I goes, he goes, they goes; I was, you was, we was
regularization of verb tenses
    I goed, I wented, I knowed, I tooked
use of subject–object pronouns
    myself, herself, hisself
use of -ly with adverbs
    he go quick

Whilst such knowledge could be useful in appraising children's written work, it is not intended that it should be used as a basis for 'correcting' children's informal oral English. It is, therefore, very important to clarify the separate contexts for oral or written activities, so that the appropriateness of different kinds of language can be judged. Teachers need to monitor the range of opportunities provided for children to explore alternative varieties of English.

The much greater emphasis on discussion – discussion about discussions, discussion about reading, about books and discussion about writing – places a serious burden on the classroom teacher. The great variety of purposes, audiences, genres and styles (identified above) which children are expected to experience and have modelled by a teacher only adds to this burden. Hence the need for rigorous monitoring of all such classroom provision becomes increasingly urgent.

(ii) Appraisal and feedback

Children spend a great deal of time writing in the classroom. An important aspect of that writing is how it is received by the audience for whom it was intended. Informally, this can operate through the way other children in the same class, or other classes, respond to the writing. But there is also the formal appraisal by the teacher which is important to the child. The child very quickly picks up the real agenda for writing through the teacher's marking policy. It is this, which, as we saw at the beginning of this chapter, affects children's attitudes and perceptions of the nature and function of writing.

It is important to appraise what is written, how it is written, why it was written and for whom it was written. With so many variables there have been very many suggestions for alternative ways of how to appraise children's writing, e.g. from the analytic to the impressionistic, from the quantitative to the qualitative. There are also differences in the emphasis which can be accorded specific features, e.g. the clarity with which the writer has constructed and conveyed meaning, and above all its appropriateness in terms of purpose and audience.

Coupe (in Harris and Wilkinson, 1986) notes that teachers' response to children's writing was predominantly to make a general evaluatory comment. In fact 25 per cent of the sample put 'Well done' or something similar. The second most frequent category was a comment which referred to content. Punctuation, spelling and structure were a low third. Very rarely was there any advice given: where this did happen it was more likely to relate to paragraphing, grammar, presentation and length. Children did not therefore receive much help in 'storying'.

Crystal (1981) identified a range of 'pre-language' factors that teachers noted in their response, such as lack of confidence, erratic attention, no imagination, poor memory. The majority of reactions focused on what was not there, i.e. problems 'by omission'. These included limited expression/vocabulary, no development of ideas, little use of adjectives. (Adjectives seem to be a favourite linguistic feature upon which to comment: an adjective is a readily identifiable part of speech to which exercises are frequently addressed.)

The issues identified by teachers can be categorized in the following way:

- psycho-social : attention, confidence, imagination
- omissions : limited vocabulary, undeveloped ideas
- usage : unable to communicate ideas effectively
- structural : unable to adopt appropriate forms

Crystal suggests that the nature of an 'error' must first be discovered: whether it is consistent or inconsistent, frequent or infrequent. After all we can easily make 'careless' mistakes if we are tired or haven't read through and edited the work before handing it in. Secondly, it must be examined as to how serious the 'error' is in terms of how badly it affects the communicative purpose of the piece of writing: whether it is a possible, permissible or impossible alternative. For example, 'punctuation' could be spelt phonetically as pung-chew-asian, even punk-jew-aishun, but not pontuicun.

Thirdly, an 'error' should be seen in the light of how important it is: whether it alters the intended meaning and how pertinent it is to the general coherence of the piece. Fourthly, an 'error' may be due to a confusion between the use of language in a spoken as distinct from a written mode, or be due to a failure to adopt a conventionally appropriate register or style.

The use of language in informal oral conversation may be considered inadmissible in formal written language; for example, linguistically incomplete sentences, ambiguous use of pronouns, considerable redundancy and repetition, filler phrases and tags like 'you know'. In such situations it is the demands being made upon the writer which have been mistaken. Finally, the 'error' may be due to illegible presentation rather than the quality of the composition.

It is important that both teachers and children know what are the criteria for marking. Because there are so many different features it would seem sensible to vary the emphasis, so it is particularly important that children are told/decide on what they are expected to focus for this specific piece of work. In this way they know what they are trying to improve and what they are learning. Hence, the overall purpose must be made clear and the expected means of achieving that purpose should be identified.

Further, Crystal suggests that the process of appraising work should include:

- identifying the specific problem
- describing its features in a coherent way
- judging the typicality of the difficulty
- comparing children to establish norms
- selecting teaching points for future action

The debate concerning what and how to assess written work already has a long history. The two ends of a possible spectrum are represented by Hartog and Rhodes (1935, in Wilkinson *et al.*, 1980) who advocated a strictly analytic and quantitative approach in an attempt to set objective procedures, and at the other extreme, Wiseman (1949, in Wilkinson *et al.*, 1980) who advocated an impressionistic approach which might catch the 'feel' of the writing from a qualitative stand point.

Further alternatives range between those who emphasize the linguistic components, such as length and variability of sentence structure, range of adjectives, etc. (T-unit method), a cognitive emphasis (Moffett, 1968), or the complex model of appraisal put forward by Wilkinson (1980) in the Crediton project, which included criteria in five categories (cognitive, linguistic, affective, moral, stylistic).

Whilst none of these methods has any ultimate claim to being 'better' or 'worse' than any other, it could well be that each has particular advantages for teachers to draw upon to help them to focus on a wide range of different aspects, on different occasions, for different children, in order to help them diagnose strengths and difficulties and thus devise strategies for future development.

The problem is not merely of what to monitor, or how, but also when to intervene and in what way. One of the difficulties that teachers have in trying to help children become writers is that they are not usually writers themselves. They may also find it difficult to analyse a story and pinpoint what exactly makes it good or bad. It is even more difficult to be able to suggest what might make it better. Further, the 'creative process' has become so wrapped in mystique and writing is regarded as so 'personal' an affair – and the writer as so potentially vulnerable – that teachers may well respond to their task in an inhibited way.

A practice which has developed in recent years (and one promoted in the National Curriculum) is that of involving the children in their own self-appraisal, often through the use of response partners. The results of this kind of collaboration have not, as yet, been fully researched. Bereiter and Scardamalia (1987), in a study of 10-year-olds, did uncover some of the ways in which partnered children were using a drafting and re-drafting procedure. For example, many of them, when making preliminary notes, still wrote in full sentences. Having once committed their ideas to paper, most were reluctant to make any but minor changes. The majority of these changes (42 per cent) were further elaborations (gory details, colourful embellishments), 29 per cent were remedying omissions found in the original text (where perhaps the child's mind had raced ahead of their hand), 15 per cent were additions of new information to the story-line. Re-ordering, dividing, and combining sentences made up 5 per cent each.

This data demonstrates that for these children at least, re-drafting was mostly 'content generation' not 'conceptual re-organization': only the three least-used categories indicate any awareness of refining how the content was expressed.

In helping to encourage children to become response partners, Newkirk and Atwell (1988) found that children, initially, were 'proto-critical' and focused on the handwriting, spelling and quality of the picture rather than the content of the written message. Later, children commented on the experience/adventure depicted (what was written) and only very rarely on the text itself (how it was written).

Clearly, if the peer response approach is to be used, there must first be time spent on helping children to know what to look out for and what to consider in their comments. However, it is important to develop such skills if we share the belief that 'a child without the ability to make evaluative judgements [about the written word] is still only partially literate' (Olson, 1984).

In contrast to how children react in a re-drafting situation, Kress (1982) found that teachers focused on different features. The main forms of intervention were:

- changing topic (semantic) connectedness to explicit (syntactic) connectedness,
- changing the cognitive model from primal causes (the hero/ child) to specific and immediate logical causes,
- changing form of speech conventions to written conventions indicating awareness of reader's need,
- changing from a collection of statements to a unified cohesive whole.

Each of these moves could help to re-focus the child on the issue of how to express ideas (structural) rather than what ideas to express (content). Such moves can be seen to help in developing children as writers rather than assessing their current performance.

The practice of weekly story-writing is changing, as researchers question the benefit there might be to the child by churning out yet another 'story' every week on the assumption that practice will make perfect. After all, how many adults could turn out a 'creative' story each week? The work of Donald Graves and others in America, and the transfer and development of their work in this country, has led many to believe that a more considered approach to the process of becoming a writer – through conferencing – could be more profitable. In this interactive social context, the emphasis is on exploring the writing, its content and impact, on communicating a message to readers. The form of monitoring is less reactive (a comment on what the child has achieved) and more pro-active (looking forward to where the child might go next). It is a monitoring process which is both diagnostic and developmental.

Such an approach needs plenty of discussion at the beginning (stimulation), middle (drafting) and end (response and conferencing) and can be a vital component in forwarding the writing process. Despite encouragement for such social support structures, writing remains, in most instances, a solitary and individual pursuit. A sense of audience and the sure knowledge of a supportive partner (whether adult or child) can help to make writing a more meaningful and worthwhile experience for many young writers, and one from which they actually learn something.

ACTIVITY

Self-evaluation Checklist

Begin to devise a set of criteria (with the children) which would encourage them to evaluate themselves, and which would also serve as a means by which you can evaluate their progress.

Remember, the process begins long before the writing begins so, include the
   pre-language attitudes,
   knowledge of audience and purpose,
   skills in composition as well at the presentation stages.

FURTHER READING

The following books provide further detail on diagnostic evaluation:

Crystal, D. (1976) *Child Language, Learning and Linguistics*. London: Edward Arnold.

Crystal, D. (1981) *Directions in Applied Linguistics*. New York, Academic Press.

Harris, J. and Wilkinson, J. (1986) *Reading Children's Writing: A Linguistic View*. London: Allen & Unwin.

Kress, G. (1982) *Learning to Write*. London: Routledge & Kegan Paul.

Wilkinson, A. *et al.* (1980) *Assessing Language Development*. Oxford: Oxford University Press.

Bibliography

Adelman, C. (ed.) (1981) *Uttering and Muttering*. London: Grant McIntyre.

Aitkin, J. (1982) *The Way to Write for Children*. London: Elm Tree Books.

Alderson, B. (1973) *Looking at Picture Books*. Boscards Press.

Allington, R.L. (1983) 'Fluency: the neglected goal'. *The Reading Teacher*, 36(6).

Alton, J. and Taylor, J. (1987) *Handwriting: Theory, Research, Practice*. London: Croom Helm.

Anderson, C. (ed.) (1988) *Reading: The abc and Beyond*. Basingstoke: Macmillan (for UKRA).

Anderson, E. (1987) 'A critical look at the advice given to parents helping their children to read.' In Smith, P. (ed.), *Parents and Teachers Together*. Basingstoke: Macmillan (for UKRA).

Anderson, J. (1983) 'The writer, the reader and the text.' In Gillham, B. (ed.), *Reading Through the Curriculum*. London: Heinemann.

Andrews, R. (1989) *Narrative and Argument*. Milton Keynes: Open University Press.

Applebee, A.N. (1978) *The Child's Concept of Story*. Chicago: University of Chicago Press.

Arnold, H. (1982) *Listening to Children Read*. Sevenoaks: Hodder & Stoughton.

Assessment of Performance Unit (APU) (1982) *Language Performance in Schools: Primary Survey Report no. 2*. London: HMSO.

Assessment of Performance Unit (1988) *Language Performance in Schools*. London: HMSO.

Avann, P. (ed.) (1985) *Teaching Information Skills in the Primary School*. London: Edward Arnold.

Bakhtin, M.M. (1986) *Speech Genres and Other Late Essays*. Austin, TX: Austin University Press.

Bald, J. (1987) 'Review of research into parental involvement in reading.'

In Smith, P. (ed.), *Parents and Teachers Together*. Basingstoke: Macmillan (for UKRA).

Barnes, D., Britton, J. and Rosen, H. (1969) *Language, the Learner and the School*. Harmondsworth: Penguin.

Barnes, D. and Todd, F. (1977) *Communication and Learning in Small Groups*. London: Routledge and Kegan Paul.

Barret, T.C. (1968) 'Taxonomy of the cognitive and affective dimensions of reading comprehension' (unpublished), cited by Clymer, T. 'What is reading? Some current concepts'. In Melnik, A. and Merritt, J. (eds) (1972) *Reading: Today and Tomorrow*. London: University of London Press (for Open University).

Barrs, M. *et al.* (1988) *The Primary Language Record*. London: ILEA.

Beard, R. (1984) *Children's Writing in the Primary School*. Sevenoaks: Hodder & Stoughton.

Beard, R. (1987) *Developing Reading 3–13*. Sevenoaks: Hodder & Stoughton.

Beech, J.R. (1985) *Learning to Read: A Cognitive Approach to Reading*. London: Croom Helm.

Bennett, J. (1982) *Learning to Read with Picture Books*. Stroud: Thimble Press.

Bennett, N. *et al.* (1984) *The Quality of Pupil Learning Experiences*. London: Lawrence Erlbaum.

Bentley, D. (1985) *How and Why of Readability*. Reading: Centre for the Teaching of Reading.

Benton, M. and Fox, G. (1985) *Teaching Literature 9–14*. Oxford: Oxford University Press.

Benton, P. (1986) *Pupil, Teacher, Poem*. Sevenoaks: Hodder & Stoughton.

Bereiter, C. and Scardamalia, M. (1987) *The Psychology of Composition*. Hillsdale, NJ: Lawrence Erlbaum Associates.

Bettelheim, B. (1977) *The Uses of Enchantment*. Harmondsworth: Pelican.

Biemiller, A. (1970) 'The development of the use of graphic and contextual information as children learn to read'. *Reading Research Quarterly*, **6**.

Bissex, G. (1980) *GNYS AT WORK*. Cambridge, MA: Harvard University Press.

Bligh, D. (1986) *Teach Thinking by Discussion*. Slough: NFER-Nelson.

Blishen, E. (ed.) (1975) *The Thorny Paradise: Writers on Writing for Children*. Harmondsworth: Kestrel.

Bloom, W. (1986) *Partnership with Parents in Children's Reading*. Sevenoaks: Hodder & Stoughton.

Bolton, B. (1979) *People Skills*. Englewood Cliffs, NJ: Prentice-Hall.

Bolton, G. (1979) *Towards a Theory of Drama in Education*. London: Longman.

Bradley, L. and Bryant, P. (1988) *Rhyme and Reason in Reading and Spelling*. Ann Arbor: University of Michigan Press.

Branston, P. and Provis, M. (1986) *Children and Parents Enjoying Reading*. Sevenoaks: Hodder & Stoughton

Britton, J. et al. (1975) *The Development of Learning Abilities (11–18)*. Basingstoke: Macmillan Education (for Schools Council).

Brodzinsky, D.M. (1977) 'Children's comprehension and appreciation of verbal jokes.' *Child Development*, **48**.

Brooks, G. (1989) 'The value and purpose of APU oracy assessment: a reply to Maybin.' *English in Education*, **23**(2).

Brown, G. (1978) *Lecturing and Explaining*. London: Methuen.

Brown, G. and Edmundson, R. (1984) 'Effective questioning.' In Wragg, E.C. (ed.) *Classroom Teaching Skills*. London: Croom Helm.

Brown, G. and Yule, G. (1983) *Discourse Analysis*. Cambridge: Cambridge University Press.

Brown, G. and Yule, G. (1983) *Teaching the Spoken Language*. Cambridge: Cambridge University Press.

Bruner, J.S. (1975) 'From communication to language.' *Cognition*, 3, 255–87.

Bruner, J.S. (1983) *Child Talk*. London: Fontana.

Bruner, J.S. (1986) *Actual Minds, Possible Worlds*. Cambridge, MA: Harvard University Press.

Bryant, P. and Bradley, L. (1985) *Children's Reading Problems*. Oxford: Basil Blackwell.

Bull, N.J. (1969) *Moral Judgement from Childhood to Adolescence*. London: Routledge & Kegan Paul.

Burgess, A. (1975) *English Maid Plane*. London: Fontana.

Butler, D. (1980) *Babies Need Books*. Harmondsworth: Penguin.

Butler, D. (1986) *Five to Eight*. London: The Bodley Head.

CACE (1967) *Children and Their Primary Schools* (Plowden Report). London: HMSO.

Cairny, T.H. (1990) *Teaching Reading Comprehension*. Milton Keynes: Open University Press.

Calkins, L. (1981) *The Art of Teaching Writing*. London: Routledge & Kegan Paul.

Cass, J. (1984) *Literature and the Young Child* (2nd edn). London: Longman.

Chall, J.S. (1967) *Learning to Read: The Great Debate*. New York: McGraw-Hill.

Chall, J.S. (1983) *Stages of Reading Development*. New York: McGraw-Hill.

Chambers, A. (1973) *Introducing Books to Children*. London: Heinemann.

Chambers, A. (1985) *Booktalk*. London: The Bodley Head.

Chambers, P. (1987) *Bright Ideas Teacher Handbook: Reading*. Leamington Spa: Scholastic.

Chapman, A. and Foot, H.C. (eds) (1977) *It's a Funny Thing, Humour*. Oxford: Pergamon Press.

Chapman, L.J. (ed.)(1981) *The Reader and the Text*. London: Heinemann (for UKRA).

Chapman, L.J. (1983) *Reading Development and Cohesion*. London: Heinemann.

Chapman, L.J. (1987) *Reading from 5–11 Years*. Milton Keynes: Open University Press.

Chilver, P. and Gould, G. (1982) *Learning and Language in the Classroom*. Oxford: Pergamon Press.

Clark, E.V. (1978) 'Awareness of language: some evidence from what children say and do.' In Sinclair, A. *et al.* (eds) *The Child's Conception of Language*. Berlin: Springer-Verlag.

Clark, M.M. (1976) *Young Fluent Readers*. London: Heinemann.

Clark, M.M. (1988) *New Directions in the Study of Reading*. Basingstoke: Falmer Press.

Clarricoates, K. (1981) 'The experience of patriarchal schooling.' *Interchange*, 12, 185–205.

Clay, M. (1975) *What Did I Write?* Auckland: Heinemann.

Clay, M. (1979) *Reading: The Patterning of Complex Behaviour*. London: Heinemann.

Colby Poindexter, J. (1967) *Writing, Illustrating and Editing Children's Books*. New York: Hastings House.

Colwell, E. (1980) *Story-telling*. London: The Bodley Head.

Cook, E. (1976) *The Ordinary and the Fabulous: Myths, Legends, Fairy Tales* (2nd edn). Cambridge: Cambridge University Press.

Corcoran, B. and Evans, E. (1989) *Readers, Texts, Teachers*. Milton Keynes: Open University Press.

Cowie, H. (ed.) (1984) *The Development of Children's Imaginative Writing*. London: Croom Helm.

Croll, P. and Moses, D. (1985) *One in Five*. London: Routledge and Kegan Paul.

Crystal, D. (1976) *Child Language, Learning and Linguistics*. London: Edward Arnold.

Crystal, D. (1981) *Directions in Applied Linguistics*. New York: Academic Press.

Crystal, D. (1988) *The English Language*. Harmondsworth: Penguin.

Cyran, E.W. (1990) *A Linguistic Analysis of Children's Language*. Lublin: Czytelnik Press.

Dale, N. (1983) *On the Teaching of English Reading*. London: Dent.

D'Arcy, P. (1973) *Reading for Meaning*, Vol. 2. London: Hutchinson (for Schools Council).

Davies, A. (ed.) (1982) *Language and Learning in Home and School*. London: Heinemann (for SCRE).

Davies, F. and Greene, T. (1984) *Reading for Learning in the Sciences*. Edinburgh: Oliver & Boyd (for Schools Council).

de Bono, E. (1976) *Teaching Thinking*. Harmondsworth: Penguin.

DES (1975) *A Language for Life* (Bullock Report). London: HMSO.

DES (1978) *Primary Education in England: a Survey by HMI*. London: HMSO.

DES (1982) *Education 5–9*. London: HMSO.

DES (1989) *English Working Party Report* (Cox Report). London: HMSO.
Dickson, W.P. (1981) *Children's Oral Communicative Skills*. New York: Academic Press.
Dixon, J. (1975) *Growth Through English* (3rd edn). Oxford: Oxford University Press.
Dixon, J. and Stratta, L. (1986) *Writing Narrative and Beyond*. Sheffield: National Association for Teachers of English.
Donaldson, M. (1978) *Children's Minds*. London: Fontana.
Donaldson, M. (1989) *Sense and Sensibility*, Occasional Paper no. 3. Reading: Reading and Language Centre, University of Reading.
Donaldson, M. *et al.* (eds) (1983) *Early Childhood Development and Education*. Oxford: Oxford University Press.
Doughty, P. (1971) *Language in Use*. London: London University Press (for Schools Council).
Dougill, P. (ed.) (1990) *Developing English*. Buckingham: Open University Press.
Dougill, P. and Knott, R. (1988) *The Primary Language Book*. Milton Keynes: Open University Press.
Durkin, D. (1978) 'What classroom observations reveal about reading comprehension.' *Reading Research Quarterly*, **14**(1), 481–533.
Ede, J. and Williamson, J. (1980) *Talking, Listening and Learning*. London: Longman.
Edwards, A.D. and Westgate, D.P.G. (1987) *Investigating Classroom Talk*. Basingstoke: Falmer Press.
Edwards, D. and Mercer, N. (1987) *Common Knowledge*. Milton Keynes: Open University Press.
Edwards, V. (1983) *Language in Multicultural Classrooms*. London: Batsford Academic.
Evans, T. (1984) *Drama in English Teaching*. London: Croom Helm.
Ferreiro, E. and Teberosky, A. (1983) *Literacy before Schooling*. London: Heinemann.
Flanders, N. (1970) *Analysing Teacher Behaviour*. Reading, MA: Addison-Wesley.
Flood, J. (ed.) (1984) *Promoting Reading Comprehension*. Newark, DE: International Reading Association.
Fontana, D. (1981) *Psychology for Teachers*. Basingstoke: Macmillan (for The British Psychological Society).
Fox, G. (1976) *Writers, Critics, Children*. London: Heinemann.
Freeborn, D. (1986) *Varieties in English*. Basingstoke: Macmillan.
Freedle, R.O. (ed.) (1977) *Multidisciplinary Perspectives in Discourse Comprehension*. Norwood, NJ: Ablex.
French, J. and French, P. (1986) 'Gender imbalances in the primary classroom'. *Educational Review*, **22**.
French, P. and MacLure, M. (1983) 'Teachers' questions, pupils' answers.' In Stubbs, M. and Hillier, H. (eds) *Readings on Language, Schools and Classrooms*. London: Methuen.
Friedman, M.I. and Rowls, M.D. (1980) *Teaching Reading and Thinking Skills*. New York: Longman.

Frith, U. (1980) *Cognitive Processes in Spelling.* London: Academic Press.

Fry, D. (1985) *Children Talking about Books.* Milton Keynes: Open University Press.

Galton, M. (1986) 'Attitudes and the infant teacher.' *Child Education* (June).

Galton, M., Simon, B. and Croll, P. (1980) *Inside the Primary Classroom.* London: Routledge & Kegan Paul.

Garton, A. and Pratt, C. (1989) *Learning to Be Literate.* Oxford: Basil Blackwell.

Garvie, E. (1990) *Story as Vehicle.* Philadelphia: Multilingual Matters.

Gentry, J. (1987) *Spel is a Four Letter Word.* Leamington Spa: Scholastic.

Gibson, E.J. and Levin, H. (1975) *The Psychology of Reading.* Cambridge, MA: MIT Press.

Goelman, H. *et al.* (1984) *Awakening to Literacy.* London: Heinemann.

Goodacre, E. (1977) *Reading After 10,* Part 2. London: BBC Publications.

Goodman, K. (1965) 'A linguistic study of cues and miscues in reading.' *Elementary English*, **42**, 639–43.

Goodman, K. and Flemming, J. (eds) (1969) *Psycholinguistics and the Teaching of Reading.* Newark, DE: International Reading Association.

Goodman, Y. (1985) 'Kidwatching: observing children in the classroom.' In Jagger, A. and Smith-Burke, T. (eds) *Observing the Language Learner.* Newark, DE: International Reading Association.

Graves, D. (1983) *Writing: Teachers and Children at Work.* London: Heinemann.

Grugeon, E. and Waldon, P. (eds) (1978) *Literature and Learning.* London: Ward Lock Educational.

Hadley, E. (1985) *English in the Middle Years.* London: Edward Arnold.

Hall, N. (1987) *The Emergence of Literacy.* Sevenoaks: Hodder & Stoughton.

Hall, N. (1989) *Writing with Reason.* Sevenoaks: Hodder & Stoughton.

Hamilton, D. and Griffiths, A. (1984) *Parents, Teacher, Child.* London: Methuen.

Hannon, P. and Jackson, A. (1987) *Belfield Reading Project Report.* London: National Children's Bureau.

Harding, M. (1990) 'The reading–writing link.' MA, Oxford Polytechnic.

Hardy, B. (1968) 'Narrative as a primary act of mind.' In Meek, M. *et al.* (1977) *The Cool Web.* London: The Bodley Head.

Harpin, W. (1976) *The Second 'R': Writing Development in Junior School.* London: Allen & Unwin.

Harri-Augstein, S. *et al.* (1982) *Reading to Learn.* London: Methuen.

Harris, J. and Wilkinson, J. (1986) *Reading Children's Writing.* London: Allen & Unwin.

Harrison, C. (1980) *Readability in the Classroom.* Cambridge: Cambridge University Press.

Hart, N.W.M., Walker, R.F. and Gray, B. (1977) *The Language of Children.* Brisbane: Addison-Wesley.

Hawkins, E. (1984) *Awareness of Language*. Cambridge: Cambridge University Press.

Hayhoe, M. and Parker, S. (1984) *Working with Fiction*. London: Edward Arnold.

Heath, S.B. (1982) 'Questioning at home and at school.' In Spindler, G. (ed.) *Doing Ethnography: Educational Anthropology in Action*. New York: Holt, Rinehart & Winston.

Heath, S.B. (1982) 'What no bedtime story means.' *Language and Society*, **2**.

Heath, S.B. (1983) *Ways with Words*. Cambridge: Cambridge University Press.

Heathcote, D. (1980) *Drama as Context*. Sheffield: National Association for Teachers of English.

Heather, P. (1984) *A Study of Use of Books and Libraries*. Occasional paper no. 11. Sheffield: Centre for Research in User Studies.

Heeks, P. (1981) *Choosing and Using Books in the First School*. London: Macmillan.

Hewison, J. and Tizard, J. (1980) 'Parental involvement and reading attainment.' *British Journal of Educational Psychology*, **50**, 209–15

Hewison, J. and Tizard, J. (1982) 'Parental involvement in teaching reading.' *Remedial Education*, **14**(4).

Hodgson, J. and Pryle, D. (1985) *A Survey of Styles of Teaching Reading*. Shropshire Local Education Authority.

Hoffman, E. (1989) *Lost in Translation*. London: Heinemann.

Holdaway, D. (1979) *The Foundations of Literacy*. Sydney: Ashton Scholastic.

Houlton, D. (1985) *All Our Languages*. London: Edward Arnold.

Huck, C.S. *et al.* (1987) *Children's Literature in the Elementary School* (4th edn). New York: Holt, Rinehart & Winston.

Huey, E.B. (1908) *The Psychology and Pedagogy of Reading*. New York: Macmillan.

Hunt, K.W. (1970) *Syntactic Maturity in School Children and Adults*. Monographs of the Society for Research in Child Development, **35**(1).

Hymes, D. (1972) 'On communicative competence.' In Pride, J.B. and Holmes, J. (eds) *Sociolinguistics*. Harmondsworth: Penguin.

Jackson, P.W. (1968) *Life in Classrooms*. New York: Holt, Rinehart & Winston.

Jagger, A. and Smith-Burke, M.T. (eds) (1985) *Observing the Language Learner*. Newark, DE: International Reading Association.

Jarman, C. (1979) *The Development of Handwriting Skills*. Oxford: Basil Blackwell.

Jarman, C. (1989) *Teaching the Left-Hander*. Oxford: Basil Blackwell.

Johnson, K. and Morrow, K. (eds) (1981) *Communication in the Classroom*. London: Longman.

Joos, M. (1962) *The Five Clocks*. The Hague: Mouton.

Keen, J. (1978) *Teaching English: A Linguistic Approach*. London: Methuen.

Kellmer-Pringle, M. (1975) *The Needs of Children*. London: Hutchinson.

Kerry, T. (1982) *Effective Questioning*. London: Macmillan.
Kerry, T. and Eggleston, J. (1988) *Topic Work in the Primary School*. London: Routledge & Kegan Paul.
Kinneavy, J.L. (1971) *A Theory of Discourse*. Englewood Cliffs, NJ: Prentice-Hall.
Klein, G. (1985) *Reading into Racism*. London: Hutchinson.
Kogan, N. (1976) *Cognitive Styles in Infancy and Early Childhood*. Hillsdale, NJ: Lawrence Erlbaum.
Kress, G. (1982) *Learning to Write*. London: Routledge & Kegan Paul.
Kroll, B.M. and Wells, C.G. (1983) *Explorations in the Development of Writing*. Chichester: John Wiley.
Lamb, P. (1967) *Linguistics in Proper Perspective*. Columbus, OH: Merrill.
Leech, G.N. (1966) *English in Advertising: A Linguistic Study*. London: Longman.
Lehr, S. (1987) 'The child's sense of theme as a response to literature.' In Anderson, C. (ed.) *Reading: The a b c and Beyond*. Basingstoke: Macmillan (for UKRA).
Lindfors, J.W. (1980) *Children's Language and Learning*. London: Prentice-Hall.
Lunzer, E. and Gardner, K. (1984) *Learning from the Written Word*. Edinburgh: Oliver & Boyd.
Luria, A.R. (1976) *Cognitive Development: Its Cultural and Social Functions*. Cambridge, MA: Harvard University Press.
McGhee, P. and Chapman, A. (eds) (1980) *Children's Humour*. Chichester: Wiley.
McKenzie, M. (1979) *Learning to Read and Reading*. London: ILEA.
MacLure, M. and Hargreaves, M. (1986) *Speaking and Listening: Assessment at 11*. Windsor: NFER-Nelson.
MacLure, M. *et al.* (1988) *Oracy Matters*. Milton Keynes: Open University Press.
McNaughton, S. (1987) *Being Skilled*. London: Methuen.
Mandler, J.M. and Johnson, N.S. (1977) 'Remembrance of things parsed.' *Cognitive Psychology*, **9**, 111–51.
Marland, M. (ed.) (1981) *Information Skills in the Secondary Curriculum*. Schools Council Curriculum Bulletin 9. London: Methuen.
Marsh, G. (1988) *Teaching Through Poetry*. Sevenoaks: Hodder & Stoughton.
Martin, J.R. and Rothery, J. (1986) 'Exploring and explaining: factual writing in the primary school.' Paper presented at the ARA Conference, Perth.
Maslow, A.H. (1954) *Motivation and Personality*. New York: Harper & Row.
Mason, B. (1989) 'It's in our CoRT now.' *Support for Learning*, **4**(3), 175–180.
Maybin, J. (1988) 'A critical review of the DES Assessment and Performance Unit's Oracy Surveys.' *English in Education*, **22**(1).

Meek, M. (1982) *Learning to Read*. London: The Bodley Head.
Meek, M. (1988) *How Texts Teach What Readers Learn*. Stroud: Thimble Press.
Meek, M. *et al.* (eds) (1977) *The Cool Web*. London: The Bodley Head.
Mehan, H. (1974) 'Accomplishing classroom lessons.' In Cicourel, A. *et al.* (eds) *Language Use and School Performance*. New York: Academic Press.
Melnik, A. and Merritt, J. (eds) (1972) *Reading: Today and Tomorrow*. London: University of London Press (for Open University).
Merritt, J.E. (1975) 'Intermediate skills: reading seven to eleven.' *Education 3–13*.
Miller, J. (1983) *Many Voices*. London: Routledge.
Mitchell, D.C. (1982) *The Process of Reading*. Chichester: John Wiley.
Mitchell, I. (1983) 'A procedure for assessing richness of story-telling.' *Journal of Reading*, **26**(5).
Mittens, B. (1990) *Language Awareness for Teachers*. Buckingham: Open University Press.
Moffett, J. (1968) *Teaching the Universe of Discourse*. Boston: Houghton Mifflin.
Montgomery, P. and Robinson, R. (1989) 'The development of oral story-telling.' *English in Education*.
Moon, C. (ed.) (1985) *Practical Ways to Teach Reading*. London: Ward Lock Educational.
Morgan, R.T.T. (1985) 'Paired reading: origin and future.' In Topping, K. and Wolfendale, S. (eds) *Parental Involvement in Children's Reading*. London: Croom Helm.
Morgan, R.T.T. (1986) *Helping Children Read: The Paired Reading Handbook*. London: Methuen.
Morris, R. (1973) *Success and Failure in Learning to Read*. Harmondsworth: Penguin.
Neelands, J. (1984) *Making Sense of Drama*. London: Heinemann.
Neville, M. (1988) *Assessing and Teaching Language*. London: Macmillan (for Scottish Education Department).
Neville, M.H. and Pugh, A. (1982) *Towards Independent Reading*. London: Heinemann.
Newkirk, T. and Atwell, N. (1988) *Understanding Writing: Ways of Observing, Learning and Teaching*. Portsmouth, NH: Heinemann.
Newman, J. (1984) *The Craft of Children's Writing*. Toronto: Scholastic.
Nicholls, J. *et al.* (1989) *Beginning Writing*. Milton Keynes: Open University Press.
Norton, D. (1983) *Through the Eyes of the Child*. Columbus: Merrill.
Olson, D.R. (1984) 'See! Jumping. Some oral language antecedents.' In Goelman, H., Oberg, A.A. and Smith, F. (eds) *Awakening to Literacy*. Victoria, British Columbia: University of Victoria.
Open University P534 (1984) *Every Child's Language*. Milton Keynes: Open University Press.
Pasternicki, J.G. (1986) 'Teaching handwriting: the resolution of an issue.' *Support of Learning*, **1**(1), 37–41.

Pearson, H. (1987) *Children Becoming Readers.* Basingstoke: Macmillan.

Perera, K. (1984) *Children's Writing and Reading.* Oxford: Basil Blackwell.

Perera, K. (1987) *Understanding Language.* Warwick: National Association for Advisers of English.

Peters, M.L. (1967) *Spelling: Caught or Taught?* (2nd edn 1975) London: Routledge & Kegan Paul.

Phillips, T. (1985) 'Beyond lip-service.' In Wells, G. and Nicholls, J. (eds), *Language and Learning: An Interactional Perspective.* Basingstoke: Falmer Press.

Phillips, T. (1988) 'On a related matter.' In MacLure, M. *et al.*, *Oracy Matters.* Milton Keynes: Open University Press.

Pugh, A.K. (1978) *Silent Reading.* London: Heinemann.

Pugh, A.K., Lee, V.J. and Swann, J. (1980) *Language and Language Use.* London: Heinemann (for Open University).

Raban, B. (ed.) (1985) *Practical Ways to Teach Writing.* London: Ward Lock.

Radebaugh, M.R. (1985) 'Children's perception of their spelling strategies.' *Reading Teacher* **38**(6).

Read, C. (1986) *Children's Creative Spelling.* London: Routledge & Kegan Paul.

Richards, J. (1979) *Classroom Language: What Sort?* London: Allen & Unwin.

Robinson, E.J. and Robinson, W.P. (1977) 'Development in the understanding of causes of success and failure in communication.' *Cognition* **5**, 363–78.

Robinson, H.A. (1977) 'Comprehension: an elusive concept.' In Gilliland, H. (ed.), *Reading: Research and Classroom Practice.* London: Ward Lock.

Robinson, W.P. (ed.) (1981) *Communication in Development.* New York: Academic Press.

Romaine, S. (1984) *The Language of Children and Adolescents.* Oxford: Basil Blackwell.

Root, B. (ed.) (1986) *Resources for Reading.* Basingstoke: Macmillan.

Rosen, C. and Rosen, H. (1973) *The Language of Primary School Children.* Harmondsworth: Penguin.

Rosen, H. (1982) *The Language Monitors.* London: London University Press.

Rosen, H. (1988) 'Stories of stories: footnotes on sly gossipy practices.' In Lightfoot, M. and Martin, N. (eds), *The Word for Teaching Is Learning.* London: Heinemann.

Rumelhart, D.E. (1975) 'Notes on a scheme for stories.' In Bobrow, D.G. and Collins, A.M. (eds), *Representation and Understanding.* New York: Academic Press.

Rumelhart, D.E. (1977) 'Toward an interactive model of reality.' In Dornic, S. (ed.), *Attention and Performance.* New York: Academic Press.

Rye, J. (1982) *Cloze Procedure and Teaching of Reading*. London: Heinemann.

Samuels, S.J. (1978) *What Research Has to Say about Reading Instruction*. Newark, DE: International Reading Association.

Sartre, J.P. (1964) *Words*. Harmondsworth: Penguin.

Sassoon, R. (1983) *A Practical Guide to Children's Handwriting*. London: Thames and Hudson.

Saunders, M. (1982) *Multicultural Teaching*. London: McGraw-Hill.

Schultz, T.R. and Robillard, A. (1980) 'Linguistic humour.' In McGhee, P. and Chapman, A. (eds), *Children's Humour*. Chichester: Wiley.

Scott, K. (1989) 'What children think about talk.' *TALK* (NOP journal) 2.

Shanahan, T. and Lomax, R.G. (1986) 'An analysis and comparison of theoretical models of the reading–writing relationship.' *Journal of Educational Psychology*, **78**(2), 116–123.

Sharon, S. (1980) 'Co-operative learning in small groups.' *Review of Educational Research*, **50**(2), 241–71.

Shaughnessy, M.P. (1977) *Errors and Expectations*. New York: Oxford University Press.

Smith, F. (1975) *Comprehension and Learning*. London: Holt, Rinehart & Winston.

Smith, F. (1978) *Reading*. Cambridge: Cambridge University Press.

Smith, J. and Alcock, A. (1990) *Revisiting Literacy*. Milton Keynes: Open University Press.

Smith, P. (ed.) (1987) *Parents and Teachers Together*. Basingstoke: Macmillan (for UKRA).

Snow, C. (1983) 'Literacy and language: relationships during pre-school years.' *Harvard Educational Review*, **55**, 165–189.

Southgate, V. *et al.* (1981) *Extending Beginning Reading*. London: Heinemann (for Schools Council).

Spender, D. and Sarah, E. (eds) (1980) *Learning to Lose*. London: Women's Press.

Start, K.B. and Wells, B.K. (1972) *The Trend of Reading Standards*. Slough: NFER.

Stefano, J.S., Pepinsky, H.B. and Sanders, T.S. (1982) 'Discourse rules for learning literacy.' In Wilkinson, L.C. (ed.), *Communicating in the Classroom*. New York: Academic Press.

Stephens, P. and Valentine, J. (1986) 'Assessing principal non-verbal communication.' *Education Research Quarterly*, **10**(3).

Stewart-Dore, N. (1986) *Writing and Reading to Learn*. NSW, Australia: Primary English Teaching Association.

Stinton, J. (ed.) (1979) *Racism and Sexism in Children's Books*. London: Writers and Readers Cooperative.

Strang, R. (1972) 'Observations in the classroom' and 'Informal reading inventories.' In Melnik, A. and Merritt, J. (eds), *The Reading Curriculum*. London: University of London Press (for Open University).

Stubbs, M. (1980) *Language and Literacy: The Sociolinguistics of Reading and Writing*. London: Routledge & Kegan Paul.

Stubbs, M. (1986) *Educational Linguistics*. Oxford: Basil Blackwell.
Stubbs, M. and Hillier, H. (eds) (1983) *Readings on Language and Class-rooms*. London: Methuen.
Stubbs, M. and Robinson, B. (1979) *Observing Language* (PE 232, Bk.2). Milton Keynes: Open University Press.
Sutton, C. (ed.) (1983) *Communicating in the Classroom*. London: Hodder & Stoughton.
Swann, J. and Graddol, D. (1989) 'Gender inequalities in classroom talk.' *Gnosis*, **14**, 31–38.
Swing, S.R. and Patterson, P.L. (1982) 'The relationship of student ability and small group interaction to student achievement.' *American Educational Research Journal*, **19**(2), 259–74.
Tann, C.S. (1987) 'Mismatch of perceptions.' *Reading*, **21**(1) 62–70.
Tann, C.S. (ed.) (1988) *Developing Topic Work in the Primary School*. Basingstoke: Falmer Press.
Tann, C.S. (1989) 'Grouping and the integrated classroom.' In Thomas, G. and Feiler, A. (eds) *Planning for Special Needs*. Oxford: Basil Blackwell.
Tann, C.S. and Armitage, M. (1986) 'Time for talk.' *Reading*, **20**(3) 184–188.
Tannen, D. (ed.) (1982) *Spoken and Written Language*. Norwood, NJ: Ablex.
Tannen, D. (ed.) (1984) *Coherence in Spoken and Written Discourse*. Norwood, NJ: Ablex.
Temple, C.A. *et al.* (1982) *The Beginnings of Writing*. Boston: Allyn & Bacon.
Thorpe, D. (1987) 'Children choosing and reading.' In Smith, P. (ed.), *Parents and Teachers Together*. Basingstoke: Macmillan (for UKRA).
Tizard, B. and Hughes, M. (1984) *Young Children Learning*. London: Fontana.
Tizard, B., Schofield, W.N. and Hewison, J. (1982) 'Collaboration between teachers and parents in assisting children's reading.' *British Journal of Educational Psychology*, **52**.
Topping, K. and Wolfendale, S. (eds) (1985) *Parental Involvement in Children's Reading*. London: Croom Helm.
Tough, J. (1976) *Listening to Children Talking*. London: Ward Lock (for Schools Council).
Trudgill, P. (1975) *Accent, Dialect and the School*. London: Edward Arnold.
Tucker, N. (1981) *The Child and the Book*. Cambridge: Cambridge University Press.
Tuckman, B. (1965) 'Developmental sequences in small groups.' *Psychological Bulletin*, **63**(6).
Tunmer, W.E., Pratt, C. and Merriman, M.L. (1984) *Metalinguistic Awareness in Children: Theory, Research and Implication*. Berlin: Springer-Verlag.
Tunmer, W.E. and Merriman, M.L. (1984) 'The development of meta-

linguistic awareness: a conceptual overview.' In Tunmer, W.E., Pratt, C. and Merriman, M L., *ibid.*

Ur, P. (1981) *Discussions That Work.* Cambridge: Cambridge University Press.

Volosinov, V.N. (1973) *Marxism and the Theory of Language.* New York: Seminar Press.

Vygotsky, L.S. (1962) *Thought and Language.* Cambridge, MA: MIT Press.

Wade, B. (ed.) (1982) *Language Perspectives.* London: Heinemann.

Wade, B. (ed.) (1985) *'Talking to Some Purpose'.* Occasional Paper 12, Education Review.

Wade, B. (ed.) (1990) *Reading for Real.* Milton Keynes: Open University Press.

Waterhouse, P. (1983) *Managing the Learning Process.* London: McGraw-Hill.

Waterland, L. (1985) *Read with Me: An Apprenticeship Approach.* Stroud: Thimble Press.

Weaver, C. (1980) *Psycholinguistics and Reading: From Process to Practice.* Little, Brown.

Webb, B (1982) 'Student interaction and learning in small groups.' *Review of Educational Research*, **53**(3), 421–45.

Wells, G. (1981) *Learning through Interaction.* Cambridge: Cambridge University Press.

Wells, G. (1986) *Meaning Makers.* Sevenoaks: Hodder & Stoughton.

Wells, G. and Nicholls, J. (1985) *Language and Learning: An Interactional Perspective.* Lewes: Falmer Press.

Whitehead, F. (1977) *Children and Their Books.* London: Macmillan.

Whiteman, M.F. (1981) *Writing: The Nature, Development and Teaching of Written Communication.* Hillsdale, NJ: Lawrence Erlbaum.

Widlake, P. and MacLeod, F. (1984) *Raising Standards.* Coventry: Community Education Development Centre.

Wilkinson, A. (ed.) (1986) *The Writing of Writing.* Milton Keynes: Open University Press.

Wilkinson, A. *et al.* (1980) *Assessing Language Development.* Oxford: Oxford University Press.

Wilkinson, A. *et al.* (1990) *Spoken English Illuminated.* Milton Keynes: Open University Press.

Wilkinson, L.C. (ed.) (1982) *Communicating in the Classroom.* New York: Academic Press.

Willes, M. (1983) *Children into Pupils.* London: Routledge & Kegan Paul.

Williams, J. (1977) *Learning to Write or Writing to Learn.* Slough: NFER.

Wragg, E.C. (ed.) (1984) *Classroom Teaching Skills.* London: Croom Helm.

Wray, D. (1985) *Teaching Information Skills through Topic Work.* Sevenoaks: Hodder & Stoughton.

Zimet, S. (1976) *Print and Prejudice.* London: Hodder & Stoughton.

Appendix

Produced by P.A.G.E., Oxfordshire

PURPOSE

- to write a story with readers in mind

- to write a traditional story, drawing on knowledge of myth and legend.

STRUCTURE

- has opening, characters, action and resolution, with detail beyond simple events.

TEXT ORGANISATION

Opening - a descriptive passage with information which sets a scene.

Action - series of events, precipitated by villagers decision to 'do' something.

Conclusion - Argold's resolution to the problem is presented but the villagers' problem is not resolved in this episode.

Argold's character has some depth but no other character is described in detail.

STORY WRITING

Long ago in the land of Cimerrica, lived an old man. A man that was so old he had seen 6 centuries float by. His name was Argold, he was a sourcera (otherwise known as a wizard) and lived on his own in a cave in a snow topped mountain. Argold was an evil minded man and the people of village at the bottom of the mountain knew this well for many a time. Argold had played tricks and set spells on them. One day, after Argold had turned their water supply into salt the villagers gathered up all the weapons they could, (wich included clubs, knifes, flaming torches etc.) and marched up to Argolds cave. Argold, hearing the row the villagers were making looked out of cave and to his surprise saw 40 or 50 men and women coming up the mountain side in a wild frenzy waving weapons over their heads. Argold raced into his cave, got out his book of spells and set to work to brew up the most evil spell that he knew of. He had just finished and bottled it and screwed on the lid (wich had a small hold in the centre) when the first of many mad minded villergers came rushing into the cave waving a club above his head screaming and shouting that he was going to kill Argold. But with one swipe in the air with the bottle a tiny drop flew out and hit the man. Instantly he stopped, no he was not dead, but blind deaf and dumb. "Go now dog, and find your way home," said Argold. This happened to all who entered his cave. The villagers went home and lived their lives for 11 years until one day a stranger walked in the village, ... but that's a different story.

(Typed with child's own spelling)

LANGUAGE FEATURES

- uses story language, 'Long ago' - sets scene 'One day' - specific event, and specific characters, Argold and the villagers

- uses past tense consistently

- uses pronouns consistently

- omits pronouns to avoid repetition and for stylistic effect, and uses literary language.

- uses action verbs for action part of the story

- uses relational verbs (e.g. 'had', 'was') to set the scene

- uses subordinate clauses

- uses parenthesis to position the reader and maintain the pace of the story

- uses a variety of sentence connectives

- changes word order for emphasis

- does not use paragraphs

- pronoun used to summarise whole of preceding action, e.g. This happened'

PURPOSE

- to write a report - classifying and describing a natural phenomenon (i.e. Barn Owls)
- to make explicit the features of a Factual Report

STRUCTURE

- has a general classification
- has description grouped under sub-headings
- includes physical and behavioural characteristics

TEXT ORGANISATION

- use of sub headings to define paragraphs
- each paragraph begins with a reference to the subject, e.g. The Barn Owls ...', 'It ...'
- use of explanation appropriately to conclude text.

JOINT CONSTRUCTION (2 children)

The Barn Owl
The Barn Owl is a bird of prey.
It is an endangered species. It lives in barns and trees. They are nocturnal.

Description
It's face is like a plate which is used as a satellite dish. The sound bounces off

The feet
The Barn Owl has tiny feet and sharp claws because it has to pick up its prey.

The colour
It has brown speckles and a white face. It has white under the wings and a white belly. There are furry-speckled feathers on its back.

Habitat
The Barn Owl lives in barns and chimneys. The Barn Owl does not make nests.

Food
It is a carnivore and it eats mice, rats, wild gerbils and baby rabbits.

Movement/Speed
The Barn Owls fly fast and silent and glides and it flies low, so that the prey can't hear it coming. The Owl is endangered because people are moving to barns and also because mice eat chemicals and the owls eat the mice and they die.

LANGUAGE FEATURES

- constant use of subject reference
- sometimes inconsistent use of pronouns with subject. e.g. The Barn Owl ... They ...'
- use of simple present tense
- use of relational 'being' and 'having' processes
- use of action processes for behaviour ('eats', 'fly', 'pick up')
- subject and verb generally consistent
- some use of technical language
- use of simple sentence structure, with some relative clauses and adverbial clauses of reason

Ways of describing
- use of nominal groups, e.g. 'sharp claws', 'furry-speckled feathers', 'endangered species'
- frequent use of very specific adjectives, e.g. 'satellite dish'
- appropriate use of simile, e.g. 'face like a plate' (an older child might write 'plate-like face')

Examples of an initial analysis of children's writing showing an application of a framework which includes purpose, structure, text organization and language features.

Name Index

Subject Index